PUBERTY AND ADOLESCENCE

Puberty and Adolescence

BARBARA BAKER SOMMER
Department of Psychology
University of California, Davis

New York
OXFORD UNIVERSITY PRESS
1978

Copyright © 1978 by Oxford University Press, Inc.

Printed in the United States of America

Library of Congress Cataloging in Publication Data

Sommer, Barbara Baker, 1938–
    Puberty and adolescence.

    Includes bibliographical references and index.
    1.   Adolescent psychology.   2.   Puberty.   I.   Title.
BF724.S58   115.5   78–2005
ISBN 0--19-502376-5
ISBN 0–19–502377–2 pbk.

For Bob and Margy

Acknowledgments

Although the choice of words and concepts is mine, the content reflects the insights and work of many researchers, writers, and educators. While their contributions form the bulk of the work, any misinterpretations or incorrect inferences are fully my doing.

I would like to express my gratitude to those who very graciously gave their time and consideration in helping me with the preparation of the manuscript: to Bob Sommer, Helen Remick, Robert Innes, and Mychelle Karlton who read the first draft and made invaluable suggestions, and to Margaret Hill who not only read it and offered editorial assistance, but also typed it. Dorian Cryer contributed the drawings for Chapter 2, and Margy Sommer gave me some insight into the myriad qualities of the 13-year-old mind. Finally, a note of gratitude to William Knowles whose interest and encouragement led to a serious undertaking of the task.

The author thanks the following publishers for permission to include previously published material:

American Faculty Press, the poems of "Thinking" and "Going Out" from *Somebody Real* by Nicholas Duva, 1972.

College of Education, The State University of Ohio, excerpts from "The Student as Teacher" by Carole Papirtis Heffner, published in *Theory into Practice*, 1974, 13, 371–5.

Contents

1 Invisible People   3

2 The Cultural Context   16

3 Changing Body   32

4 Changing Mind   50

5 Moral Development   71

6 Sex Roles   85

7 The Inner Person: Identity and Interests   104

8 The Outer Person: Social Relationships and
   Perceptions of Others   119

9 Schools   142

10 Sexuality   154

11 Delinquency, Gangs, and Drug Use   178

12 Psychopathology   202

13 Visible People   216

Glossary   225

Notes   229

Author Index   249

Subject Index   255

PUBERTY AND ADOLESCENCE

1 *Invisible People*

At thirteen, you're too old for toys and too
young to drive.

Ted S.

The prevailing stereotype of the pubescent is a negative one—pimples, fat in the wrong places, lurching gawky movements, unpredictable and hostile moods, antagonism, resentfulness, and possession of a sensitive and fragile ego. G. Stanley Hall[1] in 1904 described the period as one of storm and stress. While the strain may have been reduced since Hall's day by a more sympathetic attitude on the part of adults, a current writer described adolescence as a time of thrust and lust in a sociocultural animal.[2]

Young children and older teenagers are often portrayed on television, but rarely the 10–15 year old. The viewer is, of course, aware that there is an intermediate growth period, but the transition from toy cars to the real thing is seldom depicted, only the "before" and "after." Many a child star disappeared from the Silver Screen upon reaching puberty. Television personalities met similar fates. Seventh graders rarely make the news. Even the acne ads project an image of the older adolescent. Comparatively few novels deal with the transition from childhood to adolescence—surprising in light of its 100 percent frequency among humans. Books written for young readers about adolescence seem primarily concerned with helping the person survive a particularly painful period of life. Discovery, yes, but it is most often tinged with a bit of regret over the loss of childhood innocence. It may involve suffering the indignity of a broken bra strap or the scrutiny of fellows in the locker room. The general message is that an end is in sight and that no one is pubescent forever, thank God.

For reasons of biology and culture, the period of puberty is one of special stress. If not stressful in the negative sense of anxiety, it is at the very least a period of intense and high arousal. Pubescents are notoriously on the move. They rarely sit still. Motor movements are constant, similar in many ways to high arousal states in animals. Pubescents show a general twitchiness—foot tapping, head movements, gum chewing, repetitive hair combing, and finger snapping.

Discussions among groups of young adolescents involve more talking than listening. Attention wanders; eyes are looking everywhere. Conversation takes curious and rapid shifts in content and subject. To focus at length and in depth seems either too taxing or too threatening—perhaps both. Sustained attention to one topic may reveal an underlying chaos of thought. Emerging consciousness of self and of that self in relation to others leads to confusion and difficulty in organizing and expressing one's thoughts and feelings beyond a superficial level. A heightened sensitivity and defensiveness to criticism may be expressed by emotional outbursts or sudden withdrawal, either of which may occur with seemingly slight provocation. (A friend's 14-year-old daughter threatened to fling herself from a third-floor balcony because her slacks were about one-half inch shorter than prevailing fashion dictated.) That this is for many a period laden with emotion, tension, and sometimes anxiety is borne out by later recollections. In a survey of college students asked to rate their life stages on a scale of 1 (very unhappy) to 5 (very happy), early adolescence (puberty) received lowest rank. Detailed interviews revealed that early adolescence was remembered as a difficult period. Some students had an extremely poor recollection of puberty although they were able to recall earlier years with clarity.[3] When college students are asked what grades they would like to teach, the mention of secondary school leads to head shaking and moans of "not junior high."

ADOLESCENCE AND PUBERTY

The word adolescence is derived from the Latin *adolescere* which means to grow up. Puberty comes from the Latin *pubescere*—to grow hairy. In current usage *adolescence* refers to the life stage extending from puberty to adulthood, with adulthood generally defined as the achievement of self-governance. Adolescence thus covers the entire transition from child to adult in a psychological and sociological sense. Puberty refers more specifically to the physiological changes involved in the sexual maturation of the person—the development of the genitalia* and of secondary sex characteristics*—and of the spurt in growth leading to increased height, weight, muscular development, and alterations in body shape. These changes result from increases in circulating hormones* produced by the gonads.* Puberty consists of a sequence of changes which occurs over a span of up to eight or nine years if one measures from the very first hormonal changes early as the ninth year to the establishment of full reproductive capacity in the middle or late teens.

Puberty may be described as either an event or a process. When defined as an *event* it is quite distinct in meaning from adolescence. The observable beginnings of sexual maturation serve to mark the onset of adolescence as a developmental stage. Although the process description is more accurate because of the number of changes and the substantial amount of time involved, many people think of puberty as an event, as, for example, a girl's first menstruation or a boy's development of pigmented pubic hair. A disparaging remark in a boys' gym class is "Aw, he ain't even got a hair" as though presence of pubic hair represented the achievement of physical maturity. Others consider the first ejaculation to

---

* Definition provided in glossary.

be evidence of a boy's puberty. On occasion it becomes a verb, as in the question, "Has she pubed yet?" meaning "Has she begun to menstruate?" Sometimes the term "pubescence" is used to describe a process, while "puberty" is retained for some specific event or as describing the achievement of reproductive capacity (an event which is *not* synonymous with menarche* in girls or ejaculation in boys). However, the terms are frequently used interchangeably.

Puberty has also been conceptualized as an event independent of specific individual maturation. The twelfth birthday for girls and the fourteenth birthday for boys constituted the legal attainment of puberty in canon and Roman law, and was considered the age of eligibility for marriage. The twelfth birthday still embodies a change of status. Movie houses, bus companies, and other services demand increased tariffs. It is interesting to note that few privileges accrue at age 12, only penalties in the form of higher prices. Thus, even an increased allowance loses its rewarding properties. The 12-year-old remains under legal parental control and subject to education and child labor laws. The partial changes in social status add to the ambiguity of the age; one is neither child nor teenager.

If the *process* definition is used, the relationship between the two concepts, puberty and adolescence, changes. Puberty is then contemporaneous with pre- and early adolescence, and its role during the years from approximately age 11 to 15 is emphasized. Retaining the terms puberty and pubescence for this period underscores the very important interrelationship between the physiological process and psychological events. Although puberty often seems a particularly dramatic and rapid process, it is not unique in this regard. The development of speech in the young child in many respects proceeds at a more rapid rate than sexual maturation. The considerable linguistic skill of the 3½-year-old contrasts sharply with the one- or two-word vocabulary of the one-year-old. Just as the capacity for speech initiates new activities and experiences for the child, so puberty performs a similar role at a later age.

It seems curious that with the marked interest in human development and a plethora of books on childhood and adolescence that the period from ten or eleven to fifteen has received so little attention from social scientists. One reason for the benign neglect of pubescents is the perception of them. They are thought of as the children they were or the adults they will become. Kurt Lewin's[4] description of adolescence as a marginal status has come to be used for the person located in social space between childhood and adolescence. Today the pubescent is the "marginal person," neither child nor adolescent. An indication of the marginality is the difficulty in finding suitable clothing beyond the T-shirt and blue-jean variety. The variations in shape and size of this age group are so great that, unlike other age groups, they do not have a consumer niche of their own. Labels for the period which emphasize its transience contribute to the vagueness and absence of characterization of a very critical period. At that stage of life three to five years is too long a time to be ignored. Too often we see the individuals as who they have been, such as "the Harris girls," or we project their future, "Don't worry dear, it's just baby fat," or "Do this now because it will be of value to you later." We may perceive of this advice as reassuring but for the pubescent the issue is here and now. Psychiatrist Fritz Redl[5] has pointed out that the pubescent has two tasks. One is to "emigrate" from family life as experienced in childhood. The other is to "immigrate," not into the adult world, but into the society of the teenager. The peer group becomes the mainstay in this evolution of affiliation. The peer group becomes a refuge or place of retreat for some, and for others, a home base from which to move out into the world. The risk of confusion is high.

Among psychologists and others who study human development, there is no clear consensus as to the relationship between puberty and adolescence. Criteria as well as definitions of terms, such as latency and preadolescence, vary widely. As shown in Table 1-1, Kohen-Raz[6] and Schonfeld[7] use a physiological sequence while Muuss relies on school grade. Hurlock[8] defines puberty as an overlapping stage covering the end of childhood and the beginning of adolescence. Instead of relying on either observ-

Table 1-1. Developmental phase designations related to puberty

Sequence of maturational events associated with puberty (Tanner, 1973)	Kohen-Raz (1971)	Muuss (1975)	Schonfeld (1969)	Hurlock (1967)	
Increasing gonadotropin secretion. Beginning of height spurt in females. Breast budding in females. Pubic hair development in females. Testicular growth in males.	Preadolescence	Preadolescence ages 9–11, elementary school	Early adolescence or pre-pubescence	Last 2 years of childhood	Puberty
Menarch in females. Beginning of height spurt in males. Penile growth and ejaculation in males. Pubic hair development in males.	Early adolescence, or early puberty	Early adolescence ages 12–14, junior high or middle school	Middle adolescence or pubescence	First 2 years of adolescence	
Re-establishment of hormonal equilibrium. Regularization of menstrual cycle in females. Growth of facial hair and voice changes in males.	Puberty "proper"	Middle adolescence ages 15–18, high school	Late adolescence or post pubescence		

able body changes or chronological age, Blos[9,10] (not included on the table) uses degree of ego development and changes in sexual drive and choice of sexual object as indicators of five phases of adolescence: latency, preadolescence, early adolescence, adolescence proper, and late adolescence. None of the developmental theorists recommends using a strict calendar definition of puberty such as 12 years of age for females and 14 years of age for males.

Individual variability makes it difficult to designate a time frame for puberty and therefore for pre- and early adolescence. However, many legal statutes rely on chronological age in defining penalties and sanctions. School placement is primarily determined by chronological age, as is the time at which one may cease compulsory education, get married without parental or Court consent, join the military, and obtain the right to vote. Intelligence test scores are based on chronological age standards. The creation of the junior high school represented a recognition of the special nature of the period between the years of 12 and 15. Nonetheless, it is difficult to fit the developments of this stage into a chronological scale. Although the sequence of pubertal events, like other maturational events, is fairly fixed, the timing is individual and variable. Because it occurs at a much later age than the other maturational milestones of walking and talking, puberty is a complex phenomenon at the outset with respect to the interaction between maturational, environmental, and individual factors. Thus, chronological age is not a very precise indicator of developmental level. Further, there can be a dissonance between a person's psychological age based on experience and physiological age based on maturation, with either one outstripping the other, thus creating an asynchrony within the person.

The lack of a definite relationship between chronological age and puberty is matched by the lack of any clear social designation of puberty. The dominant American culture provides no formal puberty rites. Thus, it becomes very difficult to integrate its physiological events into the more systematic categories of age and social status. Pubescence in and of itself brings with it no formal recognition of a change of status, although there is a great deal of informal recognition as the maturational changes influence one's social interactions and self-perception. Most of the available information about pubescent behavior must be retrieved from surveys and studies which categorize children on the basis of chronological rather than biological age. We are therefore obliged to use a chronological designation of the period of puberty, recognizing that this designation in many instances does not always correspond to the actual time when the pubertal process is occurring for a given individual.

Our focus will be on the time period extending from approximately age 11 to 15 years, corresponding with grades 6 through 9, a four-year span including the junior high years. This period encompasses the most observable and dramatic events of puberty. It is a time when adjustments are required to the changes in body size, height, and shape, and the subsequent occurrence of ejaculation or menstruation. The later occurrences of ovulation, production of fertile sperm, beard growth, and voice change require less in the way of immediate adaptation. In a sense, the latter events are confirmatory and less dramatic in their impact. The pubescent years are quite different in tempo and tone from the late teen years. They are more likely to encompass personal upheaval resulting from the asynchrony of physical and cognitive maturation. The later teen years involve a somewhat different set of tasks and concerns. The focus in the earlier years is upon one's changing appearance and the shift from family orientation to the wider world and peers. In later adolescence concerns focus more upon personal identity, the meaning of life, and the future. Themes of alienation, religious commitment, vocational choice, and conflicts involving identity and intimacy in relationships with others, while sporadically present in the pubescent years, are more likely to be salient later. There is, however, a great deal of individual variation. For some, religious concerns or occupational commitment may be deep and extensive at 13 or 14 years of age. For others, such concern may never occur at any age. In general the use of the terms puberty and pubescence will cover the first two blocks of physiological developments shown in Table 1-1.

The primary developments characterizing the years from 11 to 15 are sexual maturation and intellectual growth. Other changes in personality, emotionality, sexuality, and friendship patterns; and also consolidation of gender roles and expressions of identity, intimacy, and independence are manifestations of the dynamic processes of a changing body and changing mind. They are not secondary in importance and are frequently conspicuously intense; they are termed secondary because their evolution depends in large part upon hormonal and cognitive development. The primary and secondary changes associated with puberty interact with one another to produce a very complex pattern, a pattern further elaborated by individual differences, which include: variations in chronological age at puberty and the pace or speed of development and differences in prior experience, preparation, and expectations of puberty —as well as the environment in which they occur. Puberty, the physiological process of sexual maturation, is directly responsible for the body changes of early adolescence. Its role in intellectual development is far less direct. The underlying neurological changes of intellectual development remain unspecified.

THREE MAJOR CONTROVERSIES

There is little argument about the occurrence of developmental change. However, there is a great deal of disagreement about the basis and form of transition: (1) whether change is produced by external environmental factors and hence is relative rather than absolute, (2) if it is a continuous or discontinuous process, and (3) if the components of change are reducible to more simple elements or if change reflects an alteration in the overall pattern of established components. These three persistent issues, reflecting philosophical differences, arise repeatedly in the analysis of human development. Briefly stated they are Cultural Relativism versus Absolutism, Continuity versus Discontinuity, and Reductionism versus Wholism.

Taking the first theme, the cultural relativist believes that values and behavior must always be viewed in the context of a specific culture. It follows that values are relative and there is no right or wrong for everyone everywhere. In contrast, the absolutist believes that there are forces and principles in the universe which are predictable and inevitable, and that values exist independent of time and place. The process of human development itself can be viewed from either of these perspectives. In an absolutist view, development follows a predictable and universal sequence. The cultural relativist sees events shaped by the cultural milieu.

A second major argument is whether development is a continuous process. Does psychological growth proceed in a smooth and incremental fashion or does it occur in stages, producing surges and plateaus, each qualitatively different from what has gone before? Some resolution of these seemingly divergent positions can be achieved by noting that living forms demonstrate both continuous and discontinuous processes. An individual consumes food which is incorporated into nerves, muscle, and flesh in the body. These structures are consistently being transformed, replenished, and replaced. Yet through all of the breakdown and buildup of cellular matter, the person retains the same identity. A living organism possesses its own continuity despite a series of life changes that have clear beginnings and endings. Adherents of continuity speak of changes in quantity; adherents of discontinuity emphasize changes in quality. The qualitative view implies that development is the sum total of accumulated small steps. No single step in and of itself brings about a drastic change. In the qualitative view the organism is seen as changing in a manner which makes it quite different from what it was before. A dramatic example of a qualitative change is the transformation of a caterpillar into a butterfly. By contrast the transformation of a puppy to a dog appears more quantitative and continuous.

In most cases development has both quantitative and qualitative aspects. Tadpoles and frogs are qualitatively different. The gill-breathing fish-like polliwog is a sharp contrast with the final developmental product of an air-breathing reptile-like land animal. Yet, observing the transformation more closely, one sees a whole series of small changes, none of which is dramatically different from the preceding. A visit to a local pond at the right time of year will reveal the various incremental steps in the transformation, as some of the tadpoles will be in a more advanced stage than others. Many a kindergarten class has observed over a period of weeks the gradual shortening of the tadpole tail and the budding and growth of legs. In a similar fashion the human embryo progresses through a series of structural changes in which it resembles the embryos of the entire phylogenetic sequence of the human species—those forms which are part of its evolutionary history. At one point the human embryo resembles a fish embryo, at another, a reptilian embryo, and then a mammalian embryo. This principle of ontogeny (the evolution of the individual) recapitulating phylogeny (the evolution of the species) embodies both continuous and discontinuous aspects. It is sequential and gradual; yet each stage is quite distinct from stages occurring before and after.

Both continuity and discontinuity aspects are evident as children mature. Johnny, chattering away at seven years about his dog and proudly exhibiting his drawings of airplanes, is a different person from Johnny at two years, barely walking, and unable to speak more than 20 words. At seven years he is also a different person from Johnny of 17 who is enamored of his automobile and capable of supporting it as well as his appetite for the latest stereo hits. Despite these marked changes, those who knew him as he grew up will recognize him as the same individual.

The third major controversy is between Reductionistic and Wholistic concepts of development. The reductionist believes that the whole is the sum of the parts and that in order to understand the whole, one is best advised to analyze the properties of its components. Sometimes this view is termed atomistic or elementalist. The wholistic philosophy is that the whole is *more* than the sum of its parts and that in focusing solely upon the components, one will lose sight of the qualities of the entirety. Studying individual trees is not the same as understanding the meaning of the forest, and neither hydrogen nor oxygen possess the properties found when they are combined forming water. If the whole is the sum of its parts, as the reductionist view suggests, then a change in the whole must reflect an alteration in one or more components. However, from a wholistic view the very same components may be reordered to interact in such a way as to produce a very different configuration. Thus, a qualitative change in the absence of quantitative increments becomes possible. This polarity adds another twist to the conceptualization of puberty. Are the observable changes due to the introduction of new elements or do they instead reflect simply a reshuffling of elements already present? As with the other polarities, a position between the extremes is possible. New elements in the form of characteristics of physical maturation may be introduced, while at the same time old priorities are reordered as demands from parents, teachers, and peers change.

Resolution of these controversies is impossible without looking at specific cases. Karen at age 15 is still Karen, the person who was once 11 years old. Yet she has changed in both quantitative and qualitative ways. She operates more efficiently at 15 than she did at 11. She also possesses attributes, both physical and mental, which were not present before. Their potential was present but the form was different. Thus, depending upon whether one emphasizes potential or form, one will think of change as quantitative or qualitative. The amount of time included in the analysis will affect the determination of change as well. If one described and photographed Karen at 12 years and compared it with Karen at 15, the change would be apparent. However, if Karen were described and photographed every day in the intervening period, the day-to-day change would not be noticeable.

SUMMARY

Pubescents often seem invisible. Few novelists have explored the experiences of early adolescence; it is more often than not a private business, and a stressful one as well, a stage of life to be lived through and forgotten as quickly as possible. The onset of puberty marks the beginning of adolescence. Viewed as a process it encompasses a stage of development generally characterized as pre- and early adolescence, a phase which has often been treated as marginal and transitory, yet one far too long and important to ignore. The period is a critical one of body change and intellectual growth. The exact structure and nature of these changes are unclear but their impact is marked. Virtually all areas of individual functioning are affected by puberty and its cognitive accompaniments.

2 *The Cultural Context*

Through no fault of my own I reached
adolescence.

Julius Lester

Puberty, a biological process, is universal. However, adolescence,
the lengthy period of transition from child to adult in a social and
psychological sense, is not. In many cultures puberty itself, or formal recognition or rites, are sufficient in moving a youngster from
the social position of child to adult. Adolescence, as we know it
today, is an invention. The creation of adolescence has provided
an added distinctiveness to the events of puberty, for now they
signal entry into a very particular stage of development and a well-
established culture of youth.

THE HISTORY OF ADOLESCENCE

The term adolescence was rarely used prior to the 18th century.
Early scholars from the Greek period into the Middle Ages divided the life span into stages, sometimes debating whether a six-
year or seven-year span was the more applicable.[1] Aristotle used
the latter and termed the third stage of life, the years from 14 to
21, as those of young adulthood. This characterization was com-

mon for centuries following. Although the life span continued to be viewed in segments or "ages of life" during the medieval period, the transition from one stage to the next was viewed as a gradual process. Marked qualitative distinctions were absent. Children were assumed to be miniature adults. They wore smaller versions of adult attire and participated in virtually all adult activities. The characteristics of puberty did not pass unnoticed and references are found to the growth and maturation occurring in the early teen years. However, little particular significance was attached to these developments. The passage from childhood to adulthood was determined by a transition from dependency to independence, a change having little to do with precise chronological age. Anyone in a dependent position was called "boy" or "girl" irrespective of their years.[2]

Following the Renaissance the concept of childhood began to change and more concern was expressed about the nurture and guidance, as well as protection, of the young. Philosophical views emphasizing the distinctiveness and value of the individual and the impact of environmental factors on human development began to be expressed among the learned. In 1762 the French philosopher and writer, Jean Jacques Rousseau, published *Émile*, a book proposing the proper education for youth.[3] Rousseau carefully described the period of adolescence. It was a time of new birth, of awakening sexual desire, and of increasing social expression of love; and a time of decline in self-centeredness. However, it was to be well over a century before the views of the educated were to become common. The special treatment of the young and specification of characteristics of adolescence began with the wealthy and within select religious groups. Such views spread more slowly among the population at large.

Joseph Kett[4] has traced the modern conception of adolescence in the United States from 1790 to the present. In the colonial period and following the American Revolution, family patterns were similar to those of Europe. The young American, if not subject to early mortality, passed through three important states of social development: dependence, semidependence, and independence.

Children were sent into household service or apprenticeship at an early age. During this phase of semidependence, the adult in immediate control was generally unrelated to the youngster, for example, a ship's captain, the mistress of a household, or a tradesperson. While young persons were nearly slaves in a work sense, many enjoyed a great deal of personal freedom, hence their characterization as semidependent. State of dependency rather than age continued to be a more important variable in influencing society's treatment of the individual, in contrast to the more structured age definitions we use today. Birthdays were not celebrated during the 18th century.[5] Children as young as 7 years left home, and school attendance was quite casual after the age of 12. The years of semidependence ranged from approximately 10 to 21 years on the average. Wealthier children left home later and returned more often. Girls were courted around the age of 16.

In the early 1800s the United States was a youthful society. The median age in 1800 was 16 years, that is, one-half the population was under 16. By 1950 the median age was 30.8. Many parents did not live long enough to see their youngest children reach teenage. There were large numbers of uneducated youth who, although in positions of subservience, experienced little guidance or concern. These patterns began to change as a result of a number of factors, produced directly or indirectly by the Industrial Revolution. School reform was prompted by the need for technological training along with a rising concern with the moral fiber of the young. Church groups, women's organizations, and politicians and other leaders expressed concern about the development of youth. Many reformers were influenced by John Locke's philosophical theories about the importance of environmental factors in molding character. At the same time there was a shift in population from rural to urban areas as increasingly more young people came to the cities. The concern of the reformers and the focus of rising educational institutions fell first on the 7- to 13-year-old group.

Coupled with the solicitude about moral development was the view of pubescence as the dangerous years—a period when both nurture and environmental support was essential. In both sexes, but particularly for boys, dissipation of sexual energy was a matter of serious concern. A popular view was that while boys had much energy, it was in a fixed amount. If it were drained through sexual release (masturbation being the most common), little would remain for character building. For girls, there was apprehension about the hazards of precocity and the danger of overpressure in school. Much was made of childhood innocence and the desirability of the prolongation of innocence. Victorian mores were popularly expressed, if not always practiced.

Girls had been very useful members of large families because of their roles as babysitters, nurses, and cooks. Later they became a cheap source of factory labor. However, the economic value of young women declined in the mid-19th century as a result of a decrease in family size and an increase in cheap immigrant labor, both for factories and for household service. One result was that, following the Civil War, young women spent more time in school and were often better educated than men. There was a corollary assumption of control over cultural life by women. Many of these educated women also became increasingly involved with matters concerning children and youth outside their own families.

The consolidation of the advances of the Industrial Revolution had far-reaching effects. Previously most young people had left school by age 12 and worked as servants or apprentices until around age 18, when young women married and young men began receiving adult wages. However, for the middle class to take advantage of the new economic opportunities, it became necessary to stay in school for education beyond puberty. Whereas striking out early on one's own in previous centuries had led to independence, by 1900 an early desire for autonomy and independence was a prescription for failure.[6]

Three major social movements of the late 19th century contributed to the distinction of adolescence: compulsory education, child labor legislation, and special legal procedures for juvenile offenders.[7] Compulsory education to age 16 became widely practiced in the United States. Although they varied from state to state, minimum ages of around 16 or 18 were prescribed for employment in hazardous occupations. The participation of 10- to 15-year-olds in the labor force, which had been increasing until 1900, declined thereafter. The development of the Juvenile Court and differentiation of juvenile from adult offenders further enhanced separate legal status.

In the opening decades of the 20th century two major trends were established. One was the need for extended dependency and education through the teen years, brought about primarily by economic factors. The other was the institutionalization of the view of the pubescent years as tumultuous, hazardous, and in need of adult guidance. This maturation of the idea of adolescence occurred long after the seeds had been planted, and it reached full bloom in the work of G. Stanley Hall.[8] In 1904 he published a two-volume work titled *Adolescence: Its Psychology and Its Relation to Physiology, Anthropology, Sociology, Sex, Crime, Religion and Education*. As a result of the interest epitomized by Hall's work, separate and adult-supervised activities for boys and girls became popular—scouting, Christian organizations, and similar clubs. There was an increase in manuals advising parents about the management of teenagers. Educators who were seeing many more teens in school became vocal about the special needs of the age group. While it took another 40 years to extend throughout the nation, the idea of youth as different and in need of special treatment was fixed.

At the risk of oversimplification of the welter of social change, the creation of the adolescent in the 20th century can be reduced to the confluence of two very general and major themes. One is that puberty is a period of upheaval and change. The second is that this change needs to be contained, directed, and channeled into productivity by nurturance, training, education, and character development with the goal of producing the kind of adult needed and desired by society. These views were influenced by economic as well as philosophical currents. Fueled by a declining demand for labor and a prolonged stay in school, a full-fledged culture of adolescence developed by the 1950s.

The adolescent is a social creation and even among the Western nations, one finds variations in the characterization of and behaviors attributed to teens. In the United States the creation of adolescence was an attempt to promote in youth particular qualities deemed desirable by the middle class: conformity, hostility to intellectuality, and passivity.[9] Insofar as these values are not adhered to, they reflect conflicting themes within the culture. Adolescence was not discovered in the sense that someone paid careful attention to how youth behaved. Rather, the changes of puberty—increased sexual motivation and intellectual capacity, qualities which had been recognized for centuries—came to mark a new stage of development worthy of study on its own and requiring elaborate institutions staffed by cadres of experts, professionals, and volunteers. We decided that adolescence *should* be a universal experience.

CROSS-CULTURAL RESPONSES TO PUBERTY

In humans the significance of biological events is culturally determined. Puberty as either event or process is no exception. The individual's experience of puberty results from an interaction of biological and social-cultural forces at a particular moment in history. As in the West, in many societies the period we call early adolescence is a time of transition—of an alteration in social standing. Cultural practices range from highly ritualized formal ceremonies rapidly promoting the young person to the status of adult to those with a period of role change extending over a decade, the increments so gradual as to be hardly noticeable.

The presence or absence of formal rites as well as their content is affected by social structure, history, and economics. Some anthropologists have attempted to explain the form of initiation into adulthood in terms of personality development and childrearing practices.[10] Many questions pertinent to puberty and its social implications and accompaniments in various societies remain to be explored. However, the form and speed of transition from childhood to adulthood appear to be affected more by social than by physical factors.

In Sub-Saharan Africa, Oceania, and parts of the Western Hemisphere, a wide variety of practices occurs, differing by region as well as by sex. However, three common themes are discernible: separation, transformation, and incorporation.[11] The transition from child to adult requires a severing of dependency bonds within the family. The child then must be transformed in status to an adult. Finally, the new adult must be incorporated into the society of other adults, ready to take on the rights and responsibilities of that status.

The term "rites of passage" was first used by Van Gennep[12] in 1909 to refer to ceremonies in which the child or adolescent is initiated into adulthood. Sometimes the ceremonies are termed puberty rites and defined as the means by which adolescents gain access to the sacred adult practices, to knowledge, and to sexuality —in short, how they become fully human beings in a cultural sense.[13] The rites frequently involve dramatic practices designed to develop psychological and social separation of the young person from immediate family, particularly the mother. Transformation is often accomplished by ritual death and rebirth or through other contact with the spiritual world. Finally, through means of shared ritual, hazards, and secrets combined with the learning of history and lore, bonds are forged incorporating the young person into the society of adults, particularly that of her or his own sex. These rituals provide a forceful and discontinuous entry into adulthood at a time when the person is ripe for the change—cognitive development permits an appreciation of less immediate and more spiritual considerations. The development of competence makes dependence upon the mother less necessary, and developing sexual inclinations are best deflected away from family toward opposite-sex members of the wider community.

Rites of transition show a less direct relationship to the specific events of puberty for males than for females. The more indirect relationship for males is undoubtedly due to the lack of a single event comparable to menarche. Growth of the genitals is a gradual process. The height spurt, development of facial hair, and changes in voice are variable among individuals and cover a period of six or seven years. While genital growth, height development, and body configuration changes are also gradual and encompass a period of years for girls, the event of menstruation is singular and dramatic. The sex difference may also account for the observation that male ceremonies often involve the initiation of several candidates in various stages of prepubescence and pubescence as a group. In his pioneering work on rites of passage, Van Gennep stated that for males, physiological and social puberty are essentially different and only rarely converge.[14] Female initiations often take place for the individual. The event of menstruation compels recognition of a change in status. In elaborating the sex differences, Eliade[15] has pointed out that for boys, initiation represents an introduction to a world that is not immediate—the world of spirit and culture, while for girls the emphasis is on revelations concerning the secret meanings of the natural phenomena of menstruation and childbirth.

The boy-as-candidate and girl-as-single-initiate theme is not without exception. Boys may be individually initiated and girls may be initiated in groups. Sometimes segregation at menarche overlaps with that of other girls and the individuals are initiated together. The ceremonies for both sexes may be independent of puberty, occurring either before or long after the physical changes are apparent. Given the very general characteristics of initiation rites, in many cases the term "puberty rite" is too specific. However, within the larger category of initiation rites there are those ceremonies which are more directly linked to puberty and examples of these, primarily from the peoples of Sub-Saharan Africa, Oceania, Australia, and parts of North and South America are described in the following sections. Many of the rites are disappearing under the impact of Western culture; however, some vestiges remain today. Traces of similar rites can be found among historical records of European cultures, but the practice has nearly vanished.

BOYS' INITIATION RITES

The themes of death and rebirth are particularly strong in the initiations of males. The boys are often violently separated from their mothers and families and carried off by frightening masked figures. In the Congo and Loange coast regions of Africa, boys between 10 and 12 years of age drank a potion which made them unconscious. They were carried into the jungle, circumcised, and ritually buried. On awakening they seemed to have forgotten their past life.[16]

The following account is an example of the enactment of death and rebirth in the Mano tribe of Liberia. The events took place at the entrance to a guarded area of the forest which constituted the Poro, or bush school, where eligible candidates were taken for their initiation.

> At the entrance the boys went through a ceremonial "death." In the old days they were apparently run through with a spear and tossed over the curtain. Onlookers heard a thud as he was supposed to hit the ground inside, dead. Actually, the boy was protected by a chunk of plantain stalk tied on under his clothes. Into this the spear was thrust. A bladder of chicken's blood at the right spot was punctured and spilled to make it all very realistic to other boys and women who could not resist the desire to see their sons, perhaps for the last time. Inside the fence *sa yi ge* (a ritual personage) and two assistants, all masked, caught the boys in mid-air, and dropped a heavy dummy to complete the delusion. The boys were actually unharmed and were quickly carried away into the deep forest which is the Poro grove.[17]

The bush school, a highly developed institution among tribal groups in Liberia, Sierra Leone, and adjacent countries of western Africa serves as an initiation providing the young males of the society with ordeals in which they prove their worthiness to take on the responsibilities of adult life. Every few years when there are sufficient numbers of boys to constitute a small group, a Poro is formed. The boys who pass through the initiation remain a closely knit group, functioning as a social unit throughout their lives. In those areas where it is well-established, the Poro serves both as an initiation rite and as a continuing secret society exerting power and control over its members. Similar institutions existed in Melanesia and Australia.

Among the Baktamen of New Guinea, initiation is necessary for the attainment of manhood and for active participation in religious affairs.[18] Although variable, initiations take place about every 10 years, creating a wide representation of age within a group. All participants go jointly through seven levels of initiation. A persistent theme is unpreparedness and ignorance on the part of novices, thus creating a true mystery cult whose secrets are only slowly unraveled. In a manner analogous to western African practices, the initial initiation is very dramatic and frightening for the boys. Adult men tear them from their mothers creating a substantial level of terror, and then carry them off into the woods where they undergo the secret initiation rituals.

The spiritual, the sexual, and the communal or social aspects of life are closely bound with one another in the initiation process. The spiritual contact is provided in a variety of ways depending upon the culture. In much of Australia, bull-rorarers (long, thin narrow pieces of wood attached to a string) are whirled through the air creating a terrifying, deafening roar in accompaniment with ceremonies emphasizing contact with the spirits. In other circumstances initiates are confronted with masked figures, must undergo difficult feats of strength and endurance, and are made to fear for their lives. In contrast, a common practice among many North American Indian tribes was for the youth between the ages of 10 and 16 years to leave the tribe, existing alone in the mountains or forest in order to make contact with the divine spirit.[19]

Circumcision,* a very prevalent practice, has both sexual and spiritual connotations and may serve a variety of functions: hygenic precaution, test of endurance, symbolic sacrifice, sanctification of procreation, badge of incorporation into the community, mark of subjugation, symbolic castration by a father figure, or an expression of male envy of women's menstruation.[20] The last function was proposed by Bettelheim[21] in a book titled *Symbolic Wounds: Puberty Rites and the Envious Male*. In it he presents an elaborate psychoanalytic formulation of the role of male genital mutilation and its underlying theme of envy of the female capacity for reproduction.

Often instruction on sexual matters is provided the initiate although occasionally the initiate may hold an asexual status during the period, perhaps to emphasize the quality of transformation through the rites. Frequently the initiation carries with it a clarification of sex role. Through acts of bravery and endurance a boy is able to clarify and establish his manhood. The shared hazards of initiation as well as the acquisition of secrets serve to establish and support strong communal bonds among members of the same sex. Religious and social education are provided and the initiate is prepared to assume the role of the responsible male adult.

Spindler[22] has suggested that the rigor and toughness which often characterize male initiation rites serve to convince the adolescent that he is better off joining society rather than fighting it. However, not all male rites are arduous and painful. Among the California Indians, initiates were provided with vision-producing substances. Through the events of the ceremony and their accompanying visions, they gained insight into the vocations they were most suited to pursue—such as dancer, singer, or potter.[23]

GIRLS' PUBERTY CEREMONIES

The reproductive capacity of the female and the event of menstruation are frequently the central theme of female rites. As with males, initiation rites also incorporate the sexual, the spiritual, and the communal. Female rites similar to male rites have been reported in many societies with accompanying accounts of genital operations. Generally when these occur, they include a removal of the clitoris and/or the labia minora, the inner folds surrounding and closing over the vaginal opening. As with males, these rites and operations do not always accompany puberty.

In some puberty rites girls are tortured and frightened; in others they become the focus of admiration and celebration.[24] Two frequent themes occur: those of a childbearing motif such as guarantees of feritility and easy childbirth; and ceremonies, practices, and instruction designed to further the achievement of cultural standards of beauty and sexual desirability. In the later categories are practices of scarification, changes in mode of dress, postural concerns, and information about sexual practices. The period of the puberty ceremony may also be used as a time of instruction about the facts of sexual intercourse and pregnancy. However, the spiritual is not absent. Ceremonies often elaborate the frequent association of femininity and the powers of the moon.

The consistency of the aims of puberty ceremonies for girls may reflect widespread commonalities in the adult female roles of wife and mother. Historical evidence indicates that these roles have been the predominant ones for women for centuries, even in those societies where economic and technological advances could free them from the many demands of childrearing.[25] Thus, the occurrence of more clearcut puberty rites for girls may reflect the crystallization of the female sex-role identity around themes of fertility.

In a detailed survey of the ancient puberty rites for girls in the Indian tribes of western North America, Driver[26] uncovered a large variation of practices along with some constant characteristics. Frequently there was seclusion, the presence of an attendant, restrictions on food and drink, a scratching taboo, specific work tasks at the time of menstruation or afterwards, and avoidance of hunters, fishermen, or men in general. The general beliefs about the menstruating pubescent were that she was unclean and might harm other people, animals, or crops. She was believed to be especially susceptible to harm if she did not strictly observe the various taboos. Her actions at first menstruation were believed to determine her behavior throughout life. Public recognition of girls' puberty among the American Indians appeared absent in all but western North America. The rites appear to be ancient in origin with roots established prior to human migration to the New World; the diffusion pattern follows a north–south direction with similar elements being found in the north and in Tierra del Fuego at the tip of South America. While Driver emphasized the more negative connotations of menstruation, it is not clear that it was viewed as negatively by the participants. The avoidance and isolation of a menstruating woman by hunters served the practical purpose of avoiding odor clues of human presence. The isolation also provided the women with an opportunity for solitude and meditation. Among the Indians of South California the girl, during her first menstruation, was placed in a pit of warm sand—a comfortable treatment for any attendant discomfort. She was provided with a vision-inducing herbal drink while women danced and sang around her. At that time and during subsequent menstruations she ate a low-fat diet devoid of meat, salt, and cold water. The special diet and menstrual isolation were associated with visions, often of a useful sort. She might receive wisdom by dreaming of specific animals with which to communicate, or more practically, get an idea for a new basket pattern.[27]

Clark[28] has described a puberty ceremony for Apache girls which still takes place on the San Carlos Indian Reservation in Arizona. The girl's first menstruation is recognized by a brief ceremony and is later followed by an elaborate sacred public ritual lasting as long as nine days. In the ceremony the girl represents the wife of the sun, the ever-changing woman earth. Her adolescent companion represents the moon. There are special costumes and dances involving the older women and girls of the tribe. Observed by relatives, members of the tribe, and visitors, the ritual provides dramatization and symbolic enactments of life's multiple stages and the passage from childhood into young womanhood. In one part of the ceremony a woman walks on the girl "molding her into the graceful form of womanhood." She is to become a woman with a nice disposition and good morals, who will live long and have many children. During the ceremony the pubescent is believed to possess special healing powers. After the ceremony, she is eligible for marriage. The Navaho *kinaaldá*, a ceremony commemorating a girl's first menstruation and repeated on her second, is still retained.[29] The themes are similar to those of the Apache rites.

Anthropological studies of sub-Saharan Africa and of the Pacific regions also reveal a multitude of practices. Among the Otublo-hum subgroup of the Ga people of Ghana, a girl's puberty cere-mony was very important in guaranteeing quick and easy child-birth, good health, and success as a woman. Some families took advantage of this period to educate their daughters about the sex-ual facts of life and about childbirth.[30] The Nugulu, a Bantu people residing in east-central Tanzania, emphasize proper con-duct, skill in sexual intercourse, and subsequent fertility. The ritual also serves to control what are believed to be the dangerous accom-paniments of female reproductive capacity.[31]

The theme of danger associated with female reproduction occurs also among the Maroni Caribs, an Amerindian group living in Surinam, South America. The girl at menarche is secluded in a small hut built especially for her and must omit her daily bath in the river and wear old clothes to avoid being carried off by *Oko:yomo*, the waterspirit, who cannot stand the smell. This evil spirit must be avoided during subsequent menses as well. After a confinement of about eight days, the girl participates in cere-monies designed to impress her with the virtue of hard work. When asked the function of the rite, the Caribs respond that it is good in and of itself, and that, secondarily, it serves as a means to secure fulfillment of the woman's role.[32]

In India the fear of pollution from the female during menstrua-tion, childbirth, and particularly menarche remains potent. Dur-ing such times the woman is rendered temporarily untouchable, as she is considered by herself and others as impure. Evil spirits are attracted by her impurity and she must protect others from con-tamination. At the onset of her first menstruation she is secluded from others and prohibited from eating meat and fish which are believed to be passion-raising foods. In a recent survey of 1200 In-dian women of wide range of social class, all but 23 reported segre-gation at puberty and the most common lengths of seclusion pe-riods were 15 and 10 days. The belief in pollution, while weakening slightly, still appears to be a clear feature of female life in India.[33]

SUMMARY

The responses to puberty are in large measure determined by culture. Not only is the pubescent's interpretation of what is happening subject to historical and social forces, but so are the reactions of family and members of the community. In modern culture the events of puberty receive little formal notice. However, they mark entry into adolescence, a stage of life which receives a great deal of both formal and informal recognition.

Formal or informal rites facilitate the transformation of the individual from child to adult. Their form varies from culture to culture, although three consistent themes are present: separation, transition, and incorporation. Where specific rituals occur, they are more closely tied to physical development for females than for males. Male rituals often involve themes of death and rebirth. Female initiations focus upon menstruation and reproductive matters. Sex role clarification and sexual instruction are often an integral part of ceremonies for both sexes. Underlying the concept of adolescence and many rites of passage is the recognition of the changes of puberty—sexual maturation and expanded intellectual potential.

SUGGESTED READINGS

Bakan, D. Adolescence in America: from idea to social fact. *Daedalus*, 1971. *100*, 979–95. Also reprinted in Kagan, J. and Coles, R. (eds.) *12 to 16: early adolescence.* New York: Norton, 1972.

Bettelheim, B. *Symbolic wounds: puberty rites and the envious male,* revised edition. New York: Macmillan, 1962.

Brown, J. K. Adolescent initiation rites among preliterate peoples. In Grinder, R. E. (ed.) *Studies in adolescence: a book of readings in adolescent development,* 2nd edition. New York: Macmillan, 1969, pp. 59–68.

Eliade, M. *Birth and rebirth: the religious meanings of initiation in human culture.* New York: Harper & Brothers, 1958.

Kett, J. F. *Rites of passage: adolescence in America, 1790 to the present.* New York: Basic Books, 1977.

Precourt, W. E. Initiation ceremonies and secret societies as educational institutions. In Brislin, R. W.; Bochner, S.; and Lonner, W. J. (eds.) *Cross-cultural perspectives on learning*. New York: Wiley, 1975, pp. 231–50.

Serei, C. African rites of passage. *Thought*, 1972, 47, 281–94.

Spindler, G. D. The education of adolescents: an anthropological perspective. In Evans, E. D. (ed.) *Adolescents: readings in behavior and development*. Hinsdale, Ill.: Dryden Press, 1970.

Young, F. W. *Initiation ceremonies: a cross-cultural study of status dramatization*. Indianapolis: Bobbs-Merrill, 1965.

3 *Changing Body*

We are born twice over; the first time for existence, the second for life; once as human beings and later as men or as women.

Jean Jacques Rousseau

Puberty brings into sharp focus the fact that humans come in two body types designed primarily for the purpose of sexual reproduction. We may choose to emphasize other goals, aims, and reasons for existence, but the physical developments of puberty have to do with sex—like it or not. The differences between males and females emerge shortly after conception, and sexual differentiation is a gradual and continuous process, becoming most evident during sexual maturation. In childhood the male develops a longer forearm in relation to total arm length and body length. Girls have a wider pelvic area than boys. Yet, it is puberty which brings with it a clear definition of one's female or male body. The physical changes are inescapable and the differences between the sexes are far more obvious after puberty than they were before.

A major point of differentiation arising directly as a result of puberty is the increase in strength and energy which occurs in males as a result of the increased production of sex hormones. Nationwide tests of physical fitness (sit-ups, long jump, abdominal strength, etc.) show that girls improve their fitness scores steadily until the age of 13 or 14 when their performance levels off. Boys' fitness scores continue to increase as they get older.[1] There are no differences in strength of arm thrust between boys and girls until about age 13. Then the boys show a rapid increase in strength while the girls' strength remains level. Boys have an edge over girls in power of arm pull, but the difference is not great until puberty when the boys' strength increases dramatically.[2] While prepubescent boys can throw a ball more accurately and further than prepubescent girls, the difference is due to practice rather than strength and coordination. If the children's ability and strength are tested using their nonfavored arm (the left arm for right-handed individuals) the sex differences disappear. However, differences in strength in the nonfavored arm appear at puberty.[3]

From birth through puberty and perhaps into adulthood the female has on the average a developmental edge on the male in terms of timing. Events associated with maturation such as walking, talking, and reading occur earlier in girls than boys. Girls also mature sexually earlier than do boys. However, while the growth spurt in females occurs about two years before that in males, the earliest pubertal development occurs only six months prior. Within each sex, the *sequence* of pubertal maturation is predictable, but the *rate* at which the events occur is highly variable. The differences between the sexes lie more with the order and nature of the events than with timing. It is necessary to consider the development of the sexes separately. Comparisons can be made, although close analogies in development are absent. The male shows no event comparable to menarche (the first menstruation). The rhythm, even when irregular, of menstruation is quite different from the spontaneous and unpredictable occurrences of penile erection and ejaculation in the male. Furthermore, the same physical developments, such as the height spurt, will have very different significance for the two sexes.

WHAT CAUSES PUBERTY?

While much is known about puberty, the precise events which trigger it are not fully understood. Three physical structures are involved: the hypothalamus, the pituitary gland, and the gonads (ovaries in females and testes in males) (Fig. 3-1). The *hypothalamus* is a small bundle of nerve cells in the brain which influences a number of body functions including water balance, temperature regulation, and appetite. The hypothalamus also produces a set of chemicals aptly called *releasing factor* (RF). These are secreted into the bloodstream and carried to the pituitary gland. The *pituitary gland* is a pea-sized organ located near the hypothalamus. Stimulated by RF, the pituitary gland produces its own chemical substances called *gonadotropins*. These are hormones* whose func-

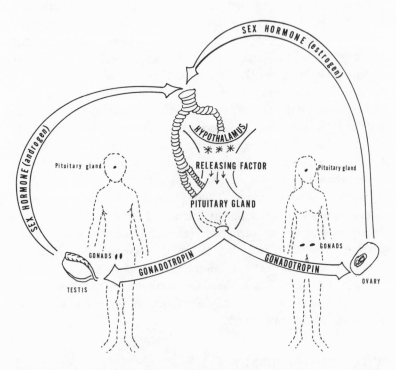

Figure 3-1. Schematic representation of the relationship between the hypothalamus, pituitary, and gonads.

tion is to stimulate the gonads. The gonads, in turn, produce and secrete into the blood system their own hormones (sex hormones) in response to gonadotropin stimulation.

For the mature female the pattern of hormonal secretion is cyclic and produces the rhythmic occurrences of menstruation. The pattern for cyclic secretion is present in the brain prior to birth. In the male fetus the presence of androgens* eliminates the neural basis for the menstrual cycle. Thus, gonadotropin secretion and sex hormone release in the male tend to be constant rather than cyclic. Although the cyclic potential is established prior to birth in the female, it remains quiescent through childhood. Until the late childhood years, gonadotropin production is very low in both sexes, as is the production and secretion of sex hormones.

For reasons not yet fully understood, in late childhood the pituitary output of gonadotropins begins to increase under the influence of the hypothalamus. As a result of the increase in this stimulation, the gonads grow and produce increasing quantities of sex hormones, particularly testosterone in the male and estrogen and progesterone in the female. These sex hormones are responsible for the development of the sex characteristics associated with puberty such as the growth of pubic and underarm hair, and changes in body shape and voice quality.

The hypothalamus is sensitive to small quantities of sex hormones circulating in the bloodstream. As the level of sex hormones increases, the hypothalamic output of RF is reduced, thereby reducing the pituitary's output of gonadotropin. Thus, a self-regulating mechanism exists among the three sets of glands—hypothalamus, pituitary, and gonads. A prevailing theory about the onset of puberty is that throughout childhood the hypothalamus is sensitive even to the very minute amount of hormones produced by the immature boy's testes or the immature girl's ovaries and that in later childhood this sensitivity to feedback is reduced. Thus, instead of shutting down RF production, the hypothalamus keeps on stimulating the pituitary which in turn stimulates the gonads, and puberty occurs. A new equilibrium is established in later adolescence.

What remains to be explained is the mechanisms of change in the hypothalamus. It is likely that maturational changes in neural growth and in other brain structures play a role.

Factors Affecting the Onset of Puberty

Most research on the onset of puberty in females has used menarche as an indicator. Very little information is available about factors affecting the onset of puberty in males. Since the triggering mechanisms involve the hypothalamus and other brain structures, we can assume that some of the generalities derived from research on the timing of menarche apply to males as well.

Genetic factors play a major role in the timing of puberty. Age at menarche is very close in identical twins and between mothers and daughters.[4] However, the genetic predisposition is modifiable by a number of environmental factors, e.g., severe stress and malnutrition delay the onset of puberty. The age at menarche has shown a downward trend from what it was 100–200 years ago. In 1860 the average age of menarche in the United States and countries of western Europe was nearly 17 years. Records of the height of English males indicate that a century ago maximum height was achieved as late as the early 20s.[5] However, the downward trend of puberty has leveled off in the developed nations. Hebrew and Roman practices and laws of ancient origin indicate an age of puberty not dissimilar from that found in United States today.[6] A combination of genetic plus environmental factors is probably necessary to account for the differences reported from historical periods.

The influence of climate in either hastening or delaying maturation is debatable and is likely to be mediated by genetic, nutritional, and possibly light exposure factors.[7] Research findings indicate that the onset of puberty is earlier in urban areas[8] and at lower altitudes.[9] Hints of a possible relationship between season and menarche have been provided, but are far from clear.[10,11]

A "critical weight" hypothesis of the onset of puberty in females has been developed by Frisch and Revelle.[12] They hypothesize a direct relationship between weight and menarche. According to their hypothesis, when weight reaches a critical level, the metabolic rate is altered, thereby disturbing the equilibrium between the hypothalamus and the gonads, or perhaps weight and menarche reflect the effect of a third set of factors. Using data from three longitudinal growth studies, they found that the mean weight at menarche was 47.8 kilograms (about 105 pounds) and that it remained constant despite differences in age at menarche. Animal studies have also indicated that age at puberty bears a closer relationship to body weight than to chronological age. The critical weight hypothesis explains the declining age of menarche in Europe as a result of increasing body size. The association of malnutrition and delayed onset of puberty could also be accounted for by this hypothesis. On the average twins are slightly smaller than the single born and also reach menarche at a later age; obese girls tend to menstruate earlier than average. These observations support the critical weight hypothesis. In a later study[13] the mean weight at menarche of 30 undernourished U.S. girls did not differ from that of 30 well-nourished girls from the same area and race. However, the undernourished girls began menstruating two years later than the controls. The validity and dynamics of the critical weight hypothesis require further investigation. The factors controlling puberty are probably related to maturation as a whole. Pubertal development usually occurs following a certain degree of skeletal maturation, and maturation of the body and maturation of brain structures are correlated.[14]

The hormonal events described in this section bring about profound changes in physical development and appearance. The most thorough documentation of the physical changes of puberty has been provided by Tanner[15,16,17] and it is from his work and that of his associates that most of the following specific information is derived.

SEXUAL MATURATION IN GIRLS

There is great variation in the normal time of onset and completion of puberty. Growth is rapid and dramatic for some individ-

uals; for others, it is longer and more moderate in tempo. Figure
3-2 illustrates the average and normal variability in pubertal development. While one girl may be achieving her full pubertal development at age 13, a second girl may be just beginning (Fig. 3-3).

Increases in sex hormones from the ovary, primarily estrogens,
lead to the maturation of accessory sex structures—the vagina,*
uterus,* and clitoris;* and the secondary sex characteristics—breast
size increase, hip size increase, and growth of pubic and underarm
hair. Hormonal secretions from the adrenal* contribute to pubertal development. Bone and muscle development, body and hair
growth, and the thickening of the skin are influenced by adrenal
hormones in both sexes. While hormones produced by the ovary
initiate growth of the genitals and the development of secondary
sex characteristics, some time is required before hormonal activity
is sufficient to bring about menstruation.

The budding of the breasts is more often the first outward indi-

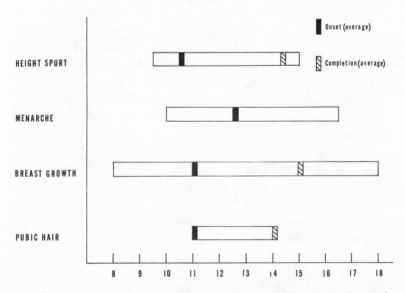

Figure 3-2.   Normal range and average age of development of sexual
characteristics in females (data from J. M. Tanner, Growing up. *Scientific American*, 1973, 229, 35–42).

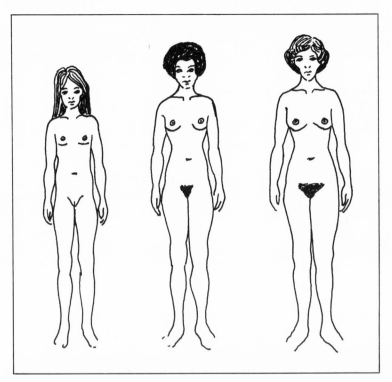

Figure 3-3.   An example of variability in degree of sexual maturation in female age-mates—all three fall within the normal range of development at age 12½.

cation of the underlying hormonal changes. However, in about one out of three girls, the appearance of pubic hair precedes breast budding. Breast growth and an increase in areola area (the pigmented area around the nipple) may begin as early as 8 years or as late as 13 years and still fall within the normal range. The uterus and vagina mature at the same time as breast growth is occurring. The labia* and clitoris become larger.

Another early pubertal event is the acceleration in growth, often referred to as the height spurt. It may begin as early as 9.5 years and results from the influence of pituitary growth hormone and androgens produced by the adrenal gland. The height spurt usually ends around 14 years of age. Children who develop early tend to show a sharper rate of increase; that is the adult height is attained more rapidly. Thus, earlier maturation may carry with it an exaggerated quality due to the suddenness of the jump in height. The increase may be perceived differently by the girl and by the boy as a result of our expectations of ideal height relationships among men and women. Men are "supposed" to be taller than women, and on the average, they are. That they often are not is obvious to any woman over 5'5" or man under 5'8".

Occurring at about the same time as the height spurt is the development of pubic hair, followed shortly by underarm hair growth. The appearance of pubic hair is variable in the sequence of changes of puberty in both sexes, despite its status in the naming of the phenomenon, L. *pubes*—hair.[18]

Menarche, generally beginning around age 12 or 13, always occurs after the growth spurt has peaked. For most girls menarche is a late event in the sequence of pubertal changes. Early menstrual cycles are often, though not always, anovulatory—no egg is released from the ovary.

Data from the National Health Survey, 1966–70,[19] are available for age at menarche, based on the parent's report. A breakdown of the data by race for blacks and whites is presented in Table 3-1.

Blacks show a somewhat earlier menarche than whites in that among 11 year olds, nearly twice as many blacks as whites were menstruating. The racial difference in timing of menarche was found within various categories of family incomes and places of residence (urban vs. rural, geographical location, etc.). Data obtained from older women about their age at menarche drawn from another segment of the survey also indicated the age difference by race.

Following menarche, girls may grow a bit taller, 6 centimeters on the average, but a major increase of height does not normally occur, probably as a result of the effect of circulating estrogens in bringing bone growth to an end. Of all the various indices of developmental age, skeletal maturity (the stage of bone growth) is

Table 3.1. Cumulative percentages of girls at each age whose menstrual periods had started (age at last birthday). (From MacMahon, B. Age at Menarche. *National Center for Health Statistics. Vital and Health Statistics.* Series 11: Data from the National Health Survey, no. 133.)

	Age at last birthday							
Percentage reaching menarche	6–9	10	11	12	13	14	15	16–17
Whites	0.2	0.8	11.6	41.7	72.9	91.4	98.2	99.6
Blacks	0.2	4.0	21.2	51.2	74.1	93.5	98.7	100.0
All girls in survey	0.2	1.2	12.8	43.3	73.2	91.7	98.3	99.7

the most accurate. An analysis of a radiograph of the bones in the hands and wrist provides a precise prediction of developmental age—of how much more growth will occur. Skeletal maturity correlates closely with the other developments of puberty and is a more accurate indicator of impending menarche than is chronological age.

SEXUAL MATURATION IN BOYS

Boys also show a high degree of variability in maturation and timing of pubertal changes. The first external sign of puberty for boys is increasing growth of the testicles with a reddening and wrinkling of scrotal skin and in some cases the development of pubic hair. The accessory internal structures, such as the seminal vessicles* and the prostate,* enlarge. Beginning testes development is followed in about a year by an acceleration of penis* growth and the height spurt. The *beginning* of the penis growth spurt occurs normally between the ages of 10.5 and 14.5 years. In the technologically developed nations of the West the age for *completion* ranges from 12.5 to 16.5 years. One sees again the tremendous variability which can constitute normal growth (Fig. 3-4). One boy may have reached adult levels of genital develop-

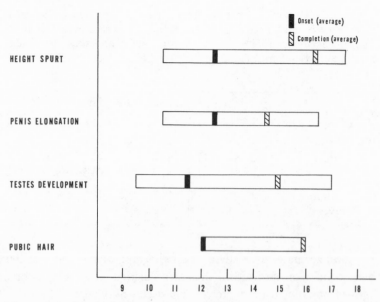

Figure 3-4. Normal range and average age of development of sexual characteristics in males (data from J. M. Tanner, Growing up. *Scientific American*, 1973, 229, 35–42).

ment before his age-mate has even begun the pubertal sequence (Fig. 3-5). Ejaculation of seminal fluid generally occurs about a year after the acceleration in penis growth. A boy may have previously experienced erection and ejaculation as a result of genital manipulation. Erections in the absence of stimulation become more frequent as a result of the hormonal increases associated with puberty.

While for girls an acceleration in height is a very early sign of puberty, for boys the peak velocity in growth, the "shooting upward," occurs fairly late in the sequence of changes. The variability in the normal range of the beginning and end of the acceleration of growth is shown in Figures 3-2 and 3-4. While boys are on the average somewhat taller than girls before puberty, from ages 11 to 13 years girls tend to be taller and heavier than boys. The shift is due to the earlier onset of height acceleration for girls.

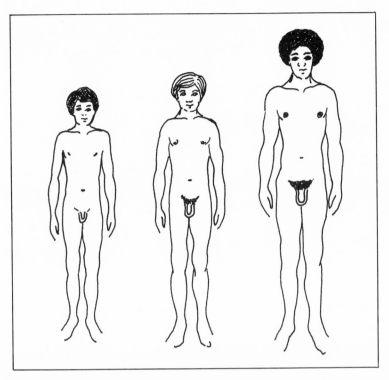

Figure 3-5. An example of variability in degree of sexual maturation in male age-mates—all three fall within the normal range of development at age 14½.

Breast development occurs to some extent in boys. The areolar area grows and sometimes an enlargement in one or both breasts occurs. The swelling eventually disappears but can be a source of concern to a boy who isn't aware of its temporary nature. The appearance of underarm hair is variable. However, it generally appears a couple of years after pubic hair and is accompanied by increased body hair and facial hair. The moustache, a later development of puberty, first appears at the outer corners of the mouth, and subsequently develops across the upper lip, on the cheeks, then below the lips, and finally along the edge of the chin. Facial and body hair patterns and amount are related to genetic factors. The deepening of the voice in males is a late pubertal event resulting from growth and changes in the larynx.

OTHER ACCOMPANIMENTS OF PUBERTY

Complexion problems and acne are common concerns for many adolescents. The increased production of androgen hormones accompanying puberty in both sexes leads to an increase in skin thickness and stimulates the growth of the sebaceous glands— small glands in the skin which produce oil. Often these small glands grow more rapidly than do their ducts to the surface. The result is clogged pores, inflammation, and infection with the appearance of blackheads and pimples and in severe cases acne, an inflammation of the sebaceous glands. A survey of 6768 American youths ranging in age from 12 to 17 years indicated that one-half of all interviewed reported they had blackheads, pimples, or acne.[20]

Figure 3-6 shows the differences by age. Among the 12, 13, and 14-year-olds, 19 percent of all boys and 27 percent of all girls were using some sort of acne medication, a sizeable group of consumers for such products. Girls expressed more concern about their complexions than boys in the pubescent age group and the degree of concern for both sexes increased with age, with boys expressing more concern than girls in the later teen years (Fig. 3-6). Because androgens contribute to sebaceous gland activity, boys on the average have more severe cases of acne than girls.

The height spurt of puberty is often accompanied by an increase in body fat. This is due in part to hormonal changes and to increased appetite accompanying the rapid rate of physical growth. The fat usually disappears as hormonal balance is restored and as height increases. As part of the same survey from which the acne data were obtained, respondents were asked whether they felt they were overweight, underweight, or about right. There was a declining satisfaction with self-perceived weight with age through the years of puberty. Being heavy was of increasing concern for the girls. The boys showed an increasing dissatisfaction with their

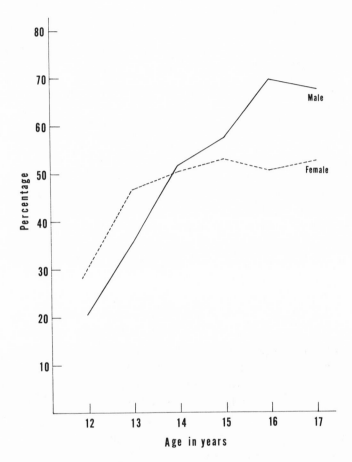

Figure 3-6. Percentage of U.S. youth reporting acne, pimples, or blackheads, by age and sex (from J. Scanlon, Self-reported health behavior and attitudes of youths 12–17 years. *National Center for Health Statistics, Vital and Health Statistics, Series 11,* Data from the National Health Survey, #147).

height. By age 14, 48 percent of the girls interviewed wished they were thinner, while 50 percent of the boys wished they were taller. Only 21 percent of the girls wanted to be taller, and only 16 percent of the boys wanted to be thinner.[21] Thus both sexes show an

increased as well as differential concern about their body throughout puberty.

Body Image and the Timing of Puberty

In the process of growing up people develop a body image which
is a mental representation of how they look. The degree to which
this reflects physical reality is highly variable. Some previously fat
people retain a fat body image long after becoming thin. Body image is more than a mirror reflection. The labels and responses provided by others are incorporated into it. If told by a parent that
we are plain, that quality may be incorporated into our body image. While a body concept includes objective physical attributes,
the positive or negative interpretation of each attribute is highly
subjective and influenced by cultural ideals. Wide lips and wide
hips as well as massive and light builds are differentially valued by
various groups and cultures.

By puberty the average person has a fairly stable body concept.
Thus, maturational changes produce an inevitable discrepancy between body image and actuality. The psychological impact of the
body transformations will depend upon the rapidity of the change,
the degree of preparation for it, social expectancy, stereotyped images projected by the culture, and one's own social and psychological security. Based upon her cross-cultural observations, Margaret
Mead[22] has stated that bodily preoccupations seem to be greater at
puberty than at any other time. The body changes intensify self-
awareness and comparisons with peers. Difference resulting from
variations in the timing of puberty may be equated with inferiority
and bring dissatisfaction with physical appearance. In general,
rapid pubertal change has a more pronounced effect on behavior
than a more gradual one. Also, changes in body size and shape are
likely to be more salient for girls than boys in Western culture because of the greater emphasis on female beauty. Awkwardness
rather than handsomeness is more of a concern for the young
male.[23]

In one longitudinal study, early puberty carried with it social advantages for boys but no immediate ones for girls. Early-maturing

boys were more popular with their peers and teachers. Both early-maturing boys and early-maturing girls were later found on the average to have more favorable self-concepts than those who reached puberty at a later age.[24,25,26] In another study involving the retrospective reports of college students, males who described themselves as late maturers scored lower on dominance and higher on succorance. The differences among the females were less clear, although for both sexes, late-maturers scored higher on a measure of anxiety than did early-maturers.[27]

From a psychoanalytic perspective, Peskin[28] assuming a fairly direct relationship between rising hormones and sexual impulses, has suggested that early puberty shortens the period in which the child develops impulse control and expands cognitive function. With early puberty energy either is taken up with sexual expression or becomes absorbed in overcontrol and inhibition of sexual impulses. In either case less energy remains for the pursuit of intellectual mastery and competence. Late-maturing boys were more "motorically purposeful and cognitively skillful" when compared with the early maturers. While the cognitive advantages may accrue as a result of a longer latency phase, it is possible that increased cognitive development serves as a compensatory mechanism for a delayed maturation. A different dynamic is offered for girls. Early onset of puberty brought stress and a turning away from social contacts, coupled with an increased receptivity to inner feelings. The late-maturing girls, in contrast, were more attuned to the demands of the external environment. According to Peskin, delayed puberty provides a lengthened period of freedom from confrontation with sexuality in social relationships; while a negative aspect of the delay is development in a climate which is "too safe" for true competence to emerge, an inference based on follow-up of these same individuals in adulthood and the finding that in later life the early-maturing females were the more self-possessed and self-directed adults compared with late-maturing females. Most of the evidence demonstrating a relationship between the timing of puberty and personality comes from the Berkeley and Oakland Growth studies which were begun in the late 1920s.

However, other longitudinal studies made in Denver, Colorado, and in Cambridge, Massachusetts, have not revealed a clear relationship.

How one responds to the events of rapid body change, the development of secondary sex characteristics, and menstruation or nocturnal emissions will be influenced not only by their timing, but more importantly by the individual's perception of them. This in turn depends upon the attitudes of those around and on preparation for these changes and events. While in general one would expect an early maturer to experience more difficulty in coping with puberty, one cannot predict this on an individual basis. Chronological age does not measure psychological maturity. A well-adjusted 10-year-old who views physical growth and change as natural can often accept menarche with less trauma than an older girl who is fearful of her sexuality and its accompanying body changes and social demands. For most pubescents, the transition has both positive and negative aspects. The confidence and competence developed during the grammar school years may be shaken. Some security and dependence must be forsaken as one is faced with the inescapable fact of maturation. On the other hand the powerful and positive features of being a teenager are inviting.

It is very important to recognize and respect the variability in maturational rates. Students whose physical development is vastly different may be found in the same school classroom. A mature-looking young man of 14 will be expected to show an analogous maturity of emotion and deportment whether or not he is psychologically ready. A physically well-developed young woman of 13 may be in no better position emotionally to cope with the sexual approaches of male adolescents than her undeveloped age-mate. The late developer is often still temporarily free of such pressures. Further, perception of one's own early physical maturity may lead to the assumption of a more mature social role in general. A more adult social role entails both positive and negative outcomes depending upon whether one chooses to emphasize adult responsibilities or adult prerogatives.

SUGGESTED READINGS

Berenberg, S. R. (ed.) *Puberty: biologic and psychosocial components.* Leiden, Netherlands: H. E. Stenfert Kroese B.V., 1975.

Grumbach, M. M. and Mayer, F. E. *Control of the onset of puberty.* New York: Wiley, 1974.

Malina, R. M. Adolescent changes in size, build, composition and performance. *Human Biology,* 1974, 46, 114–32.

Money, J. and Ehrhardt, A. A. *Man & woman: boy & girl: differentiation and dimorphism of gender identity from conception to maturity.* Baltimore: Johns Hopkins University Press, 1972.

Tanner, J. M. Growing up. *Scienctific American,* 1973, 229, 35–42.

4 Changing Mind

> I think that I think
> when I think, "do I think?",
> yes I think!
> That's what I think.
> I think.
>
> Jose, age 12

The pubescent is on the verge of becoming conscious of being conscious, of thinking about thought. Younger children think. However, they are not likely to introspect upon the thought process itself. Nor does the younger child express abstract ideas about intangible objects and events. God is a big person in the sky and Fairness means giving everyone equal portions. The child's ideas are derived from immediate experience grounded in present or fairly recent perceptual reality. Dreams reported by the child are of imaginable animal and human figures. Fear, hostility, and anger are presented in tangible forms rather than existing as vague forebodings. In contrast, the pubescent can consider a less immediate and more abstract intangible reality, a reality less directly tied to the senses. However, this capacity remains limited and represents only the crude beginnings of an articulation of new levels of self-awareness. As is often the case, understanding precedes the facility for clear expression. Children understand the meaning of words prior to using them. A name is more easily recalled when heard than when it must be dredged from memory. In a similar sense the pubescent may comprehend intangibles before being able to clearly express them in symbolic form—through words, gestures, or drawings.

The developing capacity for abstraction, being less bound to immediate reality, makes possible awareness of subtle differences of mood—the distinction between elation and happiness or between sadness and depression, for example. Yet, in the beginning the awareness may be fleeting and the feelings changeable.

> I think that I am a nice person. I'm not mean. I'm a Jesus be-
> liever therefore I try not to do bad things. I'm the kind of girl
> that worries a lot, over everything. I'm a very sensitive girl. I'm
> very emotional. There are days that I get into funny moods. My
> moods change like the weather. One day I may be in a bad mood,
> the next a good mood, a funny mood or a depressed mood. I care
> a lot about other people. I search to find myself. When I have
> nothing to do I write poems on whatever I feel at the moment. It
> helps me to find myself more. I think I'm an okay person.
>
> A ninth grader

Feelings and experiences become more differentiated and complex. With increasing awareness of both self and the world beyond self, ethical concerns grow more pronounced. Thus, new outcomes of thinking are a notable aspect of the pubescent period.

Three general factors contributing to changing thought are the cumulative effects of experience and education, the current demands of the environment, and the possibility of underlying maturation changes in the brain. There are a number of theories about intellectual growth and most include the three general influences listed above. However, theorists differ in their emphasis on the relative impact of each and disagree about the continuity or discontinuity of intellectual growth. Some theorists imply that there is a "mind adolescence" analogous to the body changes of puberty, while others insist that intellectual growth occurs in a smooth and progressive manner.

INFORMATION PROCESSING AND
CONCEPT FORMATION

Given the three factors influencing cognitive* development, one would expect that the conceptual abilities of the pubescent would be intermediate to those of the younger child and the adult. This does appear to be the case. Short-term memory span, which is generally measured by immediate recall, shows a rapid increase through childhood, leveling off at preadolescence with a continuing, but gradual, increase through adolescence.[1] Using an auditory task to assess memory capacity and information storage and retrieval, Friedrich[2] found that accuracy of recall was lower for 7- and 10-year-olds than for 14- and 17-year-olds. While both age groups used similar strategies for recall, the adolescents showed a greater memory capacity and a more efficient approach to learning. These studies and others like them in the area of information-processing[3,4] support a view that the pubescent-age child is conceptually operating as an adult but at a less efficient level.

A similar situation exists with respect to concept* formation, which shows a marked improvement during the pubescent years. Students from grades 2 to 10 were asked to identify the defining attributes of an equilateral triangle. They were to pick out correct examples of an equilateral triangle and state the basis for their decision. None of the sixth graders identified and correctly labeled all examples of the concept. In the eighth grade group 30 percent and in the tenth grade group 45 percent correctly identified, labeled, and explained their choices.[5]

Another approach to studying concept formation is to assess whether or not the person is using hypotheses.* For example, a person is presented with a series of objects which vary in size, shape, and color. The task is to figure out the criterion that the experimenter has chosen for grouping the objects. Using a hypothesis would be to say to oneself, "Perhaps it is *red*, now let's see if all the instances where red is present are correct choices."

In one study 88 percent of the children aged 10–12 years and 90 percent of the college students were using hypotheses of a predictable sort.[6] The older group performed considerably better on the tasks because a greater percentage used a trial-and-error selection and rejection of possible but incorrect hypotheses. Also, their memory was more efficient; they were better able to recall earlier outcomes. While both groups employed similar strategies, the older group used them more effectively.

CLASSIFICATION

The average 9-year-old is able to sort flowers into groups on the basis of color, size, or color plus size, as well as general petal shape, and still comprehend that all the elements fall within the larger category of "flower." A younger child has difficulty keeping in mind these hierarchical classifications. However, the categories used by the older child are still based on directly observable aspects of objects and events. Around the time of puberty youngsters show an increasing use of more abstract and superordinate* categories.[7] For example, Elkind, Medvene, and Rockway[8] compared the responses of middle- and upper-middle-class fourth and ninth graders who individually were shown a series of pairs of pictures and asked to describe ways in which the two pictures were alike (Fig. 4-1). Younger children were much more likely to respond to perceptual qualities, "They are both yellow," or to describe a function, "You can eat both of them." On the other hand, the ninth graders were more likely to use an abstract categorical concept,

PEACH   BANANA

Figure 4-1.   Example of pictures used to investigate concept formation.

"They are both examples of fruit." They were more likely to use superordinate categories which encompassed the entire object rather than relying upon a single attribute such as color or shape as a basis of commonality.

A similar trend existed among fifth and eighth graders from a much lower socio-economic background.[9] However, overall these students were more likely to utilize perceptual attributes rather than abstract superordinate categories. The development of more highly differentiated abstract concepts is linked to verbal learning; the ability to use words improves the classification process. Further, the use of abstract modes of thinking is also related to life experiences and to schoolwork such as mathematics. Thus, any variable* such as social class which influences verbal and numerical learning can be expected to affect concept formation and the development of abstract thought.

REASONING AND LOGIC

The child as young as six to eight years of age can deal in a logical manner with real, observable events.[10] These children can also handle conditional reasoning (if, . . . then) and class reasoning (all . . . therefore . . .):

> If this is Room 9, then it is fourth grade.
> This is Room 9.
> Is it fourth grade?
> (a) yes   (b) no
> All of Ted's pets have four legs.
> No birds have four legs.
> Does Ted have a bird for a pet?
> (a) yes   (b) no

While some children possess a clear understanding of the meaning of connectives such as *if* and *then*, many do not. Errors may reflect a misunderstanding of *then*, for example, rather than an inability to reason in a logical fashion.[11]

Age differences in reasoning ability become more apparent as the problems become more abstract and less dependent upon perceptual reality. Between grades six and eight students become more skilled in abstract reasoning on the following type of problems:[12]

1. All $ are *'s.
   This is a $.
   Therefore, this is a *.
   (a) yes   (b) no

2. If there is an X, then there is a Y.
   There is a Y.
   Therefore, there is an X.
   (a) yes   (b) no

3. All pittles are cloots
   This is not a cloot.
   Therefore, this is a pittle.
   (a) yes   (b) no

They are also better able to disregard perceptual reality in assessing logical correctness, as illustrated in the following problem:

All ants that can fly are bigger than zebras.
This ant can fly.
Therefore, this ant is bigger than a zebra.

One may wonder what experiments with extracting similarities among pairs of pictures, equilateral triangles, four-legged pets, cloots and pittles, and giant flying ants, have to do with getting along in the world. These logical and conceptual tasks are rarefied situations designed to tap into general thinking processes. The assumption underlying their use is that they bring out in a more clear and measurable fashion the processes which are used in making everyday decisions. Peel[13] has used examples which may help bridge the gap between the esoteric hypothetical* situations described above and day-to-day judgments. He asked students to pass judgments on situations that were more realistic:

All large cities have art galleries and Italy is exceptionally rich in art treasures. Many people travel to Italy, especially to enjoy these old paintings, books, and sculptures. Floods in the Florence area recently damaged many of these great works. Old paintings are rare, valuable, and beautiful and should be kept safely stored.

Question: Are the Italians to blame for the loss of paintings and art treasures?[14]

The responses to this question and others like it can be categorized on the basis of the reasoning employed—whether it is inadequate reasoning and is based on irrelevant aspects (Level 1), whether it is adequate reasoning but remains highly specific to the circumstances (Level 2), or whether the thinker went beyond the immediate content and considered possibilities based on past experience or generated from other situations (Level 3). The flooding responses and their categorization provide examples of different levels of reasoning.

No, not really, it's not their fault, they only had to keep them. (Level 1)

No, because they've got lots of treasures. (Level 1)

I don't think they are, I think it was just the weather, and the rain had to come. (Level 2)

Well, I should't think so, not really, because of the floods, I mean, they didn't let the flood come did they. (Level 2)

Well, not entirely, but they were partly because they could have put them somewhere where they weren't damaged by the floods, but if there was nowhere to put them then they were not to blame. (Level 3)

Well, not completely, they could have been kept safe, unless the floods took them completely by surprise. I suppose they did, but it might be best to protect them in glass cases. (Level 3)

Peel found a dramatic transition from content-dominated thought of the first and second levels to possibility-invoking thought of the third level around the ages of 13–15 years. Prior to this age, the youngsters' answers were characteristically limited to obvious descriptive and circumstantial aspects of the proposed situation. They showed very little capacity to imagine extenuating circumstances and showed little grasp of intentionality.* Even after age 15, there remained a group whose thinking remained at the restricted and circumstantial levels of 1 and 2.

The shift from concrete to abstract thought is not without its hazards. There is much to be said for concrete thinking with its emphasis on perceptual qualities. Over-reliance on abstract qualities can lead to a diminution of sensitivity to detail as well as an overlooking of important distinctions. While peaches and pears are both fruit, they remain quite distinct from one another. A reliance on abstract categories can lead to a decline in awareness of the individual and specific. In more gross forms abstraction can lead to insensitive responses such as "if you've seen one redwood tree, you've seen them all," or thinking of the deaths of hundreds of people as insignificant if some larger goal is achieved. There is a great deal more to successful living and learning than the application of abstract principles and logic. However, our school system is most concerned with the latter objectives. Thus, abstract reasoning correlates highly with school achievement; it is for this reason that IQ tests, which are specifically constructed to measure abstract skills, are good predictors of academic success. The so-called solid courses are mathematics, science, English, history, and the like. They rely heavily on abstract concepts. Courses in which good performance reflects skills of a more concrete nature such as auto mechanics, shop, drafting, painting, and musical performance are often either downgraded or seen as frills by educators. It is very important that abstract skills be developed, particularly in light of their importance for work and survival in our complex society. However, it is of equal importance that we cease downgrading valuable skills and abilities of a more perceptual and concrete nature which contribute greatly to successful problem solving and expression.

THE BASES OF COGNITIVE CHANGES

Continuity

Many psychologists, particularly those in the United States, believe the changes in intellectual performance of early adolescents are part of a continuous process of cognitive growth, a process which in large part is the result of learning. Sudden shifts or discontinuities in intellectual growth are attributable to environmental influences. Differences between age groups in cognitive development are assumed to arise from variations in efficiency of learning rather than in the kind or type of learning. Efficiency in turn reflects prior experience, training, and reinforcement. A general assumption is that learning is the same for all species and does not differ in form from one period to the next within the life cycle.

Discontinuity

In contrast, Jean Piaget and his associates, particularly Barbel Inhelder, acknowledge the importance of the environment but also place a great deal of emphasis on the role of maturation in intellectual development. In their view intellectual development is discontinuous and progresses in stages. The events characterizing each stage are invariant; that is, the stages always occur in predictable order; however, the timing of the stages varies from individual to individual and by culture because of both genetic and environmental influences. Piaget's conception of the stages of intellectual development is presented in Table 4-1. The latter phases of the stage of concrete operations and the early phases of the stage of formal thought are most pertinent to puberty.

During later childhood, the grammar school years, the child acquires the capacity for *concrete operations* (see Table 4-1). An *operation* in a broad sense refers to any type of action in which categories or propositions are manipulated. More specifically, the term *operation* applies to actions which are integrated in one's mind with internalized versions of other actions. An awareness of these internalized operations permits manipulation, particularly

Table 4-1. Piaget's stages of intellectual development

Sensory-motor stage (0–2 years). Material for thought is provided by muscle movements and sense impressions. Associations made between action and its effects form the beginning structure of the intellect.

Stage of preoperational or intuitive thought (2–7 years). With the acquisition of language, objects and actions may be represented by symbols, thus permitting internalized action or thought. An object may represent something else—a tricycle may serve as a horse, or a doll represent a baby. However, while much of the child's play is symbolic in that it is imitative and includes much pretending, concepts and rules are not used in accordance with a logical system of a series or of categories. Seeing Santa Claus on every street corner poses no problem for the preoperational child, as reason is dominated by perception.

Stage of concrete operations (7–12 years). The child is now able to think of actions and events in a series and understands that a chain of actions may proceed forward or in many cases be reversed. This capability permits an understanding of the principle of conservation, that altering the shape of a piece of clay does not affect its quantity, for example. The operational child understands principles of seriation, that 7 is more than 4 and 2 is less than 5, and can classify objects and events into hierarchical categories. While symbolic manipulation is greatly increased, thought tends to remain concrete; symbols represent tangible objects and events.

Formal operations (12 into adulthood). The capacity for formal operations is the ability to manipulate hypotheses or propositions in the absence of concrete referents, to think in an abstract manner. Formal thought is also characterized as systematic and rational. One can now think about thought.

---

reversibility. Thinking about an action in one direction permits thinking about a reverse action. Changing a clay ball into a flat pancake can be contemplated as well as returning the pancake to a round shape, as illustrated in Figure 4-2. This capacity to think about actions without actually doing them reduces the immediate dependency of cognition* upon direct observation. It permits thought in the absence of action. To an older child or adult it is

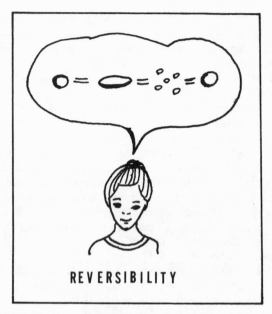

Figure 4-2.   An example of understanding the concept of *reversibility,* providing the basis for concrete operational thought.

difficult to imagine not possessing this capacity for reversible operations. However, it does not appear to be present in the very young child. Prior to the development of operational thought, the child relies heavily on immediate sensory experience. Judgments and decisions are often based upon a single quality or dimension as demonstrated in problems of conservation.* When asked which of two glasses of water contains more, the preoperational child generally selects the taller, though narrower, of the two, even when it has been demonstrated that the same amount of water has been poured into each (Fig. 4-3). The association of height and quantity has been learned, but the compensating factor of width has not yet been integrated with that of height. The child is not mentally reversing the observed action of pouring the water from one glass into the other and thereby recognizing that the amount of water remains constant despite the direction of the action.

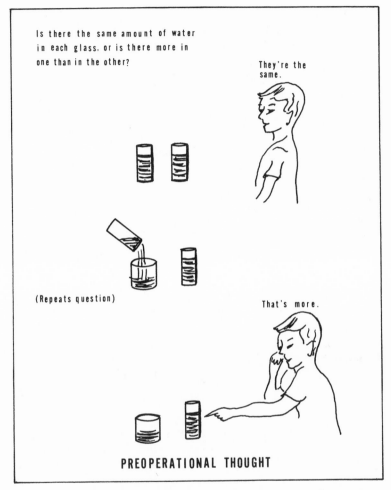

Is there the same amount of water in each glass. or is there more in one than in the other?

They're the same.

(Repeats question)

That's more.

PREOPERATIONAL THOUGHT

Figure 4-3. An example of the failure to conserve and reliance upon intuition; thus the child's thought is described as preoperational.

Thus, the child is not yet performing an operation with respect to the amount of liquid.

With development, the child masters the principles of conservation and reversibility and is able to manage the logic of classes and relations. Ideally she can then manipulate series of numbers (a basic necessity of arithmetic), knows that one can create more or less by adding or taking away, and that these are reversible procedures. These operations can be made on a number of dimensions such as the *size* of a piece of clay, the *amount* of liquid in a glass, or the *number* of marbles on a table. At the same time the child learns serial relationships, the idea that 9 is more than 7 but less than 10. She can also classify objects according to particular attributes and can understand superordinate classes, for example, fruit, flower, square, and animal. Such a child has entered the stage of concrete operations.

Equilibration

The biological principle of *equilibration* has been suggested by both Piaget[15] and Werner[16] as the basis for cognitive development. The living organism, providing its own energy, acts and moves; and, relying on feedback, regulates its own adaptation. In the case of the child the influence of feedback depends upon the mental representations she has available. These representations or mental structures, which can also be considered as ideas or thoughts about the world, have been derived from actions and the mental representations of prior actions. Maturational processes may also provide a potential for new mental structures. Disturbances in the equilibration produced by maturation or by environmental events activate the self-regulatory process leading to alterations in mental structure. In the process of adapting to the environment, the person establishes an equilibrium with it. Small failures of logic or failures of one's existing mental structures interfere with adaptation and disrupt equilibrium. In so doing, these failures promote intellectual growth which occurs as new structures are formed to more adequately meet environmental and internal demands. However, if the discrepancy between the environmental reality and the person's existing mental structure is great, change is unlikely because the feedback is unrecognized. The establishment and disruption of equilibrium produces the various stages of development. In middle childhood, with the acquisition and mastery of concrete operations, equilibrium is established. The child has solved the discrepancies between amount and appearance by comprehending the principle of reversibility.

Around the time of puberty an increased capacity for abstract thought emerges, which Piaget has termed the capacity for *formal operations* (see Table 4-1). *Formal* differs from *concrete* in that it refers to the ability to manipulate abstract concepts, to perform operations by means of symbols, and to use *propositions** and *hypotheses.** The materials for thought need no longer be restricted to observable and tangible object characteristics.

Culture and education play an important role in the disruption of equilibrium and the development of *formal operations*. Piaget[17] suggests that in the Western nations a majority of people achieve formal operations by the age of 20. Depending upon the aptitudes and specialized training of the individual, full maturation of thought may not occur in all areas. For example, a mathematician may think of the workings of a car engine in a simple and concrete manner. Formal structures, once developed, may be used in different ways, as in deductive* and inductive* logic. Thus, the stage of formal operations does not possess the same degree of consistency and invariability associated with the stage of concrete operations.

In a similar vein Vygotsky[18] points out that during grammar school years the child becomes conscious of and thereby able to control a great many intellectual functions, primarily attention and logical memory, memory guided by meaning rather than mechanical memory. What the children only later become conscious of, and hence able to develop volitional control over, is the intellect itself, or in Vygotsky's words the "consciousness of being conscious." He suggests that a gradually increasing awareness of one's own mental workings leads to the capacity for increased symbolic representation. Competence in the skills of attention and logical memory, for example, would be necessary before symbolic manipulation is done with ease. Both Piaget and Vygotsky utilize Claparède's law of awareness, ". . . that the more smoothly we use a relationship in action, the less conscious we are of it; we become aware of what we are doing in proportion to the difficulty we experience in adapting to a situation."[19] As we master skills we are then able to turn our awareness or consciousness into other domains. In Vygotsky's view growing awareness rather than a disruption in equilibrium becomes the mechanism involved in the advent of formal or symbolic thought. By puberty the person has developed sufficient skill in concrete operations, serial reasoning, classification, and simple logic, that these no longer require the effort and attention they once demanded. Hence, the pubescent is more free to focus on new realms of inquiry. As thinking becomes less tied to directly observable events, one can think about thoughts, contemplate the unobservable, and mentally structure whole series of "as ifs," "what ifs?" and "why nots?"

During pre- and early adolescence, thought expands from the consideration of *what is* to *what might be*. The domination of thought by perceptual processes is weakened. In Jerome Bruner's[20] terms, thought becomes less *ikonic* and more *symbolic*. Ikonic thinking involves a matching of external events or objects with their internal representations, a mental manipulation of images derived from sensations and experience. Symbolic representation requires breaking away from dependence upon images resembling external objects and events. The child begins the road to symbolic representation long before puberty with the development of language. However, language begins as more sign than symbol, as words reflect tangible characteristics. Mathematics and logic represent more abstract thought less dependent upon imagery. At puberty much thought remains ikonic in nature, although symbolic representation is increasing.

DISCUSSION

The contradictions among the views presented remain to be resolved. It is very difficult to settle the continuity-discontinuity argument, which may be a pseudoproblem. There is good evidence in support of both views and, as pointed out in Chapter 1, degrees of continuity or discontinuity may reflect the level selected for analysis. It is also possible that specific abilities vary, with some being more continuous in their development than others. Unfortunately, the distinction and tension between the two views remain because they each suggest very different approaches to education. The continuity assumption implies that (1) education should focus on the learning system, which does not differ greatly among age groups and (2) acceleration is desirable. The view of intellectual development as continuous and incremental (proceeding by small steps embodied in learned associations) has been a guiding notion in U.S. public education. The use of drill and graded examinations reflects the view of quantitative development, and, in the past, grade level was independent of age. In contrast, the discontinuity assumption suggests that educational programs need to be different for persons at different levels of mental growth and that acceleration may be neither possible nor desirable. A view of curricula development over the years show a pendulum-like fluctuation between the two approaches. Currently many schools attempt to incorporate both assumptions, using a more continuous model in the early years with the introduction of unique topics and more conceptual material in the junior high years.

There has been some evidence of a positive relationship between the maturational changes of puberty and mental development. However, this evidence is based on correlations obtained in very large samples. In surveys of hundreds of people the earlier maturers were found to be cognitively advanced over their later-maturing age-mates.[21] However, as these results reflect *average* differences, they have little applicability to the individual. A similar result has also been obtained in small samples where other factors such as social class are carefully controlled.[22] However, other researchers have claimed that the obtained relationships between pubertal development and mental growth are simply coincidental.[23] Peskin[24] has even suggested that a late maturation in boys is associated with increased intellectual competence in later years. These contradictory impressions imply that while the changes of puberty might have some effect upon the brain, thereby influencing mental development, the effect, if a true one, is only one among many determinants of mental growth and is probably by no means the most critical. None of the theorists disregards the importance of interactions between individual and environment and the effects of prior experience. Puberty plays a role in intellectual development by serving as a source of new experience. It disrupts one's previous adaptations to the world and with oneself.

AN EXAMPLE OF COGNITIVE CHANGE
IN PRE- AND EARLY ADOLESCENCE—
POLITICAL IDEOLOGY

The evolution of political attitudes provides much insight into the cognitive development occurring through the late childhood and early adolescent years and sheds light upon the moral workings of the intellect as well. A number of factors influence political attitudes: family attitudes, education, and prevailing social beliefs. Comparisons of children of different social class and ethnic or racial backgrounds indicate the same general trends which are found in adults of these groups. Most youngsters support the party of their parent's choice. While there is an increase in skepticism and critical evaluation with age, in general positive feelings toward the government remain quite strong.[25] Past studies have shown boys expressing more political interest and knowledge than girls. However, a recent survey of children and adolescents in grades 4 through 12 found sex differences to be less marked.[26] Political ideology remains fluid, if present at all, throughout early and middle adolescence. Children who were expressing highly favorable and compliant views about the president and the government in general in the late 1950s were vigorously protesting and often engaging in defiant acts in the 1960s, underscoring the influence of situational variables—in that case an unpopular war.

The various environmental influences are filtered through the individual's developing cognitive patterns. Adelson and his associates have studied political views of preadolescents and adolescents by analyzing explanations and judgments made in response to questions about political processes and institutions.[27,28,29] The following quotations are examples of responses of 11-year-old and

13-year-old boys to the question, "What is the purpose of government?"

Age 11 Years

> To handle the state or whatever it is so it won't get out of hand, because if it gets out of hand you might have to . . . people might get mad or something.
>
> Well . . . buildings, they have to look over buildings that would be . . . um, that wouldn't be any use of the land if they had crops on it or something like that. And when they have highways the government would have to inspect it, certain details. I guess that's about all.

Age 13 Years

> So the people have rights and freedom of speech. Also so the civilization will balance.
>
> To keep law and order and talk to the people to make new ideas.
>
> Well, I think it is to keep the country happy or keep it going properly. If you didn't have it, then it would just be chaos with stealing and things like that. It runs the country better and more efficiently.

The answers of the 11-year-olds were consistently very concrete. Those of the 13-year-olds were varied, sometimes like those of the older adolescents and at other times like those of the preadolescents. Theirs were the most difficult to classify as concrete or abstract because they often used a mixture of the two modes of thought. The 15-year-olds showed a good grasp of formal thought, and there were few ideas expressed by 18-year-olds that weren't available to the 15-year-olds. While the 18-year-olds knew more, the form of thought of the 15-year-olds was just as mature.[30]

Drawing upon a sample of 11- to 18-year-olds of both sexes from the United States, West Germany, and Great Britain, questions were posed regarding the hypothetical situation of setting up a new society on a Pacific island. It should be noted that the three countries show many cultural similarities, particularly with respect to present form of government and systems of formal education. Thus, the findings remain specific to the small range of culture sampled. The young people were interviewed on a number of issues relating to the proposal. Age differences in the growth of political concepts were far more distinct than differences of sex, intelligence, social class, and nationality. Adelson found that between the ages of about 12–13 years and 15–16 years, a marked shift in the character of political thought occurred. The young adolescents became more abstract in their views. They shifted from a mode of personalizing the institutions of society expressed in comments about policemen, admirals, and teachers as individuals, to discussions of law enforcement, armed forces, and education as more abstract entities. Along with the capacity for abstraction the researchers found an extension of time perspective. The middle adolescent showed a deeper comprehension of the effects of history, although it still remained undeveloped. The pre- or early adolescent showed little sense of either past history or future consequences in evaluating various social and political proposals. Adelson wrote:

> Furthermore, one must reckon, in this age group, with an occasional descent into sheer confusion. What is one to make of the following statement? The young man, thirteen years old, has been asked why a certain law, forbidding the smoking of cigarettes on the island, has proved difficult to enforce. "Because people who are used to it now . . . well, if you say that you can't drive cars around, well that would be awful. Then people would go ahead and drive around, but you could see it. Well maybe you could have no newspapers, but then all the people in the newspaper business would go bapoof."[31]

Unable to handle the abstract logic often required in making political judgments, the pubescent may remain silent or produce a very unclear chain of associations. The muteness easily mistaken for defiance may stem from the realization that the simplistic, sometimes smug, answers confidently blurted out a year earlier are inadequate. Unfortunately the next level of cognitive sophistication has yet to be articulated. Under pressure from adults the subsequent confusion may lead to withdrawal or hostility on the part of the young person, or the "I don't know" response which really means "Don't ask me those kinds of questions." Yet it is the recognition of the inadequacy of earlier constructs which reflects a growing maturity and also leads to its furtherance, unless the adolescent retreats into a permanent know-nothing style.

Adelson described young adolescents in the United States, West Germany, and Great Britain (all of which have democratic forms of government) as showing little sensitivity to minority rights, being indifferent to claims of personal freedom, and possessing a rigid absolutist morality. Their attitude toward treatment of law-breakers was that if punishment doesn't work, punish harder. A powerful anti-idealistic attitude with a high degree of skepticism about human goodness was also expressed, particularly by the older adolescents.[32] The latter finding raises questions about adolescent idealism. With the development of formal thought the person becomes capable of distinguishing between ideal and real. However, this does not produce an automatic flood of idealism. Inclinations toward idealism appear linked to factors other than age and cognitive maturation alone. A clear understanding of the relationship of the state and the individual and an appreciation of the meaning of political philosophy occurs long after puberty.

While the family and school are powerful socializing agents affecting attitudes and idealism, they are not alone in their influence. Young people are very vulnerable to the influence of external events since attitudes are not crystallized and are subject to modification as a result of cognitive development as well as changes in the political arena. Hence, the important and potential role of education on political issues is obvious. However, the direct effect of political education as indoctrination at this age will probably be less potent than is feared by those who object to any political attitudes expressed in the classroom.

SUGGESTED READINGS

Arieti, S. The role of cognition in the development of inner reality. In Hellmuth, J. (eds.) *Cognitive studies, Volume 1.* New York: Brunner/Mazel, 1970, pp. 91–110.

Bruner, J. S. et al. *Studies in cognitive growth.* New York: Wiley, 1966.

Elkind, D. and Flavell, J. H. (eds.) *Studies in cognitive development: essays in honor of Jean Piaget.* New York: Oxford University Press, 1969.

Elkind, D. *Children and adolescents: interpretive essays on Jean Piaget.* New York: Oxford University Press, 1970.

Inhelder, B. and Piaget, J. *The growth of logical thinking from childhood to adolescence: an essay on the construction of formal operational structures.* New York: Basic Books, 1958.

Mischel, T. (ed.) *Cognitive development and epistemology.* New York: Academic Press, 1971.

Peel, E. A. *The nature of adolescent judgment.* London: Staples Press, 1971.

Piaget, J. Piaget's theory. In Mussen, P. (ed.) *Carmichael's manual of child psychology, Volume 1,* 3rd edition. New York: Wiley, 1970, pp. 703–32.

Vygotsky, L. S. *Thought and language.* Cambridge, Mass.: M.I.T. Press, 1962.

5 *Moral Development*

I feel like a fool when me and my friends
go out. They go into a store and steal everything they can and I feel very bad, because
it feels like I did it. I feel like a dog that's
been sick as a dog for years.

Michele, age 13

Moral development is very much a part of intellectual growth, and
concepts of morality show adaptations through the pubertal years
corresponding to emerging levels of cognitive insight. Injustice for
a six-year-old is getting spanked for someone else's mischief, while
the 15-year-old may clearly recognize the injustice inherent in
racial discrimination. The 15-year-old's moral concepts are more
complex, more differentiated, less egocentric, and more universal,
covering more instances of application than those of the younger
child. In addition to cognitive growth, parental identification, cultural values, patterns of reinforcement, and situational factors
also contribute to the morality of young adolescents. The evolution of moral judgment as well as the determinants of moral behavior form the substance of this chapter.

MORAL JUDGMENT

"I forgot." "It's not my fault." "I didn't mean it." "I was just kidding." These are frequently heard statements issued defensively by accused teenagers and to a lesser degree by prepubescents as well. They reflect a common understanding of the role of intent in the evaluation of right and wrong. The younger child judges the morality of acts on the basis of their consequences rather than on their intent—breaking a dish accidentally is as serious as doing it on purpose. According to English Common Law and the Catholic Church, the capacity for true moral judgment (distinguishing between right and wrong) is not present until the age of seven years.[1] Stated in the more modern terms of developmental theorists, by the age of seven, the concept of intent is generally understood and it is also about this age that the average child has a grasp on concrete operations. However, moral development does not cease at seven years, nor does puberty bring it to a close. The bases on which acts are evaluated as right or wrong continue to change long past early adolescence. While both the 9-year-old and the 18-year-old may consider it wrong to strike another person, the reasoning which leads them to the same conclusion might be quite different. The work of Lawrence Kohlberg[2] and his associates deals with these changes in the logical process of making moral decisions. Building on the views of Piaget, they have asserted that children and adolescents show invariant stages of moral development corresponding to cognitive or ego development.[3,4] Much of their research involved presenting persons of differing ages with moral dilemmas and asking for solutions. One of the most frequently used examples is that of a man who steals an expensive drug in order to save his dying wife. The person is quizzed as to the correctness of the man's act. Should the husband have stolen the drug? Why, or why not? Based on the administration of similar problems to people of all ages, Kohlberg has identified three levels of moral orientation, each of which has two sequential stages[5] (Table 5-1). The first level is the *Preconventional* (premoral) level in which control of conduct is external and motiva-

Table 5-1. Stages of moral development postulated by Kohlberg. (From L. Kohlberg, Moral development and the education of adolescents, in R. F. Purnell, ed., *Adolescents and the American High School.* New York: Holt, Rinehart and Winston, 1970.)

Level I—Preconventional level
        Stage 1. Obedience and punishment orientation
        Stage 2. Instrumental-relativist orientation
Level II—Conventional level
        Stage 3. "Good girl—nice boy" orientation
        Stage 4. "Law-and-order" orientation
Level III—Postconventional level
        Stage 5. Social contract, legalistic orientation
        Stage 6. Universal-ethical priniciple orientation

---

tion is hedonistic.* In the first stage, characterized by an obedience and punishment orientation, moral decisions are subordinate to superior power or prestige. One seeks reward and avoids punishment. At this stage responsibility is evaluated in terms of consequences rather than intent. Stage 2 reflects an instrumental-relativist orientation. Acts defined as right are those which satisfy the self in some instrumental way (as opposed to satisfying one's conscience). A social element may be introduced "you scratch my back and I'll scratch yours," but the basis for such judgments remains external.

At the *Conventional* level, morality consists of performing good acts and maintaining the social order. While control of conduct remains external, motivation becomes largely internal; that is, behavior becomes less dependent upon external reward or punishment. Stage 3 is characterized by a "good girl-nice boy" morality where the maintenance of good relations with others is of utmost importance. Intentions begin to play a role in moral judgment. In Stage 4 retaining good relationships is superseded by the need to do one's duty in maintaining the given social order. Obedience to authority is paramount. Injustice is a violation of the rules of the land. Kohlberg calls this the "law and order" orientation.

When control of conduct is internal, the person has reached

the *Postconventional* level. The standards to which one conforms are one's own and decisions to act reflect inner processes of thought and judgment. In Stage 5 a contractual and legalistic orientation prevails. Morality reflects shared standards and rights for all. Law, a social contract serving the general good, influences moral judgment in a contractual sense rather than as something requiring blind obedience as in Stage 4. Stage 6 represents a move to adopt universal ethical principles. Conduct and moral judgment are based on internal values irrespective of the actions of others.

According to Kohlberg this sequence is invariant but the timing is not; nor is intelligence a good predictor of moral stage, although mental retardation would be associated with less mature moral development. Many adults of average and above-average intelligence function at Stage 2—where right action consists of whatever works. Combining Kohlberg's data with Piaget's stages of cognitive development, we can infer that pubescents are most likely to provide moral judgments at the Conventional level with a mix of Preconventional judgments and an occasional Postconventional decision. In a study of 13-year-old middle-class urban U.S. boys, most of the solutions to the dilemmas fell within the Stage 3 category with Stages 4 and 2 the next most frequent, in that order.[6]

In articulating these stages Kohlberg helps to clarify direction and goals which may guide educational processes and social planning in the area of moral development. Experience and culture affect the rate and how far one progresses through the stages. Kohlberg specifically rejects the cultural relativist view that virtue is determined solely by the culture in which one lives. Rather, he sees his stages as reflecting a universal system of character development of all humans and quotes his longitudinal studies in support of this view. In response to the question "Should a doctor 'mercy kill' a fatally ill woman requesting death because of her pain?" the following answers were obtained:[7]

> At age 13, Richard said about the mercy-killing, "If she requests it, it's really up to her. She is in such terrible pain, just the same as people are always putting animals out of their pain," and in

general showed a mixture of Stage 2 and Stage 3 responses concerning the value of life.

Compare the above with the following response of the same person three years later:

> At 16, he said, "I don't know. In one way, it's murder, it's not a right or privilege of man to decide who shall live and who should die. God put life into everybody on earth and you're taking away something from that person that came directly from God, and you're destroying something that is very sacred, it's in a way part of God and it's almost destroying a part of God when you kill a person. There's something of God in everyone."

The latter response was classified as Stage 4, primarily because of the emphasis on external authority, the primary authority of God, rather than on autonomous human values.

Kohlberg's theory is important, complex, and controversial. Because of the recency of his formulations, much work remains to be done in testing out its applicability. A prime contribution is the recognition that the answers to moral dilemmas provided by the child and adolescent are very much in a stage of transition. The response of a 15-year-old should differ greatly from the response that same person gave some years earlier, and we should be concerned that subsequent moral development does indeed take place. The potential for moral development clearly extends beyond childhood and adolescence.

Sometimes a difference between pubescent and adult in an assessment of a moral issue may not be one of a conceptual nature, but instead reflect a misunderstanding of the terms used. For example, an apparent inability for logical thought may simply be a matter of not clearly understanding the precise meaning of the connectives, *if* and *then*.[8] Terms and phrases, like concepts, may remain ill-defined, though frequently used. Such linguistic ambiguities serve to obscure the actual level of cognitive development, as illustrated in the following account:

> "How about lending the cause some money for a hamburger and a coke tonight." "Okay," I said, handing her two one-dollar bills.

"Are you babysitting tomorrow?" "Yeh," she replied, as she gave her hair a final pat and headed for the door. Three days later there were cries of moral outrage and indignation at the two dollar deduction from her allowance. "It's not fair," she cried. "What do you mean," I asked. She slammed the door. I was indignant, too—about her failure to pay back the loan. After all, hadn't I tried to impress her with the value of money? It was not until two weeks later, when asked to "lend to the cause" again, that we both realized what had transpired. "Lend?" I said, "wait a minute, what do you mean?" "You know," she replied with some annoyance at my denseness, "a contribution." "Aha," I exclaimed, bouncing with recognition, "a semantic* error." "Huh?" she said (wincing because living with a psychologist isn't easy). "A loan you have to give back. A contribution, you keep," I told her. "Ah!" she said.

MORAL KNOWLEDGE AND INTERNALIZED VALUES

Descriptions of the evolution of moral judgment, while illustrating the role of cognitive maturation, do not account for the process by which a person comes to hold the moral values dominant in the culture. One must consider how moral knowledge is acquired and the extent to which a person acts upon those learned moral precepts. An enduring and popular belief is that moral acts follow the dictates of one's conscience. Moral development is in this view equivalent to the development of conscience, the internalized representation of values and principles. The young child is very dependent upon parents for affection and care. In order to gain parental nurturance, the child identifies with them and internalizes their value system. In psychoanalytic theory, internalized social values and ethical systems constitute the superego, one of the structures of personality. Modification of the classical psychoanalytic theory has led to the conceptualization of the conscience as a part of the ego, incorporated into one's view of self.[9] In any case conscience, derived from the process of identification, comes to represent a set of internal principles assumed to guide behavior.

Further enforcement of morality is provided by social institutions of law, government, and religion. Marriage and other legal sanctions serve to keep sexual expression within bounds. Religion rewards good behavior with promises of paradise and reduces sin through threats of purgatory and damnation. Such curbs on the expression of sexual and aggressive drives were seen by Sigmund Freud as essential to the development of civilization.[10] The ego defense mechanism of sublimation, channeling a basic urge into a socially acceptable and constructive purpose, makes civilization possible by redirecting our innate hedonism.* While the parents play a central role in superego development, the church and state have served to influence and support the parents in their resolve in enforcing prevailing standards and prohibitions.

Many nonpsychoanalytic theorists also recognize the role of identification and they have placed additional emphasis upon early experience and patterns of reinforcement. Through identification and internalization the child adopts the parental modes of responding as well as their value systems, or those of other significant adult figures. As these identificatory behaviors are reinforced they become the child's own. Adding the notion of cultural relativity, that right and wrong and culturally determined values, the study of morality and character development becomes largely the study of social learning from this point of view. While the psychoanalysts describe moral behavior as the outcome of the relative strengths of the id, superego, and ego processes, the social learning view is that different behaviors reflect different learning conditions.[11] A number of studies have examined the ways in which parents dealt with their children's transgressions. When parents asserted their authority directly and used punitive measures and material deprivation in dealing with transgressions, they produced in their children a moral orientation based on external sanctions. In contrast when parents asserted authority less directly in subtle expressions of anger and temporary withdrawal of love and approval, children tended to show a morality less dependent upon external sanctions and support.[12]

SITUATIONAL FACTORS

The fact of having acquired moral knowledge, that is, knowing right from wrong, is not a sufficient guarantee of moral behavior. Despite the importance of identification, behavior is dependent on much more than one's internal or expressed value system. There is a wide disparity between what individuals say is right and what they do. Studies of delinquents revealed them to be quite clear and conventional in their stated beliefs about good and bad. These findings mesh with the earlier ones of a famous study made by Hartshorne and May in 1930.[13] They found that whether or not a child chose to cheat on a test had more to do with opportunity and consequences than with conscience. Thus, determination of moral behavior was seen to lie more with situational circumstance than with the individual's expressed beliefs and attitudes.

Partly in response to the 1930 Hartshorne and May studies, Peck and Havinghurst[14] and a team of researchers in 1943 began a longitudinal study of children in "Prairie City," a self-contained midwestern town. They selected all the children who had been born in 1933, a total of 120. A smaller sample of 17 girls and boys was studied intensively from 1943 to 1950, from age 10 through 16 years. The researchers found a very high degree of stability in the pattern of motives and actions shown by these individuals during the seven-year period of observation. The persons who showed a high level of self-control at 10 years of age showed a high level of self-control at age 16. This is not to say that no changes occurred. At age 16 the young people exhibited more self-control than at 10, but the changes were maturational in nature and the aspects of character *relative* to peers remained the same. The findings of the Peck and Havinghurst studies argue against the likelihood of dramatic personality and character change as an accompaniment of puberty. Yet, the study clearly points out the occurrence of maturational and developmental changes in moral behavior. About one-fourth of the persons studied showed a transition from what the researchers termed the "conforming and irrational-conscientious" mode of middle childhood to the "rational-altruistic" behaviors attainable in adolescence and adulthood.

At first glance the Hartshorne and May study emphasizing situational factors and the Peck and Havinghurst results showing individual consistency over time may appear contradictory. However, they are not since both internal and external factors interact with one another to influence behavior. A quiet, shy person may be loud and raucous at a rock concert. Another may be assertive enough to speak in front of a large group of people despite stage fright. These behaviors do not belie the more typical quality of shyness if that is the person's more accustomed style. Controversies about moral development reflect the number of factors which influence it. Morality is not entirely a matter of conscience nor solely a matter of external opportunity; it involves both of these factors. The three major emphases—cognitive development as illustrated in moral judgment, internalized values, and situational factors—are not contradictory. They represent the numerous facets of morality.

EMPATHY AND AUTONOMY

Empathy and autonomy also play important roles in moral behavior. Various theorists have pointed out the biological underpinnings of moral behavior; that as a species humans are inclined to possess altruistic feelings, to be sensitive to others, to be generally amenable to accepting social regulation, and capable of self-regulation.[15,16] Cooperation was necessary for humans to have survived early hazards to existence. The biological propensities coupled with the extreme and long-lasting dependency of human young provides the basis for the processes of moral development, particularly identification and empathy. Empathy has its roots in childhood and refers to the ability to put oneself in the position of another, requiring a diminished degree of egocentrism. The pubescent is still a fairly egocentric individual. However, the growing responsiveness to others, seen in the close relationships with peers, reflects a further increase in empathy which continues well beyond puberty.

Autonomy generally refers to one's own will and is reflected in the independence of moral decisions. However, it seems obvious that moral choice may in fact be little more than a result of socialization, of an internalization of what were initially external values. Nonetheless, one can talk about a personal or subjective sense of duty which has become relatively independent of external pressure. While steps toward autonomy are being achieved by the pubescent with respect to family, independent judgment comes under new pressure from peers. Baumrind[17] indicates that a full development of individual autonomy does not emerge until the postadolescent years. Although the antecedents of autonomy lie in early childhood, the developmental process of becoming one's own person is not complete at puberty. Autonomy is facilitated by the development of personal competence. Both overpermissiveness and overrestrictiveness on the part of family can inhibit the sense of autonomy. Parents who are themselves autonomous and reward like conduct in their children, and who engage in verbal give-and-take, explaining rules and in general helping the child develop a personal set of values contribute to the development of autonomy.[18] This pattern would certainly be an important one to continue through the pubertal and adolescent years—with the young person being given more control over decisions and choices as well as being held accountable and responsible for the outcome of those decisions.

The learning and internalization of moral precepts (socialization), the development of empathy, and the development of autonomy are relatively distinct and independent of one another. The degree to which each is achieved in relation to the other two gives each person a unique character structure.[19] A highly socialized individual with a fair degree of empathy and little autonomy would probably be a conformist. Poorly socialized individuals possessing little capacity for empathy may behave in an antisocial manner if it suits their needs. By the time a child reaches pubescence, we would expect the process of socialization to have occurred and to see aspects of empathy with the bare beginnings of true autonomy. Thus, the conformity characteristic of early adolescence is not surprising. In summary, the moral behavior of the pubescent will reflect the level of cognitive development achieved, values learned and internalized in childhood, current situational factors, and degrees of empathy and autonomy. The provision of education and opportunity for continued cognitive growth plus the encouragement of empathy and autonomy are particularly important in understanding and guiding moral development through these years.

MORAL DEVELOPMENT IN THE USSR AND THE USA

Urie Bronfenbrenner[20] has pointed out the contrasting ways in which the societies of the Soviet Union and of the United States approach the moral development of children and how they use or fail to use the shift from family to peers as a vehicle for a perpetuation of social values. In the USSR as a result of very explicit, early, and consistent child-rearing and educational practices, the peer group becomes a vehicle for adult values. The principles of cooperation and the collective are stressed early in life. Responsibilities for one's fellows as well as oneself are inculcated. Older children are encouraged to set good examples for the younger ones. In the grammar school years, small groups or "links" are established in each classroom and each link member is responsible to and for every other link member. Long before puberty, the peer group begins to play an ever-increasing part in one's life. While parental responsibility for the child's behavior remains, it is not the sole responsibility, as is far more likely to be the case in the United States. V*ospitanie* or character education is everybody's business in the Soviet Union. Strangers do not hesitate to criticize parents who allow their children to misbehave.

In the United States the family is the main provider of education in morals, ethics, and character. The function of the school is restricted to nurturing the intellect and promoting skills and abilities. However, the family is becoming less potent in its ability to influence the child's character. A number of factors account for its declining influence. The extended family, as we once knew it, hardly exists in many urban areas. Aunts, uncles, cousins, and grandparents at one time served surrogate parent roles. While perhaps one's behavior was not the business of the neighbors, it certainly was the concern of relatives who by and large felt few compunctions about interfering. However, with our great geographical mobility and our ever-increasing age segregation, it is not at all unusual for many families to move every few years, weakening links with the extended family. As distance, both geographical and social, increases and contact decreases, there is an increasing reluctance to involve oneself in matters of the character education of other people's children. One doesn't want to meddle in the affairs of strangers. Hence, the total responsibility for the inculcation of values comes to rest on the parents. However, while they may have the responsibility, they are not necessarily the agents of character development. A survey of 766 sixth graders showed that on the average the children spent only two to three hours a day with their parents on the weekend.[21] As they approach puberty, children spend increasingly less time with their parents. The majority of their time is spent at school, with their peers, and in front of the television set. As mentioned before, the schools do not devote time and effort to the training of character. To a large degree the school is explicitly excluded from the realm of moral education because of the legal separation of church and state, as many moral values reflect religious ones. Television hardly provides a clear guide to responsible behavior. Thus, as one nears pubescence and begins the transfer of loyalty from family to friends, there may be little solid grounding in matters of principle and character. Additionally, one encounters a group of peers in much the same situation. This is not to say American children grow up without moral values. They often have internalized a number of values from the adults around them on the basis of modeling. However, the models often present inconsistent versions of which values are important. Consider the contrast between the junior high school faculty and the adults on the current detective series. While parents play a large role in value formation during infancy and early childhood, that role is sharply diminished as the grammar school years progress. Thus, with the decline in family influence and the presence of contradictory models, there is a great deal of discontinuity in the development of moral character. Religious institutions and organizations such as Scouts, the Y, and 4-H clubs attempt to fill the vacuum and do influence some, but by no means all, children. The separation of the various agents of social values would not constitute a problem if consistent value systems were being promoted. However, the American value system is not a consistent one; one is taught to be honest and obedient, but not to be a tattletale or a snitch. Helping others is okay, but don't be too eager because that's not cool; TV heroes and beautiful heroines are almost always cool. As adults we can weigh conflicting values for ourselves and not experience a great deal of conflict over them. However, while growing up, each of these ambiguities had to be sorted out and worked through in some manner. Given the discontinuity and contradictions in values, it is no wonder that pubescents may evolve concerns which are at odds with those of their parents. In many respects character development in the United States is left to chance and the television set.

Discontinuity between family values and peer values is very great in America and Western Europe. This does not reflect an innate quality of the pubertal process, as we have seen in the Soviet example where conflict is less frequent. Although we may not wish for the homogeneity of viewpoints which allows such continuity to exist, we still need to be concerned about having allowed a situation to arise where we no longer take necessary steps to achieve the development of internal guides to behavior in our children which are positive and productive and reflect a concern for others. We risk leaving the young subject to the potential destructiveness and alienation which result from an absence of commitment to a system of values and ethics. This is not an argument for reducing the young person's interest in peer society. Rather, we should insure that the pubescent has a proper grounding in moral principles in order to make the transition successfully.

SUGGESTED READINGS

Aronfreed, J. *Conduct and conscience.* New York: Academic Press, 1968.

DePalma, D. J. and Foley, J. M. (eds.) *Moral development: current theory and research.* Hillsdale, N.J.: Lawrence Erlbaum, 1975.

Hoffman, M. L. Moral development. In Mussen, P. H. (ed.) *Carmichael's manual of child psychology,* Vol. 2. New York: Wiley, 1970.

Hogan, R. Moral conduct and moral character: a psychological perspective. *Psychological Bulletin,* 1973, 79, 217–32.

Kurtines, W. and Greif, E. B. The development of moral thought: review and evaluation of Kohlberg's approach. *Psychological Bulletin,* 1974, 81, 453–70.

Loevinger, J. and Wessler, R. *Measuring ego development, Volume 1.* San Francisco: Jossey-Bass, 1970.

Turiel, E. Developmental processes in the child's moral thinking. In Mussen, P. H.; Langer, J.; and Covington, M. (eds.) *Trends and issues in developmental psychology.* New York: Holt, Rinehart & Winston, 1969, pp. 92–133.

6 *Sex Roles*

> A part of every woman is the little girl who
> dreamt about the day someone would find
> her and love her and give her a ring.
> A diamond is forever.
>
> Advertisement

There has been much research and argument on the topic of sex differences in determining sex roles. Sex *roles* refer to the expected behaviors associated with gender; other roles may be based on age, occupation, or status such as parent, teacher, or leader. The documentation of consistent and reliable differences between the sexes is substantial. The arguments usually focus on the sources of these differences—whether they are caused by biological factors or by social forces. The debate is unresolvable to some extent as one's gender is obvious at birth and immediately affects the responses obtained from the environment. Many aspects of today's sex roles arose at a time when women as nursing mothers were required to remain accessible to small children, were pregnant for much of their adult lives, and probably didn't live long beyond the reproductive years. The male role was of necessity one of protection, and to some degree provider depending on the availability of the food supply.

Female roles often reflect the secondary accompaniments of gender such as pregnancy, lactation, and menstruation. These are secondary because pregnancy and lactation are not inevitable, and while menstruation is a common female characteristic, it does not occur throughout life. While biology plays a part, sex roles are more than a simple outcome of anatomical and physiological sex differences.

Male dominance is a clear pattern found in human society. Males are more likely to make decisions for the group, whether it be family, clan, tribe, or nation. Those activities which have high status are generally performed by males. Whether this is because males can perform high-status activities more competently than females or because what males do is automatically assigned a high status, does not affect the conclusion that in most societies maleness and high status occur together. While not all males in a given society have higher status than all females, the top place on the hierarchy of power is generally held by a man. The rare exceptions—Catherine the Great, Elizabeth I, Queen Lileokalani, Indira Gandhi, and Golda Meir—serve by their uniqueness to illustrate the extent of overt male social dominance.

It is often argued that the social dominance of males over females results from their superior strength and a greater degree of aggressiveness. Gonadal testosterone is responsible for the muscular strength of men and has been associated with mating and aggressive behavior in numerous species. The assertiveness and dominance of male humans thus has been attributed by some theorists to hormonal influences. Again, the directness of the effect is difficult to determine. Simply put, the question is whether testosterone predisposes fighting behavior because of a direct influence on the brain—or do males fight because they have the necessary equipment provided by the hormonal enhancement of muscular development? The question has generated simplistic and inadequate answers—ranging from the assertion that men are inherently aggressive to the view that sex differences are solely artifacts of childrearing practices and that if boys and girls were raised identically they would be behaviorally indistinguishable. Genetic, maturational, and experiential factors must all be taken into account in attempts to understand social behavior among human and nonhuman primates; their substantial capacity for associations, learning, and memory carries them far beyond the more basic brain and body functions of immediate survival and reproduction.

In U.S. culture the general differences between the sexes and their roles in the realm of personality function can be summarized in a relatively brief fashion. Members of both sexes possess the same traits, but these characteristics tend to be distributed in varying orders of importance or dominance. Males have been described as being more "instrumental" and females as more "expressive," terms used by the sociologist, Talcott Parsons.[1] *Instrumentality* involves objectivity, effectiveness, action, and outward orientation, a direction which extends beyond the personal and which transcends immediate interaction. The *expressive* role is one of orientation toward relationships with others, a sensitivity to feeling, an inner orientation, a personal focus, subjectivity rather than objectivity, and mindfulness to the needs of others.

In a similar conceptualization of the duality of male and female, Bakan[2] suggested the modalities of *agency* and *communion*. Agency reflects a devotion to individual goals and a concern with self-protection, self-assertion, and self-expansion. Communion reflects the organism as part of a larger whole. In our society we stress agency concerns for boys and inhibit their development in girls. Conversely, communal aspects are fostered in girls but not in boys. Hence an adult society evolves in which women tend to be more nurturant, dependent, compliant, conforming, fearful, warm, and emotionally expressive; while men tend to be strong, assertive, objective, achieving, and task oriented. In an expansion of Bakan's concepts of agency and communion, Block[3] spells out how *socialization* (the internalization of values) affects the sexes differently. Socialization of males initially emphasizes agency aspects, their being individualistic and autonomous and assertive. Later, communal aspects are enhanced in males as they take on such roles as husband and father. More importantly, ethical values which require sensitivity to the needs, wishes, and welfare of others are instilled. Thus, the male option for character development is expanded in our society. However, for women, the socialization process is continuous in its deemphasis on agentic behavior, thereby reinforcing attributes of passivity, docility, nurturance, and general conservatism. Thus, the socialization process which results in the expansion of male personality is a stultifying one for women, and we should not be surprised in finding only a small minority of women who are able to stand firm against the cultural tide and expand their agentic as well as communal concerns.

What difference does a difference make?

Many differences between groups are discussed in this book—between males and females, ethnic groups, and socio-economic classes; and between age groups. The conclusion that two or more groups differ in some way is generally based upon an estimate of the average group performance or some other characteristic. A frequently used estimate is the arithmetic *mean*, calculated by adding together the scores of everyone in the group and dividing the total by the number of individuals. This single score is then used to characterize the entire group or population under study. Sometimes the *median* is used as an average. The median is the number below which one-half of the group scored. Again, a single score is used to characterize the group. For example, early-adolescent girls on the average are taller and heavier than boys of the same age, and, on the average, the thought of 10-year-olds is more concrete than that of 14-year-olds. These generalities do not apply to *all* early-adolescent boys and girls, nor to all 10- and 14-year-olds. Averages tell us about groups; they *do not* describe individuals.

When dealing with a large number of persons there is very often an overlap among individual measures. Figure 6-1 shows the scores obtained by female and male college students throughout the United States on the quantitative section of the Graduate Record Examination (Educational Testing Service, 1966). The overlay of the two distributions illustrates the average difference

SEX DIFFERENCES AND THE LIFE CYCLE

Instrumental or agentic men and expressive or communal women represent stereotypes and seem caricatures when applied to specific individuals. Nevertheless they reflect overall patterns in the population and numerous studies document the existence of these average differences among groups of men and women and boys and girls. However, there are some very interesting aspects to observe relative to sex differences when one looks at the entire life cycle. At birth and through early childhood one finds some sex

---

as well as the overlap in scores. The average score for the men was approximately 512 and for the women, approximately 451. The difference of 61 points, while sounding substantial must be considered in light of the range or spread of scores which extends from less than 300 to over 650 for the females and over 800 for the males, a span of more than 350 points. In this context a difference of 61 points is not as impressive as it would be if the range were only 100 points.

A second major point to consider is the amount of overlap. Half the males who took the Graduate Record Examination scored over 500 points, but so did a quarter of the women. In addition, a quarter of the men scored below the average score of the women. Thus, while we can say that *on the average* men performed better than women on the quantitative section of the Graduate Record Examination, we cannot predict with confidence that any given male will have a score higher than that of any given female.

A single characteristic such as sex, race, age, or social class is insufficient in describing the properties and capacities of individuals. For this reason it is extremely important to prevent misuse of group differences when they exist. The value of investigating differences among groups is in the discovery of how factors of experience, genetics, nutrition, education, etc., interact and contribute to population characteristics. Predictions which are valid for the general case must not be applied to individuals.

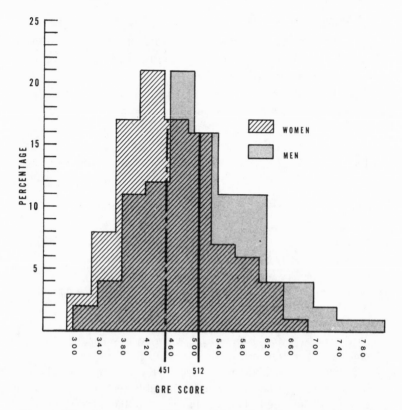

Figure 6-1. Percentage of female and male college students scoring within the various intervals of the Graduate Record Examination. Mean scores are given for the two groups (data from the Graduate Record Examination, *Educational Testing Service,* 1966).

differences—boys tend to be more active and fussy than girls, girls tend to speak sooner and show an overall accelerated pattern of development when compared to boys. However, these differences in infancy are relatively slight. Differences in sex hormone levels are practically nonexistent through early childhood, although in the prenatal phase the difference is quite distinct. While studies of the aged are far fewer than those of the young, it appears that sex differences diminish, as do the differences in the hormonal substrate. Male androgen production drops and female hormone production shows a marked decline with the involution of the ovaries and resulting menopause. In essence what one finds is a waxing and waning of sex differences occurring with the life cycle, and it would seem logical to expect the differences between the sexes to be most pronounced during the active reproductive years, which have in the past been the major period of a human's life. Following this logic we would expect sex differences to become more highly pronounced with the onset of puberty, not simply as a direct outcome of changes in hormonal level *per se* but of the effects of the hormonal changes on appearance and motivation.

Gender identity, the notion of one's own sex, has its beginnings at an early age. Any two-year-old will tell you with firm certainty that he is a boy or she is a girl.[4] Acceptance of socially prescribed sex roles is apparent by the time a child reaches preschool age. A four-year-old girl may disdainfully regard boys as rough and dirty, and boys unabashedly state that girls cannot be firefighters. The rigidity of their descriptions can be startling. However, when one considers the cognitive development of the child, the inflexibility is less surprising. Nevertheless, during the childhood years a fair amount of sex role flexibility is available for a child in our society. The roles are known but are often violated. Some boys are fearful and cry, while some girls get dirty and climb trees. Many boys keep pets and delight in being nurturant.

With puberty one confronts the inescapable confirmation of one's gender. Incomplete gender identification, which was previously overlooked as child's play, becomes more apparent, and ambivalent feelings about one's maleness or femaleness are difficult to suppress. The old rigidity connected with role stereotypes reappears in stronger form as if in response to hidden self-doubt. The fixed aspects of the perception of sex role are illustrated in the following study of students in grades five through college.[5] At all grade levels and for both sexes, examples of female success in mechanics were attributed more to luck and less to ability than was success in males. Female failure was seen as a result of the lack of ability where male failure was attributed to bad luck. Thus the stereotype of female inability in mechanical aptitude was well established by the fifth grade. Interestingly, an analogous result was not obtained for athletic performance, suggesting that prior stereotypes of female clumsiness and lack of coordination in sports are on the decline. Pubescents of both sexes expressed a strong fondness for sports participation.[6]

PERSONALITY

Assessments of personality reveal numerous differences between boys and girls in behavior, interests, and concerns. When young people from grades 4 through 11 were asked to evaluate personality traits, kindness and sociableness were more highly valued by females than males at all ages.[7] In another study girls, ages 12 to 19 years, described themselves as more sociable, nurturant, conscientious, help-seeking, and anxious than boys. The boys rated themselves higher on items reflecting qualities of detachment, self-sufficiency, and stability. While the differences were in the same direction at all the age levels covered, the girls appeared to become less yielding and more independent with age, while the boys showed increases in achievement, conscientiousness, and rule-boundedness with age.[8] From these and similar studies one sometimes gets the picture that girls at puberty are like restricted feminine stereotypes, whereas boys are like a horde of savages who later mellow and become civilized—a trend in accord with Block's description of the effect of socialization on personality.

In the California Growth Studies, a longitudinal survey which followed the same children from 21 months to 14 years of age, two periods were associated with increases in problem behavior—the preschool period and the pubescent period. Table 6-1 shows the incidence of problems reported by the mothers of one-third or more of the youngsters in the study. According to the researchers, this sample represented a normal, run-of-the-mill group.[9]

The problems shown in the 10- to 14-year-old range are those often associated with overcontrol as well as lack of control—for example, physical timidity as well as tempers, irritability, and dis-

Table 6-1. Behavior problems shown by one-third or more of the males and females (M and F), ages 10 through 14 (adapted from J. Macfarlane, K. Allen, and M. P. Honzik, *A Developmental Study of the Behavior Problems of Normal Children Between Twenty-one Months and Fourteen Years*. Berkeley, Ca.: University of California Press, 1954, p. 155.)

Behavior	10 years		11 years		12 years		13 years	14 years
Disturbing dreams	M	F	M					
Nailbiting				F			M	M
Oversensitivity	M	F	M	F	M	F	M	M
Specific fears			M	F				
Mood swings	M		M	F			M	
Shyness				F				
Tempers	M		M	F	M		M	
Jealousy	M	F	M		M		M	
Excessive reserve		F	M	F	M	F		F

turbing dreams. With respect to timing, the increased incidence of these problem behaviors corresponds with the beginnings of the pubescent process. Their extended continuity for boys may reflect later maturation for males. On the other hand, the existence of a greater number of problem behaviors among the boys at each age may reflect differential pressures on the sexes to resolve dependency conflicts. Boys experience more social pressure toward independence than do girls and may experience much conflict in this regard. This was especially the case at the time these children were reaching puberty, around 1940. While in some respects the California studies are out of date, they are noteworthy in their design, as they show the process of development among the same individuals over time.

Reports of higher anxiety among females have been a consistent finding. The question arises as to whether girls and women are in fact more anxious or whether they are simply more willing to display and report anxiety. Subjective states are difficult to assess in a way that makes them comparable. I cannot say with any certainty at all that "My headache hurts me more than your headache hurts you." In the same sense how can we know for sure who among us is the more anxious? Behavior gives us a clue, but a particular behavior often has more than one cause. More women than men seek psychological help, leading some researchers to conclude that women are more anxious. However, help-seeking and self-disclosure are part of the female role in our culture; they are not features of the male role. We have found in our own studies that pubescent males are much more likely to leave answers blank on questionnaires than are females. It is not clear whether the motive is a reluctance to answer (one could interpret the behavior as produced by anxiety) or whether there is an inability to respond to questions requiring some introspection. In any case the sex difference is quite dramatic.[10]

In a study of self-disclosure, Rivenbark[11] surveyed students from grades 4 through 12. Girls at all ages showed a greater willingness to reveal personal information than did boys. For both sexes disclosure to peers increased with age and the mother was generally favored over the father as a listener. Girls showed a greater willingness to talk to either parents and to their best girlfriend, with a decrease in disclosure to their best boyfriend. The boys in contrast showed with age a decrease in self-disclosure both to parents and best boyfriend. There was a total increase in self-disclosure to their best girlfriend, although the total amount of this was quite low. Using the same measure, Littlefield[12] surveyed blacks, whites, and Mexican-Americans from rural areas. Females in all three groups reported more total disclosure than males. However, the sex difference was not significant among the black students. The obtained order from highest to lowest disclosure rate was as follows: white females, Mexican-American females, black females, black males, white males, and Mexican-American males. For all the males the favored disclosure target was the mother and the least-favored was a friend of the opposite sex. For the black females, the favored disclosure target was the mother; for the Mexican-American and white females, the favored target was a same-sex friend. Females in all groups reported little disclosure to males.

Other sex differences in personality functioning appear in self-reports of interests and abilities. In a study of ninth graders, Wiggins[13] found that boys, more often than girls, described themselves as having more energy, being better athletes, and finding science easier. Self-ratings provided by the girls were higher on teacher-school relationships and interpersonal adequacy. The girls were more pleased with their height, considered themselves better dancers, better readers, better English students, and got along better with their teachers, and said they enjoyed committee work. While boys express greater academic aspiration, girls are more likely to indicate a liking for school. These observations are consistent with the previous description of instrumentality. Boys see school as instrumental, recognizing its role in achievement. Girls enjoy school for its own sake and for the social activity. They like the casual conversation about social topics and topics of personal significance. They enjoy visiting and family excursions far more than boys. The boys, by their own description, are far less likely to talk about intimate events of personal significance. The only topic they seem to show enthusiasm about is sports.[14]

COGNITIVE DIFFERENCES

During the pubertal years some cognitive differences between the sexes become apparent. Boys on the average show superiority in spatial perception such as visualization of two-dimensional drawings of objects in three-dimensional space. Girls show an edge over boys in verbal abilities, with the greatest difference around 10 or 11 years of age. The emerging differences in visual-spatial ability may underlie the sex differences obtained by Witkin, Goodenough, and Karp[15] on dimensions which they have labeled Field Independence and Field Dependence. They, and many subsequent experimenters, have used two general measures, the Rod-and-Frame test and an Embedded Figures Test. In the Rod-and-Frame Test, the person is seated in a tilting chair in a darkened room. An illuminated rod appears within a frame. The frame, the rod, and the chair in which the person is seated may be tilted and rotated independently. In one task the person in the chair is required through means of a control knob to adjust the illuminated rod so that it is parallel to the ground (which cannot be seen). The degree to which the person is distracted by the other stimulus cues in the field, such as the tilt of the frame relative to the rod or the angle of the chair, provides a measure of Field Dependence; the less distractability, the more Field Independence. Various tasks can be performed: to adjust one's chair position in relation to the rod-and-frame, to the ground, etc. These responses alone are not sufficient in labeling a person as Field Independent or Field Dependent because in one case the person relies on visual cues (when the chair is adjusted to match the frame or rod) and in the other on cues of balance and position derived from the sense organs of the inner ear (when the chair is made perpendicular to the ground). In both cases the person is depending on sense impressions, though of a different sort. At issue is the ability to separate elements and, for example, adjust to the rod without being influenced by the frame or body angle. What Witkin and his associates were attempting to characterize was that some persons' perceptions are dominated by the organization of the field or environment and that these individuals are relatively unable to perceive parts of the field as discrete from other parts. In these cases descriptions possess a global quality showing a limited differentiation of parts. In contrast, other persons see the various elements of the field or environment as discrete from the organized background, and perceive parts in a much more differentiated fashion. These style differences in perception and cognition can be measured on the Embedded Figures Tests. A complex figure is presented and the task is to quickly detect a more simple figure within it (see Fig. 6-2). The selection of the labels of independent and dependent was unfortunate in that independence has a much more positive connotation in our culture than dependence. In everyday life neither quality in the extreme would be desirable. A person who is extremely Field Independent might be autistic or egocentric, seeing particulars only in relation to his or her own position or attitudinal framework, or the person may be unable to detect overall patterns. An extremely Field Dependent person would be stimulus-bound, unable to counteract the influence of immediate surroundings.

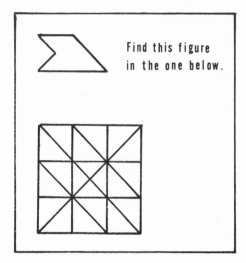

Figure 6-2.   An example of an embedded figure.

The differences found between the sexes at puberty are determined by the location of persons on a continuum as measured by the specific tasks described—the Rod-and-Frame Test and the Embedded Figures Test. On the average postpubescent males tend to be more Field Independent than females. However, neither sex as a group falls at the extreme ends of the dimension.

The bases for obtained sex differences in cognition remain controversial, with some researchers positing genetic differences and others attributing it to experience.[16] Waber[17] has suggested a third factor, maturation, as accounting for the differences in verbal and visual-spatial ability. Testing pre- and early adolescents, she found that regardless of the child's sex, early maturers scored better on verbal tasks than on spatial ones while late maturers showed the reverse pattern. Developmental measures based on the norms described in Chapter 2 were used to evaluate whether maturation was early or late. The bearing of this finding on sex differences is that perhaps the verbal superiority of females is due to their average earlier maturation, and the later maturation of males enhances visual-spatial ability.

Maturation time appears to influence spatial ability more than verbal ability, suggesting different explanations for the development of these two areas of skill. The maturational change believed to influence spatial ability is the extent of brain lateralization, i.e., the degree to which one hemisphere dominates the other with respect to a particular function. The maturation hypothesis suggested by Waber remains to be elaborated and verified by other researchers.

Thus far there is little evidence of sex differences in memory ability, reasoning, and the development of formal operations. Most cognitive differences documented with any regularity focus around the verbal vs. visual-spatial distinction.[18]

Performance and attitudes toward mathematics provide an excellent example of the interplay between cognitive and social factors. Male superiority in mathematics is an oft-cited example of a difference between the sexes. However, this common belief appears to have little validity for the early pubescent years. Both sexes perform about equally well and show the same preference patterns for math as compared with other subjects. However, many teachers expect boys to do better in math and in many families the father emerges as the parent most likely to help on math homework. By the high school years, differential performance becomes apparent with males doing better and taking more mathematics courses.[19] While emerging differences in visual-spatial abilities may play a role, understanding mathematics is not totally independent of verbal ability and the average difference in visual-spatial ability is not sufficient in accounting for the wide disparity observed between men and women in the late adolescent and adult years.[20] Changes in attitude and motivation are an important contributor to the later sex differences in performance in mathematics.

VOCATIONAL ASPIRATIONS AND EXPECTATIONS

Differences between the sexes in the numbers employed as well as differential aspirations and expectations regarding higher education exist during the pubescent years. Data from the National

Table 6-2. Percentage of youths enrolled in school who desire and expect to graduate from college, by age and sex: United States, 1966–70 (from J. Scanlon. Self-reported health behavior and attitudes of youths 12–17 years. *National Center for Health Statistics, Vital and Health Statistics,* Series 11: Data from the National Health Survey, no. 147, DHEW publication no. (HRA) 75-1629, 1975)

College completion desired			College completion expected		
Age	Males	Females	Age	Males	Females
12	59.4	47.8	12	53.4	46.0
13	53.3	40.9	13	46.9	37.0
14	49.1	38.3	14	43.5	32.9
15	44.7	30.0	15	40.6	29.1

Health Survey[21] show that in the junior high age range, 42 percent of the boys and 30 percent of the girls have employment outside the home. The desire to go to college shows a decline over the junior high years for both sexes. Table 6-2 shows the percentages for both *desired* and *expected* college completion. Boys consistently express both higher aspirations and expectations with respect to education and vocational achievement.[22,23]

Despite the women's movement, vocational aspirations among girls and women remain considerably lower than those of boys and men. Barnett[24] asked 9 to 17-year-olds to select their two most preferred and least-preferred occupations. (Children 9 years of age are able to rate the prestige of various occupations in a manner almost identical to the ratings of adults.)[25] Among males the preferred occupations correlated positively with prestige, and the correlation increased with age; that is, males preferred prestigious occupations. Among the females, there was no correlation between occupational preference and prestige; some females preferred prestigious occupations while others did not. Looking at the choices of least-preferred occupations, Barnett found that, unlike the males, the females at every age included some high-prestige occupations as least-preferred. She concluded that males learn to prefer prestigious occupations while females learn to avoid them.

In a survey of students in grades 5 through 8 at four predominantly black Catholic schools, Teahan[26] found that when asked about their vocational preferences, a majority of the girls selected lower prestige occupations than the boys. While external barriers are being removed, internal ones remain longer. Internal defenses as a means of psychological reconciliation and avoidance of frustration in response to external barriers are often found among those who have been systematically blocked from opportunities for advancement and achievement. It is hoped that as more women enter occupations and career fields formerly closed to them, girls will be less likely to internalize more traditional but less appropriate occupational goals. However, the change may not occur as quickly as one might have thought.

Patterson[27] points out the unrealistic aspects of low aspiration among women. Most girls aspire to the role of homemaker and

---

A content analysis of two Scouting magazines, Boys' Life *and* American Girl

A student of mine, Vernon K. Moore, analyzed several issues of the official Girl Scout and Boy Scout magazines, tabulating the number and content of the articles and ads presented throughout 1974. The following is his summary of the results:

Boy's Life is comprised of sports accounts; adventure stories; and history, science, and nature (environmental articles). Cover stories are predominantly sports oriented, featuring celebrities or heroes as models. Fiction is basically adventure stories or stories with a moral ending. The articles on history, science, and nature are in part educational, but they also supply some type of value lesson, usually teaching bravery or the ability to deal with the environment (maturity).

American Girl, on the other hand, focuses mainly on personal development in the physical sense. It is essentially a fashion and beauty magazine. Each issue is filled with dozens of pictures of the latest styles. However, rather than encouraging readers to stimulate the economy by purchasing their entire wardrobe,

mother. Yet according to government statistics, 44 percent of all married women work at employment outside of the home. A woman who marries and has two children can anticipate a 22-year period of employment. A growing proportion of women remain or become single. In 1975 about 40 percent of women, ages 20 to 24 were single compared with 28 percent in 1950. The number of families headed by a woman has increased by 73 percent since 1960 to 7.2 million, comprising 13 percent of all families. In 1974, there were 63 women for every 100 men in the labor force.[28] Despite these vast changes in life styles and the employment of women outside the home, girls of the junior high school age often do not make a serious psychological commitment to planning a vocation. They also show low and unrealistic expectations of future income.[29] Part of the responsibility for the limited future view rests with parents, teachers, and counselors who, reflecting tradi-

---

American Girl urges them to sew their own creations. The magazine is also replete with advice columns dealing with decorating and beauty, not to mention romantic and social problems. For all the advice given to improve a young female's appearance, *American Girl* is sadly negligent in improving her intelligence. Only a minute amount of space is devoted to education in this respect, and then it usually deals with the social aspects of the intellect.

The attitudes that are expressed in both magazines are carried in their advertising as well. *Boys' Life* advertises hobby kits, sports equipment, firearms, camping equipment, and military and religious academies. The only clothing items were rain gear and tennis shoes. In contrast *American Girl* promotes clothing, jewelry, beauty aids, modeling schools, and summer camps.

By comparing these two magazines it is possible to see how each reinforces society's indoctrination of young males and females into their respective sexual roles. In each case talents and behavior patterns that are designated for the opposite sex are omitted or minimized, while those associated with the same sex are emphasized with specific attention given to those considered the most desirable.

tional stereotypes, see a career for a woman as "something to fall back on." Another important aspect is the girl's own marriage fantasy perpetuated by prevailing cultural stereotypes. It is extremely important that the adolescent girl's developing sexuality and desires for a home and family are recognized when considering vocational training and career planning. Because of the socialization process for women in this society, family concerns, interpersonal relationships, vocation, and career are often more intimately related to one another than is the case for men. Whether we like the previous difference in sex roles or not, they persist and adequate counseling, education, and problem solving for pubescent and postpubescent youth will require more than simply treating the sexes in the same manner. However, the past double standards in vocational guidance must be eliminated such as steering a boy into dentistry and an equally talented girl into dental hygiene.

COMMENT

An acknowledgment of and respect for patterns of individual and group differences is necessary in making it possible for each person to achieve the greatest possible fulfillment and satisfaction with life. Sex roles and sex stereotypes can be stultifying and harmful when they define and limit a person's potential. Pretending everyone is the same can have limiting effects as well. The dangers to be avoided in recognizing differences are the assumptions of superiority and inferiority, and the use of irrelevant sex-related characteristics as job requirements and stepping stones to career advancement.

SUGGESTED READINGS

Deaux, K. *The behavior of women and men.* Belmont, Calif.: Wadsworth, 1976.

Friedman, R. C.; Richart, R. M.; Van de Wiele, R. L.; and Stern, L. O. (eds.) *Sex differences in behavior.* New York: Wiley, 1974.

Gadpaille, W. J. Research into the physiology of maleness and femaleness. *Archives of General Psychiatry,* 1972, 26, 193–206.

Hauck, B. B. Differences between the sexes at puberty. In Evans, E. D. (ed.) *Adolescents: readings in behavior and development.* Hinsdale, Ill.: Dryden Press, 1970, pp. 24–42.

Maccoby, E. E. (ed.) *The development of sex differences.* Stanford, Calif.: Stanford University Press, 1966.

Maccoby, E. E. and Jacklin, C. N. *The psychology of sex differences.* Stanford, Calif.: Stanford University Press, 1974.

Rosenberg, B. G. and Sutton-Smith, B. *Sex and identity.* New York: Holt, Rinehart & Winston, 1972.

Stoller, R. J. The "bedrock" of masculinity and femininity: bisexuality. *Archives of General Psychiatry,* 1972, 26, 207–12.

7 *The Inner Person:*
Identity and Interests

> It's hard to describe myself because I really
> don't know myself as much as I would like
> to. I guess I am a carefree person who
> doesn't have many serious problems. I am
> shy when I get up in front of a group of
> people because I wonder what they will
> think of me.
>
> A ninth grade student

Who am I? Rarely asked, but percolating at a less conscious level, the question underlies a substantial part of adolescent thought and behavior. Answers are found by carefully watching the reactions of others, particularly peers, but adults as well. Identity, the solution to the question, is explored in fantasy and daydreams, in imitation and identification with popular figures—Olympic stars, rock musicians, movie characters, and similar media figures. Clothing styles, a particular group of friends, haircuts, and special talk often reflect the trying on for fit of various identities.

At the same time society has an answer. You are an adolescent. The characterization carries with it a substantial number of expectations. You will be moody and unpredictable; you will sometimes behave very much like an adult and at other times like a child; you will be willful and hard to live with on occasions and a marvelous entertaining companion at other times; we will be able to talk about things and the world in new ways together. These and other expectations further mold the youngster's development of identity through the transition of the early adolescent years.

The emergence of identity as a central issue at puberty has been described in detail by Erik Erikson.[1] He developed an eightfold classification of life stages representing a sequence of developmental crises whose resolution determines the individual's personality and behavior (Table 7-1). His theory is psychoanalytic in nature but, unlike Freud's which concentrated on the family, is focused on the interrelationship between the individual and the larger cultural milieu. For Erikson, overcoming the crises produced by the interaction of individual and society constitutes a major source of psychological growth through ego* development, leaving each person with a unique combination of strengths and weaknesses. Through the life stages the person evolves from an instinctual pleasure-seeking being to one whose behavior becomes social in nature as a result of mutual interchange with others.

The concept of identity as it is being used here is not a simple attribute of a person. Rather it refers to the core of a person's character. Identity formation is a process which depends to a substantial degree on interactions with the environment and the continuity of principles and actions over time. We associate a lack of identity with a lack of guiding principles. A person who is always expedient, who is strongly influenced by others or by a single goal, such as ambition, is one whom we often describe as lacking a sense of identity.

In the United States today the process of identity formation is, more often than not, a lengthy one. Puberty initiates the process of identity consolidation as it marks the advent of maturational changes resulting in adult appearance and reproductive capacities. However, the final commitment to a particular identity may not

Table 7-1. Erikson's stages of psychosocial development (adapted from Erikson, E., Identity and the life cycle. *Psychological Issues,* 1959, *1*, monograph, p. 166).

Psychosocial crises	Radius of significant relations	Psychosocial modalities
Trust vs. mistrust	Maternal person	To get To give in return
Autonomy vs. shame, doubt	Parental persons	To hold (on) To let (go)
Initiative vs. guilt	Basic family	To make (= going after) To "make like" (= playing)
Industry vs. inferiority	"Neighborhood," school	To make things (= completing) To make things together
Identity vs. role confusion	Peer groups and out-groups, models of leadership	To be oneself (or not to be) To share being oneself
Intimacy vs. isolation	Partners in friendship, sex, competition, cooperation	To lose and find oneself in another
Generativity vs. stagnation	Divided labor and shared household	To make be To take care of
Integrity vs. despair	"Humankind," "my kind"	To be, through having been To face not being

occur until the twenties or even the thirties. One treads a precipitous route in the search for identity in our culture. At one side are the hazards of too early a consolidation leading to a premature and subsequently inadequate identity. In contrast to the hazards of premature identity formation, at the other side is a continuous postponement of identity consolidation, and the cultivation of a fluid adaptable identity. An exaggerated form is the person who seems never to grow up, remaining a perpetual adolescent where shift from role to role is easily and deliberately accomplished. A commitment to a particular and constant set of principles, values, and life style are avoided. These traits are reflected in current cultural heroes—the rock star who retains an adolescent life style of playing multiple roles in costume as well as in choice of friends, associates, and displays of material possessions. He may also cultivate a hermaphrodite-like appearance and bisexual preferences, thereby avoiding even a clear sexual identity. Kilpatrick[2] has pointed out that the maintenance of a fluid ever-changing identity is becoming a popular concept and represents an attempt to adapt to a rapidly changing world. He sees some benefits in the adaptation but suggests serious consequences which may outweigh the gains. Erikson has postulated the development of a sense of identity as a necessary precursor to true intimacy—that we cannot share ourselves with others until we know who we are, nor can there be love and appreciation of others as they are. Thus, the cost of a fluid identity may be superficial intimacy reflecting only the search for self.

The concept of mastery plays a primary role in Erikson's scheme —mastery and the pleasure of exercising it combined with social approval and recognition serve as the primary developmental forces. A similar concept, termed competence or effectance motivation, has been described by R. W. White.[3] Competence refers to an organism's capacity to interact effectively with its environment. White describes the motivation for effectance as "what the neuromuscular system wants to do when it is otherwise unoccupied or is gently stimulated by the environment." The main point is that humans have the desire to display competence for its own sake; that there is an intrinsic satisfaction provided in being active and effective. Verbal dueling, competing in school or on the playing field, dressing well, having lots of friends, being the best hustler on the block, all are expressions of one sort of competence or another. Through the pubertal years competence is expressed more and more in the extended world of peers and adults outside of the home.

Douvan and Adelson[4] have pointed out that both sexes achieve identity through task mastery. However, the areas of mastery differ. They assert that the male develops his sense of self, of identity, through a process of managing skills and tasks, and of avoiding the domination of others. In short the male develops autonomy. Further, he is more directly challenged by his developing sexuality and must learn impulse control in an immediate and direct manner. The female develops her sense of self in the process of relationships with others. Her identity development lies within the interpersonal realm. Girls, according to Douvan and Adelson, do not encounter the same press of sexuality as boys and hence need not develop an analogous set of sexual self controls. Their main point which is pertinent here is that the differences in sexual development between boys and girls differentially influence identity formation and the reworking of other elements of personality—the resolution of dependence, the development of independence, and interpersonal styles.

In the search for identity the young person often tries out various roles and engages in over-identification with movements, best friends, and media idols, particularly athletes, movie stars, rock musicians, and singers. The clue to the self-serving aspects of these identifications lies with their temporary nature. Yet, while the external attachment seems faddish and transient, the internal goodness-of-fit is important in the evolution of personality. The heroes and heroines of the culture reflect its values and these values are transmitted through the process of identification to the young, despite attempts to train them otherwise. Hence, our secret wishes and identifications as well as our more obvious ones are transmitted from generation to generation.

The creation of cliques with their stereotyped and rigid views is directly related to identity seeking. Clubs, gangs, and secret sororities nearly always constitute an underground culture of adolescence despite attempts by school authorities to discourage their existence. More informal cliques described as rah-rahs, surfers, hoods, cheerleaders, and the parking lot crowd, abound on most any secondary school campus. Participation in these groups provides an added source of identification. However, many youngsters are not included and achieve identity in other ways, perhaps through schoolwork, church participation, or even cultivating non-participation into an identity style.

Erikson described puberty as precipitating a crisis of identity because of the difficulty of maintaining a sense of continuity through change. He pointed out the difficulty of avoiding role confusion and of the possibility of losing the sense of self in the roles played. Nevertheless, for some youngsters, the crisis appears to be minimal. Puberty in and of itself need not be coincident with identity crisis. It often plays a significant role because the question "Who am I?" takes on an increased salience with the development of more abstract thought, and also because interest in others is increasing markedly. However, many adolescents are not particularly preoccupied with self-discovery. Some aspects of identity, occupational commitment, for example, often seem a long way off for the pubescent.

Self-appraisal does, however, undergo modification for most through the early adolescent years. In a study of fourth through twelfth graders, the eighth graders showed the most discrepancy between their self-rating of scholastic ability and their actual ability. The boys tended to overrate their ability while the girls underestimated theirs, perhaps reflecting the internalization of socially prescribed sex roles.[5]

Changes in self-appraisal herald a decline in egocentricism. Subsequently self-appraisal as well as the estimation of the views of others become less grandiose and more realistic. At the same time the image of one's ideal self becomes loftier with an increase in the discrepancy between perceived self and ideal self.[6]

The following self-descriptions show the increasing complexity of appraisal with age. The students were asked to describe themselves in any way they chose. The seventh graders' descriptions are noticeably more simplistic than those of the ninth graders.

From the seventh graders:

> I am a tall Handsome who likes track, baseball, basketball.
> Well, I am 5'1" and ugly. I have short hair and it's nappie around the edges and I wear earrings.

I'm 4'11". I got blond hair, blue eyes and I get emotionally upset when people get angry with me or ignore me.

I am 5'5" and am 13 years old and a male. I weigh 100 pounds. I like sports.

I am short, black and beautiful.

The eighth graders show a mix of sophistication and simplicity:

I have freckles, a round face, brown eyes, long brown hair. Very few pimples, a birthmark on my neck (middle). I'm 5'2" slim and have a good personality.

I'm short, nice build, weigh 93 lbs. brown hair, hazel eyes and most of all my mental state is sane. I have a size 7½ shoe, short hair so people can see I'm not a hippie.

I like people but I have trouble getting to know many. I like animals, sometimes better than people. I like to cook and eat. I enjoy certain sports though I'm not very athletic. I also like plants and gardening.

I am too quiet, easily embarrassed, slightly overweight, and wear glasses. I belong to the unstated middle-lower group in the student society. I'm near the top of my class, and am tired of trying for good grades because I can get them without trying.

By ninth grade the majority of the self descriptions are quite elaborate:

Emotionally I feel I can do many things and do them successfully but I don't know how to go about it. I am not a shy person and do not feel others should be shy. I like people to be open with their feelings but not too much so that they corrupt the feelings of others. I am very selfconscious about my looks (in my face) Because I feel others don't like me.

A deep person who does alot of thinking. I am a leader not a follower. I hate being number 2 when there's something to be done. I guess I'm outgoing. But around some people I tend to be quiet. I don't know why.

I am a rather tall person for my age. I enjoy adventure, challenge, school, and sports. I also enjoy studying possible future occurrences.

I am a person who loves to help other people with their problems. I don't think I'm too attractive but people say I am. I'm

not fat and I'm not skinny. I guess I'm just a little plump. I am
a very aggressive person at times and other times I'm really lazy.
I'm aggressive when I'm with the people I like and I'm lazy when
I'm with people I dislike.

I am very moody, quiet, sensitive, cautious, lazy, patient, and
overly conscious about myself. I like quiet people who are not
real loud, but have many friends and talk an average amount. I
am reserved and do not like to tell people how I feel or about
myself or anything else.

THE LOOKING-GLASS SELF

Accompanying the growing complexity of self-appraisal is an increased awareness and sensitivity to the thoughts and feelings of
others, particularly peers. There is an increasing recognition of
the differences between one's own feelings and those of others.
"No one understands me" is a statement which reflects the dawn-
ing awareness of the uniqueness of self. A new form of egocentricism replaces the old, despite the improved understanding of
the feelings of others. The young adolescent becomes overly concerned about how others feel toward him. So for the first time a
12-year-old child says "My teacher hates me" instead of the more
familiar "I hate my teacher." Elkind[7] used the phrase *the invisible
audience* to convey the sense that the young adolescent is perpetu-
ally on stage performing for an audience. Many an adolescent is
acutely self-conscious, believing that absolutely everyone is watching, appraising, and evaluating every motion, piece of clothing,
and blemish. This self-concern is not without some basis in fact.
Chances are that one's peers are paying a great deal of attention.
However, the degree of that attention is mitigated by each person's own self-consciousness. It is as though each person is intent
upon his or her own reflected image as well as the judgment of it.
They see themselves as they might exist in the mind of another
person.[8] The exaggerated concern may produce a great deal of conflict between youngster and parent. An unyielding conformity to
peers is often the most obvious—an unwillingness to wear rain-
clothes in wet weather because they look silly, extreme sensitivity

to the appearance of the parents if the family is out in public to-gether, a headlong rush into the fads of the moment—clothes, sharp haircuts, pierced ears, 10-speed bicycles of specific design, etc. Scrutinizing the reflected image and seeing oneself as others do is a major means by which identity is formed. The reflected image becomes a part of oneself. Once the internal view is con-solidated, the looking-glass self diminishes in importance.

One of the exasperating aspects for all involved—pubescents, family, and teachers—is the inconsistency with which all these changes present themselves. The behavioral alterations produced by maturation and learning are slowly consolidated through each succeeding year, the increment taking an upturn around the time of puberty. Conversely, residues of less mature behavior appear with less and less frequency over time. The increase in adult-like behaviors make the remaining childish behaviors more obvious by contrast. After all, even as adults we have our egocentric moments and carry fragments of our own invisible audiences.

VALUES, INTERESTS, AND ACTIVITIES

> I like Sue because she is a very nice person. We don't have much
> in common but we get a long pretty well anyway. She likes boys
> and I don't. She is very domestic minded too. She likes camp,
> the latest fashion and curling irons. She also likes to go shopping.
> Eighth grade student

The values of pubescents reflect in large part those of surrounding society. Although not particularly idealistic in the reformist sense of late adolescence, young adolescents express general concern for the values of a world at peace, freedom, and family security.[9] Of more immediate interest, however, are issues of money, school, and personal impact, i.e., attractiveness and getting along with others.[10] In general, being ambitious becomes more salient for boys; for girls, qualities of responsibility and being neat become in-creasingly important. As one might expect, the self-reported im-portance of being obedient declines with age. Overall, pubescents seem more concerned with qualities of character and personality than with those of an intellectual or artistic nature.[11,12] Asking young adults to free associate back to their junior high years, the first recollections and associations usually are memories of social interactions such as adjusting to school, remembrances of individual teachers, or experiences in gym.

Young people spend a great deal of time attending to the media —TV, radio, and movies. Results from a national survey show that the average television-watching time for 12- to 15-year-olds was 3 hours a day. Radio-listening time was 1 to 1½ hours per day and increased with age. The time spent reading newspapers, comics, or magazines averaged ½ hour to 45 minutes per day. More girls than boys read books and they spent more time at it. The median time spent reading books was 1¼ hours per day for girls and slightly less than 1 hour per day for boys. It is not clear whether or not this includes school assignments.[13] In another national survey the average TV viewing time for sixth graders (age 11) was found to be 4 hours per day during the week and 6½ hours on Sunday.[14] Eighty percent of those surveyed did something else while watching TV—they would eat, sketch or doodle, read or talk. Informal observation suggests that much of the casual conversation at school is about current television shows and soap operas.

Many youngsters, male and female, play in organized sports. Soccer is becoming very popular. Activities such as miniature golf, bowling, and pool increasingly engage the interest of both sexes. Of particular delight are games of pinball, air hockey, and the electronic games such as pong. A good place to find pubescents is around the games in a local restaurant or entertainment arcade. While boys may spend much of their time on the block or in schoolyard sports, girls often pass their free time wandering downtown through department stores. Moviegoing is a very popular pastime and a social event as well as one of entertainment, with most adolescents preferring to attend with peers rather than with parents. Fast-food stands also serve as popular gathering places. The presence of movie houses and snack bars, combined with enclosed yet public space, has made the shopping mall a favorite site for young people, particularly on weekends. Here one sees a perpetual movement among knots of youngsters performing and watching, with conversation punctuated with squeals, breaking voices, and talk liberally sprinkled with profanity, and much ado over lighting cigarettes, all carried off with various degrees of aplomb depending upon age and sophistication.

FANTASY

Fantasy is an internal form of make-believing play. In prepubescence make-believe play often occurs in an overt form. War games in the bathtub or impromptu puppet shows are enactments of fantasy themes where the operator is an active participant in the action, winning over all and dominating the stage. Through the pubescent years make-believe becomes less open and more private. The content also changes. A study of daydreams revealed a preponderance of adventure and lively activity among 10 to 12-year-olds. By 13 or 14, most of the youngsters of both sexes had shifted to fantasy dominated by romance, sex, and achievement.[15]

The capacity for fantasy is of inestimable importance through the early adolescent years. Daydreaming serves the functions of preparation and anticipation of future roles, the development of power and autonomy, and coping with frightening events.[16] Both adolescents and adults use fantasy as a means of trying out strategies and responses to other people and situations. Mental imaginings about winning games, constructing a go-cart, ideas for new outfits, or steps to be taken on the road to popularity are a means of working on day-to-day problems and concerns while at the same time achieving need fulfillment. In one's fantasy world, one can always be successful, beautiful, powerful, independent, possessing whatever qualities one most desires. The fantasy can extend beyond the more plausible demands of existence and into projections of the future where one may lead a revolution; become a second Helen of Troy; achieve professional eminence as a scientist, physician, or architect; or emerge as a world-famous rock star complete with cars, clothes, and adulation. Even these grandiose daydreams serve the dual function of propelling one toward achievement and of providing its satisfactions at the same time. For many young adolescents the gulf between fantasy and actuality is great. The discrepancy can be a part of the pain of adolescence. Jerome Singer has pointed out that as a person matures, daydreams move into conceivable channels becoming more attuned to reality.[17]

The degree to which an adolescent engages in fantasy depends on a number of factors. Temperament, whether one is introverted or extroverted, for example, plays a role. The extrovert is less likely to rely on fantasy and more likely to take action often directly imitative of adults in an attempt to fulfill personal needs. The degree of general satisfaction or dissatisfaction with daily life is also a factor. Fantasy serves the function of delaying gratification. As society places more demands upon the individual for postponing fulfillment of desires, the benefits of daydreaming increase. Adolescents are expected to defer sexual gratification as well as desires for money, cars, and other material goods until they finish their schooling. Many young people are unwilling to accept the delay. Sexual involvement and gainful employment frequently lead to an early termination of formal education. Fantasy can provide substitute gratification for those needs expressed more directly by the school dropout.

Some life experiences and rearing practices are more conducive to the development of a capacity for fantasy than others. Practice leads to improvement. The opportunity for play in early and middle childhood and the chance to develop a rich repertoire of imaginary devices facilitates later fantasy. A child confronted with a harsh environment which permits little opportunity for reverie is not likely to elaborate a rich fantasy life. Reading provides an opportunity for fantasy development. Projecting oneself into the world of the characters of a book expands one's range of experience. Reading preferences differ among boys and girls. Adolescent boys favor stories of adventure, nonfiction, and science fiction. Themes of power and achievement are frequently found in these works. Girls, too, read adventure stories and are interested in power also, but of a different sort. Their reading often moves more toward the romantic with themes of power of an interpersonal and less instrumental sort. All of these categories of books usually unravel a tale of coming to grips with adversity, whether it be nature, monsters from Jupiter, or overcoming heartbreak and drug addiction. Television often fulfills the same fantasy needs, as the viewer can identify with the characters. However, TV is less of a stimulant to one's own fantasy.[18] Unlike a book, television provides all the elements—action, setting, visual and auditory qualities—to a passive viewer. A person who watches TV regularly is less likely to develop a rich fantasy life with an independent existence. The fantasies will be dominated by the TV programming rather than the individual's own unique cognitive and emotional experience.

While not strictly a fantasy activity, horseback riding is a particularly favored activity of girls and they often fantasize having a horse of their own. The associations of freedom and the control of power embodied in the act of riding are heady ones. Boys often show a fascination with motorcycles, go-carts, and cars probably for similar motives. The sex difference is an interesting one. Horses are personal creatures that respond to pats and sugar lumps. The same can hardly be said for a motorcycle.

Daydreams stimulated by various media and through participation in activities involving power-evoking qualities of speed and strength also contain elements of coping with fearful situations. This theme lies beneath the fascination of adolescents with horror movies and films about the occult. Monsters, giant animals of prey, and persons with demonic power are big draws at the box office. Younger children view the figures as authentic and may be extremely frightened. However, the young adolescent can suspend belief in the immediate enough to avoid being totally overwhelmed, retaining enough imagination to be titillated and pleasurably terrified. Many adults are able to enjoy these aspects of horror films also, but for them the action often must be more realistic to have the desired effect. Those adults who no longer possess the capacity to provide their own fantasy may prefer realistic and violent scenes often with sexual overtones. The result is a restriction of the availability of the movie to a teenage audience. Needless to say the restriction enhances the desire of the young to see the film; and the habituation to violence provided by such movies is not desirable. Mystery films and horror shows for younger adolescents need not possess all the gory details of reality in order to be entertaining and to satisfy the urge to confront the fearsome and come out of it victorious having been scared to death, shrieking in half-fear and half-fun.

As a final note, fantasy is not a panacea for the problems of today's youth. An overreliance upon fantasy characterizes *autistic thought*—thought that has become totally egocentric and removed from reality leading to psychotic or insane behavior. However, fantasy in more moderate amounts is an extremely important and productive part of an individual's cognitive and emotional functions. Those who lack the capacity for fantasy possess less control over many aspects of their lives, being more subject to the direct push and pull of biological and environmental demands.

SUMMARY

The inner person becomes more complex during the pubescent years. The search for identity is a major factor influencing behavior, and concerns with self and others become more differentiated. Of major interest to the young adolescent are the development of competence, the world of peers, and social interactions with others. Activities increasingly extend beyond home and immediate neighborhood. Fantasy life also becomes richer and serves as an important source of need satisfaction, coping with anxiety, and practice for actual encounters.

SUGGESTED READINGS

Blos, P. *The young adolescent: clinical studies*. New York: The Free Press, 1970.

Cottle, T. J. *The abandoners: portraits of loss, separation and neglect*. Boston: Little, Brown, 1973.

Elkind, D. *A sympathetic understanding of the child six to sixteen*. Boston: Allyn & Bacon, 1971.

Erikson, E. *Childhood and society*, 2nd edition. New York: Norton, 1963.

Gallatin, J. E. *Adolescence and individuality: a conceptual approach to adolescent psychology*. New York: Harper & Row, 1975.

Gardner, R. W. and Moriarty, A. *Personality development at preadolescence*. Seattle, Wash.: University of Washington Press, 1968.

Kohen-Raz, R. *The child from 9 to 13: the psychology of preadolescence and early puberty*. Chicago: Aldine-Atherton, 1971.

Muuss, R. E. *Theories of adolescence*, 2nd edition. New York: Random House, 1968.

8 *The Outer Person:*
Social Relationships and Perceptions of Others

> A friend furnishes you with a thousand
> eyes, like the goddess Indra. Through your
> friends you live untold lives. You see in
> other dimensions. You live upside down and
> inside out. You are never alone, never will
> be alone, even if every last one of your
> friends should disappear from the face of
> the earth.
>
> Henry Miller

The search for identity often involves others. The shifting alliance
from family to peers gives an added sense of independence. The
price of reliance upon peers is more than offset by the return provided another set of needs—those of friendship and intimacy. The
increasing desire for closeness to others is expressed by pubescents
in numerous ways—lengthy telephone conversations, desires to
bring a friend along on family outings, incredibly long hours spent
at the drive-in lingering over cokes, and just plain hanging around.

There is often a kind of relentlessness seen in pairs and knots of young adolescents, as though they need and want to do something together, but can't figure out what. Camp counselors and scout advisers often recognize the tremendous potential for accomplishment which can be achieved if a group of puberty-age youngsters can be galvanized into action. The problem is getting that energy focused. Unfortunately, one often encounters resistance masked by a flurry of reasons for inaction. While the desires for collaboration with peers may be strong, the antipathy to direction from adults is equally so.

The affectional bonds manifested during the early adolescent years form an important and critical aspect of psychological growth, a development which was elaborated by Harry Stack Sullivan, an influential psychoanalyst.[1] According to Sullivan, the development of intimacy first occurs with like-sexed peers and stems from a need for closeness with others which arises in preadolescence. Feelings of loneliness propel the individual into attempting to establish relationships. Close attachment with members of the same sex facilitates the later establishment of intimacy with the opposite sex. In addition to the necessity of having a good friend, he pointed out the important evolution of collaborative relationships where group performance and thinking in terms of *we* rather than *I* dominate. Erikson said much the same thing when he described pubescence as a time of both being oneself and sharing oneself.

The young child accepts love and concern without deeply perceiving their source, and, while often very loving, receives rather than consciously gives. Even pubescents still talk more than they listen. Later, with maturation and experience, the young adolescent becomes capable of empathy and is in a position to give as well as receive. To give of self in a less egotistical manner is to go beyond cooperation and into collaboration. The intimacy aspects of the early adolescent period focus around the sharing of one's self with others. It is in later adolescence and early adulthood that the person becomes better able to comprehend in depth the affection offered by others. The early adolescent is still in the midst of the process of evolving a truly reciprocal pattern of intimacy.

Friendships become increasingly more stable through the adolescent years. Prior to puberty they are relatively unemotional and lack the complex love-hate tensions which begin to characterize family relationships. In early adolescence some friendships remain superficial. Others, while perhaps short-lived, are very intense. Girls appear more prone than boys to form small, exclusive, and highly cohesive groups. They pay more attention to social class in friend selection and spend more time with one another. In general girls' friendships during these years are more fervent and reciprocal than those of boys.[2] In the 14 to 16-year range they frequently desire strong loyalty and absolute security in their like-sex friendships. They often express a strong need to be similar—lots of clothes sharing occurs during these years, if parents permit it. If parents don't permit it, the clothing exchange may go on in the restroom before and after school hours. Girls tend to be more advanced than boys in interpersonal development during early adolescent years judging from their more mature conceptions of friendship and greater ability to articulate them.[3]

Friendships among boys tend to be more lasting and stable than those of girls. The stability may result from the lower degree of intensity and consequent reduced chance for conflict.[4] In general friends for both sexes tend to be from similar backgrounds and the same neighborhood. Interpersonal relationships during these years reflect the influence of sex roles. Boys rely on their peers for support in fulfilling needs for independence and achievement. Girls use them for the development of interpersonal skills and close relationships with one or two others. For boys a camaraderie and fraternal feeling within a larger group is more frequently observed, in contrast to the development of smaller cliques (exclusive groups) and pairs within a larger crowd of girls.[5] In most school settings the crowds and cliques are often obvious, as are their members who draw confidence from their group. Yet, many youngsters are not participants in any group. Programs which insure a variety of clubs and interest groups encouraging participation and the development of friendship skills, particularly of the more isolated individuals, are highly desirable.

INDEPENDENCE

Identity and intimacy are important needs. A third is independence; and it adds a complicating twist to the quest for the other two. Otto Rank,[6] an early disciple of Freud, believed that the shift from dependence to independence was a major crisis of adolescence. According to his theory the principal internal conflict aroused by puberty is the struggle for independence and the exercise of the will. The will represents conscious awareness and control. At puberty two threats to independence and the will exist. One is the threatened domination of biological urges. Sexuality directly threatens the development of the will, of self-control, and of independence by virtue of its overpowering urges for gratification. The other threat is the domination of adult authority. Adding to Rank's insight, the conflict between autonomy and submission to either internal impulse or external control is further complicated by the ambivalent attitude of the culture toward independence. Values of individuality, independence, and self-direction are stressed, while at the same time cultural conformity is approved and many aspects of individuality are punished with social disapproval and censure. The young adolescent is caught in the midst of these contradictory values.

Girls remain in a particularly ambiguous situation. They are not as strongly pushed in the direction of independence as are boys. A female can avoid establishing independence without suffering severe criticism. She can remain quite dependent upon her parents, transferring her dependency to her husband upon marriage and then to her grown children in her old age. Yet most girls experience independence strivings. Often the very bonds of intimacy, particularly with the mother, are perceived by the girl as threats to freedom. Lacking the more clear promise of independence available to boys, girls may precipitate very stormy interpersonal relationships with their family members. Issues of self-determination and control are more often sources of familial conflict for girls; while for boys, concerns and disagreements are more likely to revolve around the attainment of more specific adolescent privileges of growing up, such as having a car or taking long trips.[7,8]

Whereas for girls intimacy may be seen as a barrier to the achievement of independence, for boys gaining freedom poses a threat to intimacy. The harsh demands for the development of independence in males may contribute to an inability to acknowledge any true intimacy because of the implied dependence and threat to autonomy. The "cool" male stereotype portrays such a person. In actuality he is likely to experience psychophysiological symptoms such as ulcers and coronary problems in later life. For many young adolescent boys the cool phase is a transitory one, ceasing when defenses are lowered as needs are resolved. In the adolescent period the expression of independence may extend to persistent disregard of authority, an activity which may actually reflect a defense against more deep-seated fears of a lack of autonomy.

The ease of the development of independence and the extent to which the parental tie is severed will depend on a number of factors: the strength of the attachment to parents, whether prior training for independence occurred or whether the parents kept the child in a dependent relationship, and the child's own self-confidence. A timid, fearful youngster may be unwilling to risk alienating family by attempting to expand social relationships and assert independence. Extreme factors may result in a failure to alter the primary relationship to parents producing, for example, a man of 38 years who is still a mama's boy, or a grown woman with children of her own who feels she must telephone her mother once or twice a day.

Either neglect or parental overcontrol may result in a simple displacement of dependency onto the peer group, resulting in a shift in alliance without the accompanying development of self-direction. Even in less extreme instances of negative parent-child relationships, early adolescence may carry with it transitory instances of heedless gang behavior, conformity, and devotion to peer values.

The press for independence often carries with it a devaluation of parents; those ideas with which the parents are most closely identified may be the earliest victims of the pubescent's expression of individuality.[9] School, vocational choices, values of reliance, punctuality, and neatness may fall into disrepute. Being the butt of criticism and seeing their cherished goals ignored are enough to drive parents to despair. However, in addition they must deal with their own ambivalence about their growing child. While anxious for their offspring to develop into self-sufficient adults, this aim carries with it concerns about the loss of love and attachment which the end of dependency might bring. For parents caught in this dilemma perhaps the best advice is that offered by Gardner[10] in the phrasing of the ancients confronted with the unpredictable and uncontrollable, "It will pass. It will pass."

Attempts to assert independence and develop a more clear sense of identity while meeting intimacy needs leads to an increasing involvement with peers. In an illustrative study,[11] schoolchildren in grades 5 to 10 were asked about three aspects of interpersonal relationships: *identification*—who they felt understood them better, family or friends, and whether when they grew up they would most be like parents or friends; *association*—who they liked to spend their time with; and *normative* orientation—whose ideas (family or friends) were most like theirs. In response to the items in each category the students checked either family, friends, or neutral. The results shown in Figure 8-1 represent the percentage of students who showed a predominantly family orientation (by answering "family" to a majority of the items), peer orientation (selecting "friends" more often than "family"), and neutral orientation (either a majority of neutral responses or an equal number of "family" and "friends" answers). The most marked differences in overall orientation by age are seen from the sixth to the eighth grade. In the school system studied, students entered junior

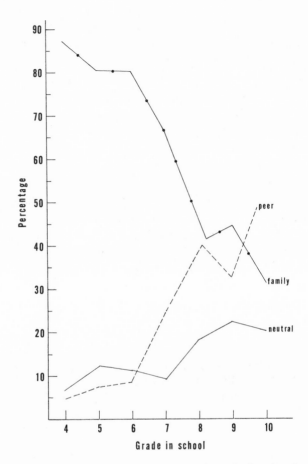

Figure 8-1. Percentage of students in each grade showing family, peer, or neutral orientations (data from C. E. Bowerman and J. W. Kinch, Changes in family and peer orientation of children between the fourth and tenth grades. *Social Forces*, 1959, 37, 206–211).

high school in the sixth grade and high school in the ninth grade; thus, the differences were not immediately contingent upon a change in school. Among the three types of orientation, the least change with age was found on the identification dimension, while the greatest age differences occurred on the association dimension.

There was a sex difference in the ages when the most marked shift from family to peer orientation occurred. The percentage of peer-oriented girls went from 4 percent in grade six to 33 percent in grade seven. For the boys the greatest difference in peer orientation was found when comparing grade seven and grade eight, 17 percent to 43 percent. The sex differences correspond with the later onset of puberty in boys.

Affiliation patterns change throughout the years of puberty. There is a trend away from membership in traditional national organizations such as Scouts and 4-H with a concomitant increase in membership in local clubs and groups.[12] Table 8-1 shows the results of a study of girls' affiliation by age. The age trends were similar for urban, suburban, and rural groups. As expected, YWCA strength was higher in the city while 4-H was more popular in rural areas. There was also less action-group membership in rural areas. National organizations have become concerned about their decline in popularity among teenagers and have made concerted

Table 8-1.   Percent of group membership by age in organized groups in the United States, for females (from Burk, B.A.; Zdep, S.M., and Kushner, H. Affiliation patterns among American girls. *Adolescence*, 1973, 8, 541–546).

	Age			
Group	9–10	11–12	13–14	15–16
Traditional national groups: Girl Scouts, Girls' Club, YWCA, Camp Fire Girls, 4-H	50.3	37.7	21.3	11.3
Local groups: school clubs, neighborhood clubs, church clubs (choir, Sunday School, etc.)	27.4	48.7	61.1	72.3
Social action groups: environmental protection, civil rights, black power, women's liberation	0	0	5.1	8.9

efforts to attract and hold members. Changes in uniforms and activities have been initiated in order to bring such organizations into the mainstream of the youth culture.

CONFORMITY

Conformity plays a part in the satisfaction of needs for identity, intimacy, and even independence. A degree of conformity is essential for a stable and mutually supportive society, and cooperation to a large degree depends upon shared goals and mutual adherence to standard rules and procedures. In the pubescent a social responsiveness to age-mates emerges in an exaggerated form. Conformity to peers increases through early adolescence and then declines in the late teen and early adult years. Testing out the assertion that conformity to peers is stronger among younger adolescents, Landsbaum and Willis[13] compared a group of 13- to 14-year-olds with college students on the degree to which they were influenced by peers on a conformity task. The task involved the judgment of the lengths of lines where conflicting judgments made by peers were presented. As predicted, the younger group showed greater vulnerability to peer judgment. They were more likely to make the same judgment as the peer partner even when it was obvious that the judgment was incorrect. There were no significant differences in measures of self-confidence between the two groups. Nevertheless, the younger students behaved as if they had less confidence in their competence by changing their decisions to match those of the partners far more frequently than did the older students.

There are differential aspects of conformity between the sexes. Boys may conform in a manner more consonant with the development of independence by being more rebellious and defiant toward authority; while girls may express their conformity in less defiant ways, focusing upon concerns of an interpersonal nature. Among 12- to 14-year-old girls, Kernan[14] found that taste in clothes and cosmetic fashions was influenced more by older girls than by mothers. However, a high degree of dress conformity is not restricted to the female sex. Male members of gangs wear almost identical uniforms such as khaki pants and white T-shirts, black leather jackets, etc.

SOCIAL ACCEPTANCE AND SOCIAL ACHIEVEMENT

Social acceptance and social achievement become increasingly important through the adolescent years. Social acceptance refers to welcomed participation in some valued group such as a social club, school activity, gang, or clique. Past studies have indicated that high grades rarely contribute to social acceptance. Accomplishment in the realm of athletics and leadership in activities contribute to a boy's social acceptability, while girls often gain social acceptance by leadership activities and by having nice clothes.[15] Physical attractiveness is also important for social acceptance. Throughout the grammar school years peer acceptance is associated with high socio-economic status, above-average intelligence, better health, and other positive background factors.[16] Pubescents favor others who are physically attractive and who have similar attitudes.[17] Thus, the payoff of being liked may contribute to conformity. Adolescent conformity in part may represent a ritual interaction which provides a basis for social acceptance.

Social achievement is attained by meeting a socially defined standard of excellence and having the achievement acknowledged in some symbolic form.[18] What constitutes achievement will vary considerably depending upon the community and such variables as social class and sex. It may or may not conflict with social acceptance. Among the upwardly mobile middle class, grades may represent achievement, while for other groups, social acceptance may in itself constitute social achievement.

Social acceptance and social achievement are sought within the context of the peer group. An analysis of group activities also reveals the connections to the needs for identity (including sexual identity), competence, intimacy, and varying degrees of independence. Jack Remick has written about male adolescents growing up in the central valley of California. He describes what he terms the male adolescent rites of getting drunk, bragging about sexual exploits (including intercourse with a cow), the first visit to a house of prostitution, and ganging up on the high school students in a nearby town in order to retrieve stolen header plugs.[19]

Highly stereotyped patterns of peer group behavior may be found in a broad cross-section of ethnic groups. Among the Mexican-Americans of south Texas and probably characteristic of other Mexican and Chicano groups of the Southwest, boys are encouraged to spend more time outside the home. Forming small loosely knit groups called *palomillas,* the youths talk about sports and sex, sharing their supply of knowledge and exchanging much-exaggerated accounts of sexual prowess. Some say that the term *palomillas* refers to the boys' resemblance to the moths that gather around the streetlights at night.[20] However, it is more likely the diminutive of *paloma,* the word for pigeon or dove—as the boys all dressed up and standing around in groups resemble innocent little birds.[21]

A practice which embodies many ritual qualities and provides a means by which a young male can demonstrate his manliness is that of "playing the dozens." Playing the dozens or "sounding" is the practice of a ritualized exchange of insults and retorts particularly popular among urban black males. While not exclusive to blacks, the practice, known on the West Coast as chopping or cutting, has been cultivated by progressively younger adolescents and is frequently practiced by pubescents.[22] Little scholarly attention has been paid to these linguistic games because they are extraordinarily obscene, and as many taboo words and references are used as possible, beginning in most cases with a reference to the opponent's mother. Some of the more mild insults recorded in a New York group of pubescent males were

Eh, eh, you mother's so skinny she could split through a needle's eye.

His mother was so dirty, when she get the rag take a bath, the water went back down the drain.

> When I came to your house, seven roaches jumped me and one
> search me.[23]

The insults need not be original. The point is to demonstrate
knowledge of both the insult and retort and to deliver them in a
flawless, unhesitating manner. This verbal jousting is exciting and
potentially dangerous. It is important that the ritual insults not be
entirely true in order to avoid offense, and insults delivered outside one's own circle often provoke a fight or revenge. The goal
of the verbal encounter is to be more sophisticated than the opponent and to eliminate the possibility of a good retort on his
part. A fascinatingly similar practice has been described by
Dundes, Leach, and Ozkök[24] among Turkish boys between the
ages of eight and fourteen. Very stereotyped openings and closings
which require linguistic skill and cultural knowledge are used. The
parrying is a strictly male activity and, again, is highly obscene in
content. There are two general principles. One is to attempt to
force the opponent into a female, passive role. Either direct insult
or insults aimed at his mother or sisters will do. The opponent,
thus attacked, will attempt to recoup with a verbal phallic threat
of his own. If he does not take an active role in these like-sex encounters a boy risks being perceived in the extremely undesirable
(to him) feminine receptive role. The second principle is that the
retort must end with a rhyme to the initial insult. While many of
the insults and replies are memorized, skill can be exercised by
incorporating editorial comments on the opponent's verbal thrusts.
As long as the content and rhyme requirements are met, the duel
goes on. As with the urban blacks in the United States, the pace is
fast, and the retort expected to be without fault and difficult for
the opponent to turn to his advantage. In one example a boy called
another a bear, a common insult indicating clumsiness and stu-
pidity. The response was "May the bow of a violin enter your ass"
with the syntax such that the sentence ended with *yayi* (bow)
which rhymes with *ayi* (bear). Many of the insults involve reference to the anus and genitals, not unlike talk among U.S. prepubescent and pubescent boys.

Verbal dueling illustrates pubescent concern with themes of sexuality, sex role, identity, and competence. The sexual theme is the most explicit and obvious, both in the content and the vigorous exercise of an active male role and an explicit disdain of female receptivity and passivity. A friend who teaches junior high school in California pointed out that calling a boy a "fag" remained the ultimate insult. Concerns with sexual identity seem uppermost and assume an exaggerated, almost ludicrous quality. The researchers who studied the Turkish verbal duels indicated that the encounters were tests of the ability to manipulate very emotional themes within the constraints of the group. By besting opponents in a dangerous and explosive situation, the young male could demonstrate his fitness as a member of the peer group. The same probably applies to verbal duels among U.S. adolescents. Beyond the sexual identity concerns and the need to ventilate emotion surrounding sexuality, there is also the aspect of knowledge display. Playing the dozens, and its various equivalents, shows that one is skilled in communication and knowledgeable, not only about obscene terms and concepts, but about current sets of insults and retorts; in short it shows that one is culturally sophisticated and sufficiently knowledgeable for inclusion in the group.

While girls show correlative increases in verbal skill and learn how to be cutting in comments, the interactions are neither as general nor as ritualized. It is likely that the boys described above experience a great deal more culturally produced conflict about their sexual identity than do the girls; hence the strong need for assertion and verification of masculinity, which in its more extreme form rests upon negation of femininity.

HOW THEY SEE OTHERS

The perceptions of others held by children up to the age of about 11 years are generally simplistic and unitary.[25] The child has difficulty understanding that positive and negative traits may exist simultaneously within the same individual. A person must be either mean or nice, rarely both. In an experimental situation where two highly inconsistent traits were insisted upon, children of grammar school age gave the person a neutral rating on a scale of likableness.[26] However, in a life situation the maintenance of a neutral attitude toward a person one encounters often is less likely, and one or the other incompatible trait may be denied.

During the early adolescent years there is a shift from an absolutist view of personality—the view of a person being all good or all bad—to a more complex and realistic perception. While the change is fairly dramatic, it is by no means complete. The young adolescent still relies heavily on concrete categories. A big step is the acceptance of inconsistencies in character, a gain which is often not achieved until later adolescence (16 to 18 years). In evaluating simple and obvious qualities of others one finds little difference between prepubescents and postpubescents. However, there are marked differences in the degree of abstraction and in the descriptions of more subtle psychological traits. Researchers have asked youngsters to describe someone they like and someone they dislike. The descriptions are then evaluated in terms of content and complexity. The increased sophistication in the descriptions produced by pubescents cannot be accounted for by linguistic development alone because the general descriptive terminology, words like nice, friendly, affectionate, and grouch, are learned by seven or eight years of age. However, these terms are not freely used, especially with additional qualifiers such as *very* nice or *sometimes* a grouch, until adolescence.

We can see examples of these trends in the responses of junior high students asked to describe someone they like very much and someone they dislike very much. The seventh graders rely heavily on physical characteristics in conveying their attitudes. The disliked person is almost invariably described as ugly. Even among the ninth graders the descriptions of others, both liked and disliked, are simplistic, though certainly more complex than those of the seventh graders.

Seventh Grade

> There is a girl I like who is in 6th grade. She's got a good personality and she's very cute. She has blond hair.

Tall, muscular, very nice black hair, runs very fast, 8th grade, likes track.

He is 5′7″ pretty ugly and is a beat.

Sam is a fat and ugly guy. He always picks on people and steals money from people.

She is tall and ugly.

Eighth Grade

About 5′3″ dark skin. Dark super fluffy hair. A excellent trumpet player. Super friendly. The biggest brown eyes, A great personality. He is easy to talk to if you have a problem.

I hate my brother because he's good looking and bright. He made a total mess of his life and is beyond repairing the damage. He never works, eats or goes places. He has no money, is entirely independent of everyone and furthermore entirely satisfied with his life.

He's ugly, stupid, and a fool. He doesn't have any pride in his uniform. He's slimed over and has a big mouth. He doesn't have pride in his work and just slimes it together. He's a real creep.

Ninth Grade

She is 5′3″ and German and Jewish. She has gold hair and an excellent figure. She likes secrets.

The person I like is about my size. He has black hair and his eyes are dark brown. He's also the same color as I am. He weighs about 122, and he is fine (a fox).

She is funny, tall and keeps me from getting depressed. She likes things that are completely different from the things I like. She comes from a large family and talks alot about them. She is quite hilarious.

I don't like one person because they talk behind my back and it gets back to me and it makes me feel bad they have a snotty attitude and have a smart mouth.

He thinks he owns the world, he brags alot, and gets loaded whenever he can. He also gets people into trouble.

People that I don't like are people that don't judge you by personality but by looks. And people that think they are too good for others.

Increasing sensitivity is a major part of the transition from childhood to adolescence. As a result the inner world and the outer world become progressively more complex.

HOW OTHERS SEE THEM

Almost everybody is aware of the growth spurt since nearly everyone experiences it. What may not be recalled by the son or daughter but probably remains memorable to parents, is the food expense spurt. Appetite at puberty can be amazing. Small wisps of girls devour copious quantities of food at this time. A lean lad of 14 years can put away tremendous amounts washed down by glass after glass of milk, only to return an hour or two later to rummage through cupboards in search of a snack. Others have been known to develop addictions to concoctions of hot chocolate and coffee liberally laced with milk and sugar; exotic teas and weird combinations of ice cream, yogurt, and fruit abound; sandwiches of lettuce, mayonnaise, and peanut butter, and other bizarre combinations and, of course, insatiable desires for junk food are evident. Chicken from the Colonel, Big Macs, franchise pizza, and other fast food fancies become the ultimate treats. Many are constant nibblers— either chewing gum or crunching life savers.

The incessant eating, even among those who are concerned about being fat, continues in the confines of the bedroom. Some youngsters become hermits and stash refreshments and entertainments in their bedrooms. The pubescent's room is generally evocative of a disaster area with clothes, schoolbooks, records, and objects of vague function strewn about. The room's inhabitant soberly claims to knowledge of exactly where everything is, and prefers the room in this state. Cleanliness of rooms often becomes a major source of contention with parents. Under adult insistence it may be cleaned weekly or even daily. However, it reverts to its former state with amazing speed. Fortunately the messy room phenomenon follows the messy clothes syndrome in its decline through adolescence. Interest in personal appearance tends to precede room neatness. The most impeccably groomed 15-year-old may reside amid a chaotic jumble of possessions, mementos, pennants, and posters.

A variety of explanations has been offered for sloppy dress and messy rooms. Psychoanalysts have described it as a regression to an earlier stage of development embodying a fascination with dirt and messiness reflective of the anal stage* of infancy. There are qualities of defiance, withholding, and self-assertion involved similar to the budding assertiveness of the two-year-old. The messiness may also reflect a preoccupation with other matters. Having to pick up in one's room is often seen as a truly arduous chore—a dull and tedious task, which in fact it is. The young adolescent is acutely aware of the negative experience of tedium and boredom and often has not yet developed means of managing them. The act of cleaning is viewed as pointless since the room will simply become messy again. One's space is an extension of oneself. The messy room reflects untapped nervous energies. Rooms will be cleaned spontaneously only after one decides that neatness counts, in and of itself, or as a reflection of one's own personality. Of course, in the face of strong insistence or punishment the room will be tidied, temporarily. However, observation of its more natural state reveals a great deal about the mental life and nervous energy of its occupant.

The general messiness of self and space which characterizes the early phases of puberty is often accompanied by a corresponding decline in manners. The formerly polite and agreeable child of nine years may be unrecognizable in the slouching, monosyllabic 13-year-old at the dinner table imperiously issuing commands for salt or butter or whatever, totally devoid of please and thank you. "Yeh," "nope," and "fine" are all that remain of a previously well-developed vocabulary. Parents often express concerns about their children's posture. Reasonable arguments appear to fall upon deaf ears. Yet, the young person is far from impervious to the views of others. Some of the apparent resistance and detachment serves a protective function. "I don't know" really means "get off my back." Youngsters at this age are a curious mix of awareness and insensitivity. It is not always clear either to them or to the observer which mode is dominant at any given time. For the adult, discerning what is on their children's minds and figuring out the best ways to communicate require familiarity and attention which were not as necessary when the children were younger. Thirteen-year-olds make 9-year-olds appear simple and transparent by comparison.

Not only are the 13-year-olds more complex, they are also more aware of complexity in others and they are quite curious about new people. Cognitive development through the intervening years provides for a reassessment and more penetrating analysis of the acts and motives of others. They can be extraordinarily irritating if not downright brutal in their observations of adults. Many a substitute teacher has been driven from a junior high classroom by the pressure as well as the antics of the students. The harassment of the teacher may in part reflect malicious intent. However, it also reflects curiosity and a desire to know how the person operates. Young adolescents are not yet sufficiently perceptive in evaluating the more subtle components of personality to be fully empathic with the feelings of others. Yet they are often sufficiently perceptive to recognize areas of sensitivity and vulnerability. The urge to push and poke and test limits becomes irresistible. There is no reason for an instructor to tolerate cruelty and disruptive behavior. However, it is often helpful to recognize the motivation and see that all such attacks are not meant to be as harmful and personal as they might seem. In surveying college students about their recollections, it was found that many of them acknowledged various dirty tricks against teachers. Yet, as often as not, they really liked the teacher. The trick was just something to do. Capers like putting tacks on chairs, hiding all the chalk, and throwing erasers often reflect a general restlessness and discontent or hostility to authority rather than malevolence intended for a specific person.

The insensitivity also extends to age-mates. While an adult may have the perspective to manage negative interactions, life for an adolescent who is made an object of derision by peers is incredibly miserable. The feeling of isolation as a result of torment and ridicule can be a devastating experience.

The inability or unwillingness to reflect upon and consider the meaning and consequences of acts corresponds with an overall restlessness. Pubescence is a period of tension which is often expressed in physical movement aptly described as twitchiness. "Movement was the standard," one junior high school teacher wrote of his students, "tapping of hands or fingers, wiggling bodies, turning heads, bouncing, jiggling, squirming. These were not the exuberant and free movements of small children, nor the coordinated display and use of body."[27] Accompanying the physical restlessness is a shortened attention span and limited periods of involvement in any single activity.

There also may be unrealistic attitudes expressed about what one can and cannot do. Simple errands may be seen as complicated and difficult, while unrealistic and elaborate plans for trips or projects may be devised. Previous behavior patterns not seen since early childhood may reappear—bedwetting, nail-biting, and anxiety of the dark and childhood fears. The resurgence of both old and new anxieties requires various coping practices such as compulsive rituals involving putting on one's clothes in a particular order or frequent bathing. Tics and other physical manifestations of anxiety are not unusual. Flashlights, knives, and other power symbols may be acquired and kept for ready use under a pillow. Collecting objects can be a means of establishing order and control and thereby assuaging anxiety. In most cases these practices are transitory and disappear in later adolescence.[28]

MATURITY PROFILES

One of the most detailed descriptions of what pubescents are like is that of Gesell, Ilg, and Ames.[29] From a longitudinal study they constructed a series of 24 profiles for consecutive ages from infancy to adulthood. Each profile represents a mini-stage of development. Using designations of Twelve, Thirteen, and so on, they described the developmental traits and trends of each year. A given 14-year-old may not fit exactly into Gesell's Fourteen, however, she'll probably be near, either having been there, or soon to arrive. She may, at 14½ years still be in a stage of 13-year-oldness in a descriptive sense. The designations have a stereotypic quality to them as they represent a composite picture of many persons. The portraits are also reflective of their Anglo middle-class composition. Their usefulness is in providing a flavor of behavior during the pubescent years and for illustrating important themes and trends. They are not to be used as rigid standards by which to judge either delayed or accelerated maturation. Following are summaries of the profiles of Eleven through Fourteen.

Eleven

The profile of an 11-year-old is of a wiggling, inquisitive, talkative, and hungry person. The former equanimity of Ten disappears as Eleven experiences new moods and impulses. Behavior reflects the immaturity of the new emotional development and may include yelling, threats, rudeness, and moodiness. The source of emotion may not be apparent to the adult, but is very real to the 11-year-old, and the acknowledgment and recognition of that emotional discomfort helps with its management. Gesell and his associates are careful to point out that emotions and tantrums at Eleven do not reflect a regression to an earlier age but, rather, reflect patterns of growth in the person. They are the result of maturational changes of the organism itself instead of reflections of the environment. Eleven is the threshold of adolescence and is characterized by movement, action, and social inquisitiveness, and, according to Gesell, Eleven is more adept at challenge than at response. At age 11 youngsters begin to see their parents as individual personalities and become critical of them. Argumentativeness and talking back increase. Social relationships with peers are peppered with transient antagonisms: quarrels are frequent. These antagonisms are reflective of the growing intensity and depth of peer relationships. In sum one gets a picture of a beginner engaging in exploration of self and the social environment.

Twelve

Twelve has become less self-centered than Eleven and shows a growing sense of humor and sociability. Twelve is trying to grow up, yet in many respects is still quite immature. Group activity is conspicuous and often boisterous. The 12-year-old is developing a capacity for insight and may occasionally grapple with an abstract concept such as justice or loyalty. Enthusiasm is often a notable characteristic. Twelve carries intimations of maturity which will require the cycle of adolescence for their realization. A major concern is that this potential for maturity be allowed to develop by the cultural shapers of personality.

Thirteen

At thirteen adolescence is well underway. Thirteen is adaptable and dependable and shows the evolution of a sense of duty. The 13-year-old may also often be quiet and moody, lapsing into periods of reverie and reticence. Thirteen-year-olds worry a lot, are detailed in their criticism of parents, and are concerned about what others think of them. The worry reflects an increasing sensitivity to inner personal concerns, an awareness representing a major maturational step. The recognition of internal thoughts and feelings is beginning to connect with external awareness. The quiet periods may reflect the mulling over of external events and experiences and their incorporation with inner responses and feelings. Thirteen is a period of reflection and appraisal. Sensitivity to criticism is heightened. Both sexes tend to withdraw from the previously more close confidential relationships with their parents. Both sexes are increasingly concerned with their appearance. Using the analogy of a mirror, Thirteen is portrayed as studying the reflected image, comparing it with internal images, and trying on new ones. The mirror fosters self discovery and, it is hoped, self assurance. Of note is that the person is becoming even more active in constructing the reality of self. The sense of self is still profoundly influenced by the group, although individual differences begin to emerge. Thirteen is described as a very complex year, one particularly characterized by change—change in body development; change in mood; and a time of increasing interpersonal demands made by family, teachers, and peers. Yet through all this a sense of identity and independence is developing. Thirteen is a time when sympathetic understanding is particularly needed.

The description of Thirteen provided by Gesell, Ames, and Ilg is a more specific embodiment of the general themes of puberty. "Thirteen" is the prototypical pubescent.

Fourteen

Life becomes easier at Fourteen. The emotional climate mellows with a reduction in shyness and touchiness. The inward absorption of Thirteen established the groundwork for an integrated and balanced self concept, and, as a result, Fourteen shows a better orientation to self and others. There is increasing interest in the opposite sex. Unless very nonverbal, Fourteen enjoys exercising a new command of language, using it to communicate ideas and assessment—of an intellectual nature or of a psychologizing sort—giving advice to friends about appearance or social skills. A broader outlook on life emerges. Fourteen is seen as an important period for evaluation as it provides a perspective on the developments of the years 11, 12, and 13. Talents and gifts are now recognizable, as are difficulties and deviations of a harmful nature. Fourteen is a pivotal year in which youth are coming into their own. Emotions are less precarious. The increased ability for logical and prepositional thought increases educability. Fourteen is often an age of finding ideals and of their taking root. Albert Schweitzer, in looking back on his own youth said, "If all of us would become what we were at fourteen, what a different place this world would be!"[30]

COMMENT

Many changes take place during the years from 11 to 15. Social relationships become more extensive and complex. Friends are of particular importance during these years, providing support as well a being a source of concern and sometimes pain. Relationships with parents may become strained as a result of yearnings for independence and an increased reliance upon and devotion to peers.

SUGGESTED READINGS

Adams, J. F. (ed.) *Understanding adolescence: current developments in adolescent psychology*, 2nd edition. Boston: Allyn & Bacon, 1973.

Brody, E. B. (ed.) *Minority group adolescents in the United States*. Baltimore: Williams & Wilkins, 1968.

Evans, E. D. (ed.) *Adolescents: readings in behavior and development*. Hinsdale, Ill.: Dryden Press, 1970.

Hamburg, B. Coping in early adolescence: the special challenges of the junior high period. In Arieti, S. and Caplan, G. (eds.) *American Handbook of Psychiatry*, Volume 2, 2nd edition. New York: Basic Books, 1974, pp. 385–97.

Kagan, J. and Coles, R. (eds.) *12 to 16: Early adolescence*. New York: Norton, 1972.

Konopka, G. Requirements for healthy development of adolescent youth. *Adolescence*, 1973, 8, 291–316.

Muuss, R. E. (ed.) *Adolescent behavior and society: a book of readings*, 2nd edition. New York: Random House, 1975.

Sullivan, H. S. *The interpersonal theory of psychiatry*. New York: Norton, 1953.

9 *School*

> Fundamentally, for most American twelve-year-olds, school is *where it's at*. School occupies the time and concerns of all the people you know—your friends, your parents, people you meet. People are always asking what you do in school and how you like school. School is often a source of contention between you and adults. Why did you get low grades? Why did you play hooky? Why don't you play school sports or join clubs or work harder or work less, and so forth? You are always telling people you don't like school, but often you don't mean it because school is comfortable and they at least want you around. Also you think school is important and even fun. But these things can't be said too openly.
>
> Edward C. Martin

A special institution has been constructed for the pubescent—the junior high school. The history of adolescence was presented in Chapter 2, and the close relationship between society's educational needs and aims and the evolution of adolescence as a distinct stage of development was described. The junior high school is an institutional embodiment of the recognition of pubescence as a special period of life.

From its earliest inception in 1896, the primary focus of the junior high has been on needs of young adolescents rather than on specific studies. This does not mean that educational concerns were absent; however, the basis for the creation of a special school was the recognition of puberty as a time of flux and an awareness of the special needs of maturing boys and girls.

For the pubescent embarking upon the journey through adolescence, school is where the action is. It is the stage upon which her interests, concerns, and conflicts are displayed. Insofar as it achieves goals of separation, transformation, and incorporation, school may be considered a rite of passage.

A BRIEF HISTORY

The first educational institutions in the United States were elementary schools patterned after European models, and there was a great lack of uniformity from town to town. The elementary school, a one-room schoolhouse committed to the "three Rs" and covering grades 1 through 8, evolved in response to the demands of life in the New World. With respect to secondary-school education, the first import was the Latin grammar school whose function was to teach Latin and Greek to boys in preparation for college careers. These schools, while supported by public funds, served only a small minority and never really caught on in the United States. In response to more practical needs, Benjamin Franklin founded the academy, a private institution. An early function of the academy was preparation of boys for careers in business and diplomacy, although such institutions occasionally admitted girls.[1]

In 1821 a high school for noncollege-bound boys was established in Boston. As the principles of universal education and local control became stronger, more high schools were established. In 1924 a girls' high school was opened in Boston, but it closed the next year because there were too many female applicants. It did not re-open for another 25 years.[2]

The demand for high school education increased greatly after the Civil War. Supplanting the private academy, the high school emerged by 1890 as a four-year school. This length was an arbitrary one. At the turn of the century there was still little connection between the elementary school and high school. In general, high school promoted democratic and comprehensive programs encompassing broad areas of study ranging through manual arts, domestic science, physical education, music, art, commercial subjects, and college preparatory courses. Despite the original breadth, the high school imitated the college with its reliance on lectures and written papers. With the developing focus on academics combined with a lack of coordination between schools, first-year high school students showed high rates of failure. Further, a substantial number of students had left grammar school by the seventh and eighth grades. Educators became concerned about these high dropout rates.

In the now-familiar pattern of stimulation for educational reform, Charles W. Eliot, President of Harvard University, in an address to the National Education Association in 1888, pointed out the advanced quality of secondary school graduates in France. In the 1888 speech and a subsequent address in 1892, he asserted that elementary education was too long and that specific areas of study should be introduced at an earlier time. These recommendations were supported in 1892 by the Committee of Ten, a group of educators appointed by the National Education Association to study the topic. The outcome was the recommendation that secondary education begin two years earlier, following six years of elementary education. This view was expressed in a report published in 1899:

> The seventh grade, rather than the ninth, is the natural turning point in the pupil's life, as the age of adolescence demands new methods and wiser direction. Six elementary grades and six high-school, or secondary grades form symmetrical units. The transition from the elementary to the secondary period may be made more natural and easy by changing gradually from the one-

teacher regimen to the system of special teachers, thus avoiding the violent shock now commonly felt upon entering the high school.[3]

A multiplicity of circumstances led to consideration of a separate school for the transition years. With the rapid growth of the population and the necessity for increased building, housing grades 7, 8, and 9 in a separate unit became feasible. At the same time the burgeoning mental testing movement emphasized the individual differences among school children and the desirability of individualized attention. A further need was to ease the transition from elementary to high school. A major consideration in the evolution of the separation from elementary school was the attempt to attract more highly trained instructors, particularly more male teachers, into the seventh and eighth grades.

One of the earliest schools designed for pubescents was established in Richmond, Indiana, in 1896 and included grades 7 and 8. The superintendent would have included grade 9 in what was termed the "Intermediate School" had space permitted. The features which distinguished this intermediate school from the elementary school were electives, promotion by subjects, homerooms, and departmentalized teaching, i.e., math teachers, history teachers, etc. Similar schools developed in Michigan and New York. In Berkeley, California, an "Introductory High School" covering grades 7, 8, and 9 was established in 1910. In the words of Superintendent Bunker, ". . . children would enter it at the beginning of the period of adolescence, when by nature they crave an opportunity to dip into a wide range of subjects and activities, which is Nature's way of insuring freedom of choice in determining occupation and of exercising somewhat of intelligence in the same."[4]

The term "junior high school" was first officially used in 1909 at Indianola Junior High School, in Columbus, Ohio. It became the most frequently used designation with "intermediate school" the second most frequent. Currently "junior high" has been criticized because of the implication that it should model itself after the high school—hence today one finds "intermediate" or "middle" school gaining in popularity. Despite the name, the junior high concept has been quite distinct from the high school, particularly with respect to its focus on the pubescents and their needs, and on generalized rather than specialized education. The primary focus on the young adolescent is a repeated theme throughout the literature. In 1911, J. H. Francis, superintendent of schools in Los Angeles, outlined the goals of junior high school education:[5]

1. More challenging approaches to teaching
2. Departmental work
3. The development of social responsibility during early adolescence
4. The attraction of male teachers to grades 7 and 8
5. Better provision for pupils who would soon terminate their education
6. More guidance for pupils as individuals, especially vocational guidance
7. A more gradual transition from elementary school to high school

In response to social change, the goals of the junior high school program have been altered over the years. Compulsory school attendance laws eliminated an earlier aim of preventing dropouts. Beginning vocational training was deferred to the later grades and the junior high school emphasized exploration, guidance, and the recognition of individual differences instead.

Two forces have shaped the curriculum of the junior high school. One is the acceleration or "economy of time" concept which emphasizes introducing academic and specialized subject matter at an earlier time. Departmental teaching stems from this view. The other force has been the emphasis on providing age-appropriate education directed toward exploration and discovery of interests with much emphasis on individual guidance and counseling. From the twenties to the fifties, the emphasis on "economy of time" diminished while the concept of providing the best education for the age group gained ascendance. In the mid-1950s a good program was one which provided a general education and integration of experience with emphasis on the development of sharing, responsibility, and self direction. The ideal program would foster the discovery of aptitudes and interests. Prevocational training and plenty of guidance and counseling were seen as desirable. The "economy of time" concept lay dormant.[6]

By 1960, during serious questioning of the effectiveness of the entire educational system, the "economy of time" notion was revived and the old arguments began anew. Critics did not denigrate the guidance function; they continued to recognize the transitional nature of the junior high school student. However, a renewed emphasis on departmental teaching, ability grouping, and earlier college preparation was urged.

THE JUNIOR HIGH SCHOOL TODAY

In many respects the junior high has become a very insular institution. It has developed its own bureaucracy. Its students are in the process of severing family ties and have not yet made connections with the larger community. Technological and economic changes as well as social change have led to a denigration of many of the more practical aspects of the junior high program. The wooden lamps, copper plaques, and ceramic ashtrays—products of shop classes—are pale heirs of earlier more vigorous occupational training programs. Classes in home economics and shop have become electives. On the positive side, more controversial issues are being incorporated into the curricula in history and government classes. Science programs are becoming increasingly sophisticated, and the intellectual capacities of pubescents for considering and dealing with controversial and difficult questions of social import are gaining recognition.

As some educators feared, the junior high has in many respects become a miniature high school—but one even more cut off from the community. Junior high students participate in their own sports events (complete with pom-pom girls and cheerleaders), their own football banquets, and their own evening dances; there is very little participation of other age groups apart from the mandatory chaperones. Concern with preparation for college has increased. Tracking systems are often employed as early as seventh

---

Experiences of a student teacher—some excerpts

Carole Papirtis Heffner did her student teaching with an eighth grade class. The following segments were selected from her account of the experience.[13]

The most difficult thing for me to adjust to was the devious way the eighth grade mind works. It was only a little less than shock to walk into home room the first day and have twenty students jumping up and down shouting "Who is she?" or asking me testily "Who are you?" At least my first reaction to the bedlam wasn't to turn and run out the door. I can't say I was embarrassed, either . . . perhaps only flabbergasted to the point of speechlessness. I can picture myself mutely gaping in the face of adversity.

Eighth graders are amazingly straight forward. After the initial "What's your name" gambit they fired an amazing barrage of personal questions. "How old are you?" "Are you married?" "Are you our real teacher?" "Are you really going to be a teacher?" "Do you smoke dope?" "Who did you vote for?" Then other mind bogglers as "Mr. Smith cheats on his wife." "Do you know Mr. Paxton?" "How would you like me to fix you up with Mr. Brown?" "My old man's name sounds like that, he's Greek. He doesn't speak English either. He's fat, too." "Hey, peace, man . . ."

What is so great about these kids is that they seem embarrassed when you get serious with them, but it really sinks in. I think right now is when they take things to heart, they're getting over play relationships with other people and are just beginning to become serious, responsible, and sensitive people. I think it kind of scares them,

grade. There is an emphasis on physical prowess among boys, clothes and beauty among girls, and early involvement in sex, alcohol, and drugs.

Like the pubescents it serves, the junior high school has its own identity problems which have persisted since its inception. The ra-

and that is why they spend a lot of time putting up an elaborate front.

Sometimes I get the urge to ask them what they eat for breakfast so I can cash in on some of that extra-ordinary energy. I've had a brief glimpse of a grandiose dream to channel it all into something great. That something is the grown-up person each one will become.

I think the reason they accept things so readily is because they don't really think about what the teacher is saying, and also because they haven't reached the stage of delving into their own beliefs and questioning them. A lot of them never will, but if any are to be reached I feel that now is the right time. Some of them are a little shocked and perturbed when I ask them to explain why they hold a certain opinion. The answer is usually "Well, I don't know why." When I ask them why they don't know, and tell them that I won't believe them unless they come up with some good reason, I'm met more often than not with a kind of bristling hostility, which I think is good. They are old enough to be taught to think, not just to memorize and call that learning.

One of the small pleasures of being an eighth grader is watching the teacher get mad. Or even better, knowing that you've played just a little part in pushing him or her to the brink of insanity. When the teacher does get mad and then rants and raves for a minute or two the entire class will be silent as the tomb. Then, just like curious little kids pulling the wings off a buzzing fly, they come up with perceptive little gems like, "I bet you feel like locking yourself in a closet and tearing your hair out," or "This is a bad class, isn't it?" or best of all "Are you sure you still want to be a teacher?"

tionale for making grades 7 and 8 part of the secondary system was the belief in an economy of time, that 12-year-olds were ready for the more specialized study provided by departmental teaching. The idea of "economy of time" is a cherished American value. It reflects a belief in acceleration, an idea (in gross form) that more is better and that the guy (or nation) who gets there first is the best. This is most evident in our attitude toward explorers and discovery. The person who arrived somewhere first is remembered; others who came later are forgotten.

If academic excellence and the achievement of specialized education were the sole aims of the junior high school, an identity conflict would not exist. However, also dating from the institution's earliest beginnings is the goal of providing a program suitable to the immediate needs of young adolescents. This goal emphasizes guidance, individualized instruction, personal contact, social development, and the maintenance of continuity. While these aims need not necessarily conflict with specialization, in practice they often do. The demands of departmental teaching often interfere with more personal contact. If a school has one music teacher, that instructor will not be able to devote long periods of time to the same small group of students. Individualized instruction can slow down a teacher who is obliged to cover a particular amount of subject matter so that the students will be where they are supposed to be in time for the succeeding year's work.

These two themes, the early introduction of academic subjects and the provision of the best education for young adolescents at their age level, lie beneath the ebb and flow of frequently changing views of junior high school. Perhaps as a result of the difficulty in resolving the practical outcomes of these trends, the junior high school has been often left in limbo. There is a great deal more research these days on the junior college than on the junior high school. Few universities and colleges provide any special training for junior high teaching despite the frequent acknowledgment of the special nature of the age group. Course work is more likely to focus on either elementary or high school teaching.

AN INVISIBLE SCHOOL FOR INVISIBLE PEOPLE

The identity problem of the junior high school also results from the identification of pubescents as marginal people. The educational literature emphasizes the transitional quality of the passage from prepuberty into early adolescence; pubescents are perceived as being in a state of transition. That this is a limited view with little explanatory potential is demonstrated by the fact that people of many ages are in periods of transition. Kindergarteners are in a state of transition between home and school. The primary grades, first and second, are important transitional phases in the development of concrete thought. Recent high school graduates are in a state of transition from adolescence to adulthood. Recognition of change is more acute for the pubescent because of the dramatic body changes, and change is a major theme of the phase. However, carrying the concept of transience to its extreme leads to the evolution of a holding institution—a place where one "waits it out." Unfortunately some junior high schools possess this quality. The hiatus status of puberty has sometimes been associated with a plateau in intellectual development as well, although this view has little support.[7] Attempts to avoid the holding pattern have vacillated between the poles of "economy of time" and "waiting with guidance and exploration." These concepts and conflicts are reflections of the underlying arguments about continuity and discontinuity in development which were discussed in Chapter 1. The junior high school program represents both a manifestation of this conflict and a valiant attempt at dealing with both possibilities. However, caught between two equally attractive alternatives, preparation and acceleration vs. "here and now" education of an age-appropriate nature, the junior high school risks the danger of doing neither.

THE EMERGING MIDDLE SCHOOL

Among educators, there is a strong movement toward changing the traditional age composition of the three schools involved in compulsory education.[8,9,10] The most frequently suggested plan is to combine the ninth grade with high school and to reduce elementary school to either kindergarten through grade 4 or kindergarten through grade 5, thereby leading to a 4–4–4 plan or a 5–3–4 plan with the *middle school*, as it is often called, including grades 5 or 6 through grade 8. The arguments in support of the change are numerous; a prime one is the recognition of the earlier physical maturation of children as well as their increased sophistication, a result of media exposure. Further, ninth-grade work involves high school and college credit and the high schools have often had a hand in determining junior high school programs. Hence, the argument is made that if ninth grade is combined with high school, the middle school will be more free to design an age-appropriate program. Again it becomes apparent that the major impetus behind the middle school movement is a recognition of the special status of pubescents. Some educators feel the departmentalization process has been carried too far and interferes with the need for breadth and exploration of various subject areas, while at the same time *some* departmental teaching is seen as appropriate for fifth and sixth graders.[11]

The main reasons underlying the quest for the development of the middle school are that the pubescent years are crucial for the development of attitudes about learning, that there is a need for specialized teaching and early presentation of new subjects, and that individual programs are desirable. There is also the hope that a program of middle school certification will attract superior teachers, and protect pubescents from the domination of the achievements of older or more mature children.[12] Other suggestions have been to eliminate delineation among class levels and to omit the assignment of letter grades in evaluation. These goals are strongly reminiscent of those set forth over 70 years ago. The tension between acceleration and age-appropriate teaching remains. However, the recognition of pubescents as a special group with special needs is uppermost and that recognition is becoming more closely allied to the physiological development of puberty than to historical and chronological considerations. The middle school supporters perceive the necessity of an institution which reaches back to the earlier stages of puberty. The current movement is not without its detractors. For some children the single-teacher classroom of grades 5 and 6 is preferable to moving from one instructor to another, and some ninth graders are vastly immature, in contrast to their potential twelfth-grade schoolmates. The dilemma is to some degree insoluble because of the inevitable variations in rates of maturation during these years. A shift to the middle school format will not be advantageous to all. The question is whether it will be of greater benefit to more youngsters than is the current junior high school.

It was the recognition of the accompaniments of puberty—concern with self, a developing ability to meet new intellectual challenges, the need for social development, and extensive individual variability—which played a major role in the evolution of the junior high school and the current trend toward the middle school. In turn, these institutions have contributed to defining pubescence as a unique stage of development.

SUGGESTED READINGS

Hansen, J. H. and Hearn, A. C. *The middle school program.* Chicago: Rand-McNally, 1971.

Howard, A. W. and Stoumbis, G. C. *The junior high and middle school: issues and practices.* Scranton, Pa.: Intext Educational Publishers, 1970.

Martin, E. C. Reflections on the early adolescent in school. *Daedalus,* 1971, *100,* 1087–1103. Also reprinted in Kagan, J. and Coles, R. (eds.) *12 to 16: early adolescence.* New York: Norton, 1972, pp. 180–96.

Overly, D. E.; Kinghorn, J. R.; and Preston, R. L. *The middle school: humanizing education for youth.* Worthington, Ohio: Charles A. Jones, 1972.

Silverman, I. and Shaw, M. E. Effects of sudden mass school desegregation on interracial interaction and attitudes in one southern city. *Journal of Social Issues,* 1973, *29,* 133–42.

Thompson, L. J. Benchmarks for the middle school. *Theory into Practice,* 1976, *15,* 153–5.

10 *Sexuality*

> To suppose that children have no sexual life
> —sexual excitations and needs and a kind of
> satisfaction—but suddenly acquire it be-
> tween the age of twelve and fourteen, would
> (quite apart from any observations) be as
> improbable, and indeed senseless, biologi-
> cally as to suppose that they brought no
> genitals with them into the world and only
> grew them at the time of puberty. What
> *does* awaken in them at this time is the re-
> productive function which makes use for its
> purposes of physical and mental material
> already present.
>
> Sigmund Freud

Sexual behavior on the part of pubescents is variable, reflecting a combination of maturation, inclination, and opportunity. Factual information about sexual behavior is scarce. The insights of psychoanalysts and novelists have constituted the bulk of our information buttressed by the retrospective interviews provided by the work of Kinsey and Pomeroy[1,2] and by the more recent studies on adolescent sexuality by Schofield[3] and Sorensen.[4] While behavioral information is limited, there is even less knowledge about imagery and feelings of eroticism, an area where inquiry remains on the fringes of social acceptability. Much of the information presented in the following pages is drawn from a recent study of adolescent sexuality made by Sorensen.[5] Information was obtained by means of anonymous questionnaires answered by a carefully drawn sample selected to be representative of the entire adolescent population of the United States, based on the 1970 Census. In the final analysis there were 411 completed questionnaires which could be tabulated. While only a small proportion of the 27.1 million adolescents between the ages of 13 and 19 were represented, the responses reflected a wide range of geographical regions, ethnic groups, and social classes, thereby insuring some confidence in the generality of the findings.

COITAL* ACTIVITY

There is very little factual information on the degree to which pubescents engage in sexual intercourse. While many pubescents become sexually experienced, many others are not yet involved in the full range of sexual activities. In the Sorensen sample, among the 13- to 15-year-olds, 44 percent of the boys and 30 percent of the girls reported having coitus* on one or more occasions. Of the remaining youngsters of both sexes 24 percent were in the beginning stages, such as petting, and the remaining 39 percent reported little or no sexual activity with others. In a given ninth grade class, it is not unlikely that one-third of the students will be sexually experienced while another third may be quite naive—another example of the high degree of individual differences that exists during these years.

NONCOITAL ACTIVITIES

The increasing sexuality of pubescence takes many forms of expression—masturbation, homosexual and heterosexual sex play, and sexual fantasies.

Masturbation

Masturbation, the act of manipulating one's own sex organs to induce sexual pleasure without the participation of another person,[6] has received a bad press over the ages. Consider Kellogg's[7] ominous warning published in 1888:

> If illicit commerce of the sexes is a heinous sin, self-pollution, or masturbation, is a crime doubly abominable. As a sin against nature, it has no parallel except in sodomy. It is the most dangerous of all sexual abuses because the most extensively practiced. The vice consists in an excitement of the genital organs produced otherwise than in the natural way. It is known by the terms self-pollution, self-abuse, masturbation, onanisms, manustrupration, voluntary pollution, and solitary or secret vice. The vice is the most extensive because there are almost no bounds to its indulgence. Its frequent repetition fastens it upon the victim with a fascination almost irresistible. It may be begun in earliest infancy, and may continue through life . . . Even after being solemnly warned, he will often continue this worse than beastly practice, deliberately forfeiting his right to health and happiness for a moment's mad sensuality.

Despite the dire warnings, masturbation remains a frequently practiced activity among humans of both sexes. Estimates range from one-half of all male and one-third of all female adolescents[8] to 95 percent of the males and 66 percent of the females—a report based on a college sample.[9] Table 10-1 gives Sorensen's findings on the incidence of age of first masturbatory experience.

The age and incidence suggest masturbation is more clearly associated with the pubertal changes in boys than in girls, and more girls tried it at a younger age. Of those masturbating on a regular basis, one-half claimed they rarely or never experienced feelings of guilt in relation to masturbation. About 80 percent believed they masturbated about as much as others their age. Boys not only masturbate more frequently than girls, they also seem to enjoy it more (Table 10-2). Despite the acknowledged enjoyment, masturbation remained a source of concern. Few had discussed the topic with their parents, and many were extremely defensive about it. They were concerned with self-esteem and expressed embarrassment and

Table 10-1. Age at which males and females with masturbation experience first masturbated. (From R. C. Sorensen, *Adolescent Sexuality in Contemporary America: Personal Values and Sexual Behavior, Ages 13–19.* New York: World, 1973, p. 130.)

Age	All (%)	Males (%)	Females (%)
10 years or under	20	12	33
11 years	11	12	8
12 years	14	15	13
13 years	29	36	18
14 years	18	17	19
15–19 years	8	8	9

a sense of personal disgust. These feelings were the major source of the youngsters' attempts to inhibit masturbation.

Homosexuality

Much of the so-called homosexuality of early adolescence might be more aptly labeled *mutual masturbation,* in that while there is involvement by members of the same sex, such activity does not reflect an enduring sexual orientation. Although Sorensen's definition of masturbation as self stimulation was used in the preceding section, the term has also been defined as any sexual stimulation

Table 10-2. Assessment of enjoyment of masturbation by boys and girls, ages 13–15 years, currently masturbating, in percentages. (From R. C. Sorensen, *Adolescent Sexuality in Contemporary America: Personal Values and Sexual Behavior, Ages 13–19.* New York: World, 1973, p. 130.)

Response	Boys (%)	Girls (%)
Enjoy a great deal	16	6
Enjoy somewhat	53	35
Enjoy a little	24	52
Enjoy not at all	7	7

apart from sexual intercourse which produces orgasm.[10] Mutual masturbatory experiences often occur in childhood and adolescence among persons of either the same or opposite sex. Sexual play and exploration with members of the same sex often represent a satisfaction of curiosity and an extension of knowledge with persons more familiar and less frightening than those of the other sex. Segregation of children and young adolescents by gender often leaves them with only members of their own sex with whom to experiment. This segregation need not be as drastic as that found in boarding school and summer camp. Children are generally warned not to play too intimately with children of the other sex. The hazards may not be spelled out, but the intimations of fearful consequences reduce occurrence of cross-sex experimentation. Homosexual fantasies are not at all rare during pubescence and reflect a broad range of motives. Pubescents often have crushes on persons older than themselves—teachers, camp leaders, athletes, etc. The object of the crush may be male or female. Infatuation with an adult of one's own sex provides a model, a sort of anchor in the rough sea of maintaining a clear notion of self through a period when one's self concept is being challenged by rapid changes in body as well as the experience of new sensations and impulses. In a similar sense the like-sex grouping of prepubescence and early adolescence facilitates the consolidation and learning of sex roles. These like-sexed orientations may be very intense in their quality, yet they are often transient and do not reflect a stable homosexual orientation.

The interpretation that much like-sex activity is not perceived as homosexual is born out by the very low number of reported incidences of homosexual experiences. (An alternative explanation is that homosexual activity is viewed as shameful and thus is not reported.) Among the 13- to 15-year-olds, Sorensen found only a small percentage (5 percent male and 6 percent female) who indicated having had one or more homosexual experiences. Approximately 80 percent of the pubescents agreed with the statement that they would never want to. The 13- to 15-year-old boys were less tolerant of homosexuality than were the older teenagers.

While 40 percent of the entire adolescent sample agreed that homosexual activity was okay if both persons wanted to do it, legislation against homosexuality received a great deal of support.

PRINCIPLES OF EROTIC DEVELOPMENT

Sigmund Freud laid to rest the ill-conceived though culturally satisfying notion of puberty as the beginning of the sexual life. His insight was based in part on the recognition that human sexuality is not synonymous with reproduction. With genital maturation the young person arrives at a time in life when sexuality and issues surrounding it become primary sources of interest and concern. Puberty brings with it an acceleration of sexual development. Psychoanalysts see puberty as ushering in the final stage of psychosexual development, the genital stage (Table 10-3). Successful resolution of this stage occurs when mature sexual aims are directed to persons outside of the family and the early pleasures of self-stimulation are put aside.

Puberty is conceptualized as a time of increased sexual energy derived directly from the increase in sex hormones and accompanied by a general increase in drive level including aggressive as well as sexual impulses.[11,12,13] According to Freudian theory these unconscious instinctual forces are collectively referred to as the *id*. Infants function primarily on the basis of id processes directed toward achieving pleasure and avoiding pain. The psychological means by which the child later adapts to reality and function in the world are called *ego* processes. Ego processes include learning, perception, and cognition. With maturation and experience, ego processes exert control over the primitive and pleasure-oriented demands of the id. By middle childhood the dominance of the ego is fairly well established. In general, school-age children show good impulse control and are quite competent in getting along in their world. With intellectual growth and new skills, ego strength increases. The ego process has an ally in its control over the id in the conscience or *superego*. The superego represents an internalization of cultural values, rules, and prohibitions—the "thou shalts" and

Table 10-3. Stages of psychosexual development hypothesized by S. Freud

Stage	Approximate ages	Characteristics
Oral	First year of life	Mouth as primary source of pleasure through sucking activity. Auto-erotic—pleasure derived from own body.
Anal	Second year	Anal preoccupation and development of control over excretory processes. Autoerotic.
Phallic	Ages 3–5 years	Interest in genitals as source of pleasurable sensation. Replaces interest in anal region. Still auto-erotic but Oedipal situation arises —erotic attraction to parent of opposite sex.
Latency	Middle childhood years	Sexual impulses are quiescent or latent as a result of repression brought on by Oedipal conflict.
Genital	Puberty	Resurgence of sexuality, now directed to members of opposite sex.

the "thou shalt nots" of society. During the years from about six to ten, the instinctual urges are quiescent after a period of intense activity in early childhood. During this period of latency, an equilibrium among the three personality processes, the id, ego, and superego, is established. However, with puberty this balance is disturbed by the increasing activity of the gonads and sex hormones in generating instinctual energy. The pubescent, faced with powerful urges of a sexual and aggressive nature, is not without resources. Ego and superego processes rise to the occasion and an internal conflict ensues.

Anna Freud, daughter of Sigmund Freud, elaborated a more detailed psychoanalytic view of puberty and the early adolescent years.[14] She saw two basic sources of upheaval at puberty. One source is the increase in id strength produced by the functioning of the sexual glands, the physiological change. The second upheaval stems from psychological maturity, independent of physiology. These are changes in object relations—of the shift of attachment from parents to peers and other adults outside the family. That the change in physiology accompanies the psychological maturity does not mean one causes the other. A. Freud underscored years ago the point that cognitive change is as much a part of puberty as sexual change. She did, however, delineate a connection between sexual development and intellectual function, stating that two ego defenses are employed in controlling id impulses at puberty. These are *asceticism* and *intellectualization*. Asceticism refers to a renunciation of instinctual gratification. The young person may, however, show a marked vacillation between renunciation on the one hand and indulgence and gratification on the other. These swings often characterize the pubescent's approach to masturbation. Intellectualization refers to modes of employing the intellect in dealing with the upsurge in the instinctual drives of sex and aggression. The intellect of the pubescent functions more in the service of daydreams than in the realm of planning and reality. This process may contribute to asceticism by allowing the person to *think* about expressing sexual and aggressive impulses rather than actually doing it. Once again we see the themes of fantasy and cognitive development in yet another theoretical perspective concerning puberty. Piaget described the intellectual developments of early adolescence as the outcome of a series of disequilibrations and alternations of cognitive structures by means of assimilation and accommodation between organism and environment. Erikson outlined the process of ego development (and cognition is one of the processes comprising the ego) as it emerged from the interplay of personal history and social forces. A. Freud stated that the effect of the physiological changes of puberty is to bring attention to the mastery function of the ego, a function which has been operating through childhood but which is now brought to bear in controlling the instincts. In this view latency-age children have no need to indulge in abstract thought. It is the danger posed by the increase in instinctual impulses which contributes to the development of the intellect. While the three theorists emphasize different mechanisms of intellectual development, all share in common the assumption that disruption of previously established equilibrium is an impetus to growth and changes. However, it must be borne in mind that too great a disruption may seriously interfere with development.

The high energy level of pubescents, the fluctuation in moods, the resurgence of anxiety as well as incidences of cruelty and vandalism are attributed to the effects of disequilibrium. In the psychoanalytic model, puberty is an inevitably stressful and crisis-like period of development. The form and extent of the crisis will reflect prior ego and superego development. By preadolescence the person has acquired a wide variety of defense mechanisms which influence the form which behavior takes in response to the stress of sexual maturation. Some psychiatrists have gone so far as to view the disequilibrium as analogous to a temporary psychosis. With time a new equilibrium is established among the three psychological processes, which provides the basis of the adult personality.

There are three general problems with the psychoanalytic conception of sexual development. First, the scientific utility of the hypothetical constructs of the id, ego, and superego has often been questioned. Second, the observations upon which the theory rests were drawn from a particular population—persons of an upper-middle class and culture who had problems and consulted a physician. Third, most of the information about their sexual development through childhood and adolescence was subject to the bias and distortion of memory.

Sexuality reflects a broad and variable set of feelings and emotions and patterns of behavior which convey different qualities of experience and varied meanings at different stages of developments. Acts in and of themselves cannot be termed sexual. A gynecological examination is not a sexual act. A rapid beating of the heart does not automatically indicate the emotion of lust. Events have psychosocial meanings attached to them which give them their sexual quality, and these connotations are learned. This has led some to argue that the expression of sexuality need not necessarily follow a prescribed pattern of development, nor should it be conceptualized as a drive.[15]

The role of hormones in the physical maturation of the primary and secondary sexual characteristics is clear. Their role in generating sexual feelings is less so. Androgens* are associated with sexual feelings in both males and females. A woman's sexual arousal is more likely to be altered by changes in levels of her androgens produced by the adrenal* than by alterations in the ovarian hormones of estrogen and progesterone. Thus maturation of the adrenal may play an important role in the development of female sexuality. However, it is very difficult to find direct relationships between levels of circulating hormones and levels of erotic interest for humans of both sexes. Limited research on young people with aberrant hormonal development indicates that sexual interest follows a chronological rather than a purely physiological pattern. Children who show *precocious puberty*† tend to share the immature sexual expressions of their age-mates. Teenage girls who fail to reach menarche for genetic or organic reasons display many of the behaviors associated with sexual maturation such as the occurrence of romantic fantasies accompanied by an increased interest in appearance and in the other sex.[17] The latter example may also serve to confirm the role of adrenal androgens in female sexuality, assuming that the subjects' adrenal system was relatively normal.

The increase in sexual interest in pubescence results in large measure from the indirect effects of hormones. Increasing hormonal levels bring about body changes associated with adult sexuality which in turn alters self-perception and the expectations of others. The physiological changes focus attention upon those psychological and social factors which have to do with sexuality. For

---

† In industrialized societies puberty is considered to be precocious when it occurs earlier than eight years of age in girls and earlier than ten years of age in boys.[16]

example, in a culture where female breasts are regarded primarily as a sexual stimulus, their development will carry a stronger sexual connotation than would be the case in a society where breasts were less often associated with sexual attractiveness. A physically mature boy may be expected by his peers as well as by his father or older brothers to begin developing his sexual skills. As one acquires the body configuration of an adult, one will be expected to take on the behaviors and attitudes characteristic of adults as well.

Sexual expression in males shows a greater variability across social class than is the case with females. This difference may reflect a greater consistency in the female role, that of wife and mother. In general, male development moves from a specific genital orientation to a more general social one. In contrast, female development generally shows a progression from a social and interpersonal orientation to a more genital one.[18] Sexual development, like physical maturation and sex role, must be described specifically for each sex.

Male Erotic Development

Due to increases in the size and responsiveness to stimulation of the penis in the early stages of puberty, erection occurs in response to indiscriminate sets of stimuli—strong emotional arousal of many sorts—fear, anger, virtually any sort of genital contact, and also in response to accumulations of semen. Hence, the male is possessor of a conspicuous and spontaneously active appendage and one from which many pleasurable sensations are gained. Of course, the pleasure is of a mixed sort in that social taboos dampen enthusiasm with guilt, and erections often become a source of embarrassment as well as a prelude to the pleasure of orgasm.

Possession of a penis by males provides a particularly strong genital focus. Masturbation provides a means of producing and hence, to some degree, controlling one's own sexual responsiveness. In males masturbation is often accompanied by a host of progressively more elaborate and complex fantasies. These fantasies are comprised of many associations which have been established prior to puberty. Humans are symbolic creatures and symbolic association accompanying sexuality is as likely as in any other realm of thought, feeling, and action. Thus it is no surprise that while the sexually precocious boy may masturbate more because of the growth and development of his genitals, his fantasies resemble those of his less mature age-mates.[19]

The incidence of masturbation by males is fairly constant across social class, although its use varies considerably. Middle-class males evolve more elaborate and complex masturbatory fantasies than do working-class males. The socio-economic differences are due to educational factors as well as a tendency for working-class youth to move earlier into the realm of heterosexual relationships. In lower socio-economic groups, masturbatory behavior may serve as a fairly brief prelude and training for heterosexual behavior without providing an overlay of fantasy development.[20] Erotic overlay such as sexual fantasies and behaviors other than coitus, show very little cross-cultural consistency and represent learned components of sexual behavior. Elaboration of masturbatory fantasies may serve as a vehicle for the evolution of a more variable and wider-ranging eroticism. Sexual feeling becomes attached to a variety of situations and circumstances through the process of associative learning. Fantasies in the head become linked to pleasurable stimulation derived from the penis. The possibility for variations in sources of sexual satisfaction in adulthood is greatly increased.

The fantasies of the masturbating male pubescent will reflect qualities learned from adults, peers, and the media. For him, genital stimulation is a fairly frequent experience and his sexuality will extend through a process of learning to nonsexual motives and needs for achievement and autonomy, the expression of aggression, and a sense of power. Orgasm associated with these fantasies serves to reinforce them and leads to a further consolidation of fantasy aims. The fantasy life itself may subsequently come to be satisfying in its own right and later be associated with other nonmasturbatory behaviors.

Masturbatory fantasies also connect sexual pleasure to genital activities which are not heterosexual. The potential for broad symbolic association provides a basis for what has been considered deviant sexual development, where orgasm is achieved from activity other than coitus.* Thus while masturbation does not cause blindness, madness, hairy palms, or pimples, it facilitates the association of elements other than coitus with sexual satisfaction. Perhaps it is the recognition of this potential which lies beneath the long and largely unsuccessful history of attempts to limit mastur-

---

The following is an adult male's recollection of his adolescent experience of erections, fantasies, and masturbation:

My first public hard-on occurred in the swimming pool. I didn't know what to make of it except that my suit was being stretched out of proportion. I remained in the water until the crisis passed. Neither of my parents had ever talked with me about erections or masturbation or anything to do with sex. From reading novels and discussion with my friends, I had some idea of what sex was all about. My favorite masturbatory fantasies had a sadistic flavor. They would include beautiful blond busty women tied to racks with their hands tied above their heads and blouses open or torn. All sorts of degrading things would be done to them with pokers or hands or whips. Nothing specific, and no blood was drawn or bruises left. It was the cry of pain and the anguished "please stop, please stop, you're hurting me" that provided the turn on. Virtually all of my fantasy women came from movies (Jane Russell with her torn blouse in *The Outlaw* provided innumerable trips to orgasm) or from comic books or novels I read. I was much more interested in breasts which at least had some form than in the cunt which I didn't know anything about. I should add that I had no sister and dated very inactively until my twenties.

I masturbated frequently and worried a great deal about it. I knew it was wrong, not from anything my parents had told me or what I had learned in school (there was no sex education at that time) but from the jokes about jerking off and the obvious resemblance to bed-wetting. During my

bation. A less ominous interpretation of masturbatory fantasies is that they may serve to enhance aspects of male–female interaction which are associated with courtship, romance, and foreplay.

Puberty for the male accentuates the development of sexuality. Sexual assertiveness becomes essential to subsequent gender identity and sex role development. Society expects the adolescent male

adolescence both of them would be cause for shame . . . I fought to control them (ejaculations) during junior high school years. I am not sure what I felt would happen if I did it too often, but I didn't want to risk finding out too late. I set goals for myself for reducing the number of times I would jerk off. I remember putting up a weekly calendar above my bed and X-ing the times I masturbated. If I were particularly aroused, I could masturbate two or three times a day. It was a hand-drawn calendar with the days on top and X's for the occasions when I succumbed. I recall an average of three X's per week. I am not sure what my mother or brother thought of my sophisticated code but they never remarked upon the significance of the X's. I did everything I could to keep the sheets from getting sticky with coagulated scum (another fine term!) or "cum" as we called it, I had a terrible time with those sheets. Fortunately the stuff didn't stain indelibly but I always thought my mother would notice. I noticed. I usually shared a room with my brother. We have never talked of these matters to this day nor did my mother or anyone else in the household give any sign they noticed the encrusted sheets. The linen was collected at the end of the week and new sheets put on the beds.

I am sorry I was so guilt-ridden about it. Luckily I was never caught masturbating in the park or at camp. I knew that it was wrong, that I should be discreet, but I would not have known how to handle discovery or ridicule. No one prepared me for the changes that took place during my adolescence. Like most of my friends, I guess, I survived. That's about the most I could say.

to begin the business of learning how to perform sexually. Not only are a whole batch of sexual expectations posed by adults and peers, but sexual expression becomes directly linked to being assertive, strong, independent, competent, achieving, and the embodiment of all these—manliness.

Female Erotic Development

The female treads a very different path to adult sexuality. The routes of the two sexes cross in some places. Sometimes they join and run together, and often they are separate. In any case the sexes seem light years apart at puberty with respect to sexuality. For the female, expressions of sexuality are muted by social expectation and enmeshed in the marriage ideal. More immediate expressions of sexuality may be generated by the responses of males toward her. However, despite changing roles, social pressures continue to direct her toward the dual goals of marriage and motherhood. Menstruation is associated with the capacity to bear children rather than the capacity for sexual enjoyment derived from genital stimulation. Girls are surrounded with prohibitions about sexual expression from the very early age when warned against talking to strangers to adolescence when cautioned about the hazards of pregnancy. Sexual control of the female occurs within the greater context of control in general. When dating, she is rarely told explicitly "don't have coitus." More often she is cautioned about ominous and inexplicit dangers, questioned about her choice of boyfriends, warned about places not to go, and told to be home by a certain hour. She may be advised that boys have difficulty controlling themselves and that therefore the responsibility is hers. Even in this day of liberated women, girls are not advised to sow their wild oats. While boys may no longer be explicitly so advised, the message remains implicit. Long before puberty, female sexuality is contained and channeled by a broad system of control and is consistently directed toward the social roles of being a wife and mother. Females masturbate far less frequently than males and masturbation increases after they have become more sexually experienced, instead of serving as an early substitute in anticipation of sexual relations with others. While both sexes are actively discouraged from masturbation, the prohibitions are probably more effective with girls. First, the female genitalia do not respond with the same obvious and visual qualities provided by the male penis. The penis, by its anatomical nature, is more conspicuous, obvious, and readily accessible to stimulation than is the female clitoris. Anatomy may account for general sex differences throughout infancy and childhood in masturbatory behavior, with boys engaging in more masturbation than girls. A second factor is that at puberty, girls seem to shift their sexual interest more rapidly and strongly to the other sex than do boys. It is not clear whether this difference in timing between the sexes is a part of the maturational programming of development or is a result of social factors.

The socialization of the female with its emphasis on qualities of obedience and conformity and passivity also extends to the sexual realm. Female sexuality is consistently directed into the service of interpersonal and social relationships. The close association of sex with love and long-term affection remains a part of female sex socialization even though the marriage requirement may be less stringent today. Emotional emphasis and romantic ideals serve to establish and reinforce a less genital concept of sex for the adolescent girl. Sexual development is very closely linked to sex role. Male needs for achievement and power become linked to a genital focus at the time of puberty or soon thereafter. "Having balls" with its implications of daring and fortitude is as much a part of being man as possessing testicles. It is later in male sexual development that social concerns precede the genital ones. While both sexes at puberty spend most of their time with like-sex peers, boys with a lot of help from the media, are seeing girls as potential sex objects. However, girls are seeing boys as potential romance objects, ultimately lovers or husbands—again with the assistance of the media. Female eroticism is associated with being attractive and being sexually *reactive* rather than assertive in a genital sense. The female shift to achieving sexual pleasure from genital stimulation generally occurs *within* the confines of a reasonably secure and pleasant relationship.[21]

Just as the resolution of the dependence and independence conflicts differs substantially for the sexes, so does the evolution of
sexuality. In the independence–dependence dimension, female development often involves a transfer of dependence rather than a
shift to independence. In a similar sense, female sexuality is shaped
into a reactive mode early in development and remains so, thereby
contributing not to autonomy in the sexual domain but rather to
female contingency upon male initiative. There are, of course,
exceptions, and the sexual role of women is currently being questioned and may alter. Because general patterns of socialization of
the sexes are deeply imbedded qualities of a society, change is
likely to be incremental and slow for the majority.

HAZARDS

In both sexes sexual maturation may be accompanied by feelings
of shame and of a loss of control. Often the young person lacks a
clear concept of what is happening. While today girls are generally provided with some knowledge of menstruation, the information may not be fully assimilated until they reach menarche. Girls
are often very ignorant about their genitals, referring to their various sexual parts as "down there" or "it" and using "vagina" to
refer to all of the genital structures. Menarche brings with it a
number of emotional associations—the absence of voluntary control, the association of menses with excretory functions, and accompanying feelings of disgust or shame. At another level the onset of menstruation may accelerate and consolidate taking of the
female role. It can be seen as a time when one gives up an active
orientation, becoming more careful and ladylike.[22]

Whereas girls may be ill-prepared for the impact of puberty,
their knowledge of menstruation appears almost encyclopedic
when contrasted with the information possessed by boys about
seminal emission. Men may have more difficulty in talking about
ejaculation than women have discussing menstruation.[23] While
the girl may feel shame over the uncleanliness associated with
menstruation, the boy often experiences a sense of disgust and

guilt over the content and involuntary quality of his sexual fantasies. The content may incorporate familiar females such as mother or sisters, or might be homosexual. Guilt over sexual dreams or daydreams, the occurrence of spontaneous erections, and the effect of acne on appearance all contribute to feelings of shame and loss of control. The guilt may impel the boy more strongly into early heterosexual activity. If the prospect is threatening, he may cope by dehumanizing the object of his drive—the female. Much of the exploitive bravado and gross references directed by men toward women may reflect conflict resulting from mixed emotions of desire and fear and its resolution through the process of dehumanization.

The act of coitus when compared to other motor behaviors is an easy one to perform. It is quite another matter for it to be a psychologically satisfying experience. Sexual learning requires going through some preliminary steps having to do with coupling. Two individuals must learn how to transcend ego barriers, to sense one another, to be emphatic and sympathetic in order that a physically intimate act becomes one of sharing rather than one of exploiting or producing feelings of being violated. Because of the physical proximity of sexual contact and due to social conditioning, sexual behavior carries with it a very high degree of arousal and emotion.

The lack of assistance and training in this area is appalling. Many still carry the naive notion that with sexual development nature will take its course; these same individuals spend vast amounts of time, effort, expertise, and money on other aspects of development—school, sports, and talent. Nature *has* taken its course, clearly demonstrating that healthy sexual development and understanding is not an automatic achievement of human maturation. Every day hundreds of people approach physicians, clergy, educators, psychologists, social workers, and newspaper columnists in search of advice on sexual matters. Pregnancies among young adolescents are increasing in number. Venereal disease has become an epidemic because of ignorance and associations of dirtiness and shame which block adequate treatment and control. Assaults, injuries, and death have in many cases been the outcome of sexual inadequacy, frustration, or fear. All of these instances cannot be explained away as the sexual impulse going awry; the sexual impulse is to a great extent nurtured and cultivated by the social milieu.

Our increased permissiveness in sexual matters has led to disdain for those fumblings so characteristic of beginners. Yet those very fumblings are essential to the full development of one's sexual potential and competence. Because it is often assumed that a sexual interaction must culminate in coitus, some youngsters have a very frightening first experience of sexual intercourse. A little experience and practice at foreplay paves the way for more satisfying and less frightening coital experiences. Beginning sexual activities such as kissing games, necking, and petting should not be denigrated. Further, a greater emphasis on the commonality of feeling between males and females would encourage and enhance sensitivity toward the sex partner.[24]

For a child who has been raised with a belief in the evil of sexual behavior, including masturbation, the resulting guilt may be very strong and influence other behaviors. Masturbation still remains a sin in the official pronouncements of many religions. The young person may engage in rebellious or anti-social behavior in order to obtain "deserved" punishment and achieve some alleviation of guilt. Further, puberty carries with it a degree of fluidity of identity. It is a period during which both positive and negative elements may be incorporated, thus increasing the hazards of the consolidation of a negative identity. Making much of sexual behavior may facilitate the development of a deviant identity where the person internalizes a negative self-image and continues to act in accord with it. Extreme conflict can result in pathological conditions such as *anorexia nervosa,* a cessation in eating which is observed occasionally in adolescent girls. At a symbolic psychological level, the anorexic can be seen as regressing to infancy where feeding must be imposed from an outside source. A failure to eat also accomplishes the aim of avoiding an acknowledgment of puberty, since starvation results in less fat and reduces the size of the breasts and buttocks.

Venereal Disease

Medical and public health authorities claim the incidence of venereal disease has reached epidemic proportions. Large-scale public education programs have been launched both in and out of the schools. However, these programs have had only limited success in affecting the attitudes and behavior of many young people. Much of the problem seems to be the image of VD as disgusting and disgraceful, hence unthinkable in one's own circle. A general attitude is "It won't happen to me" or "My sex partner is not that kind of person."[25] The use of scare tactics and horror stories to prevent the spread of VD is clearly ineffective. A factual approach emphasizing positive steps which can be taken to reduce the chances of contagion combined with information about early detection and the value of treatment makes much more sense.

Pregnancy

The possibility of pregnancy during adolescence is a serious one for many young girls. In light of the emotional, cognitive, and social development of young adolescents, many are not ready for parenthood in modern society. While the rate of birth appears on the decline for all of adolescence, the birthrate is increasing for early adolescents. The increase in early out-of-wedlock pregnancies is occurring at all socio-economic levels. Further, as a result of poor prenatal care and marginal nutrition, the pregnancies of young adolescents are characterized by a greater incidence of sickness in the mother and of premature birth. A younger mother is by no means a healthier mother.

Over 50 percent of those who are pregnant by 14 years of age are pregnant again by age 18. Experiencing pregnancy does not serve to deter subsequent pregnancies; and, in fact, early pregnancy is associated with a greater likelihood of a subsequent and still early (with respect to the age of the mother) pregnancy. Early pregnancy has been associated with factors of external focus of control, societal rejection, and acting out.[26] An external focus of control is the view that external forces beyond personal control direct one's life. The societal rejection factor reflects a conflict on the part of the adolescent between the values of society in general and those of her peer group. Many young pregnant girls identify with a subculture of peers in which pregnancy is tolerated and may even carry a degree of status. The third factor, acting out, refers to the correlation between early pregnancy and specific delinquencies.

Young adolescents are also not likely to practice birth control. Failure to use contraception reflects a lack of information, lack of availability, and opposition in principle, or religion. A major problem blocking the reduction of pregnancy among the young is a motivational one. It is here where we see most clearly the ambivalence and ambiguity which is so prevalent in areas of sexual conduct. Despite a fairly high degree of sexual activity, many youngsters are unable to face the potential outcome of sexual intercourse —pregnancy. Contraceptives, when available, are not used because of carelessness, unwillingness to take the trouble, or because one's sex partner disapproves. Of great impact is the fear of discovery by parents. The issue of spontaneity also looms large. Many adolescents believe that if a girl uses birth control pills or other methods of contraception, it makes it seem as if she were *planning* to have sex. A major block to contraceptive use is the "I'm not that kind of girl" response which one often hears from unwed pregnant teenagers. Here we see the outcome of the clash between sexual permissiveness and opportunity on the one hand, with the traditional values of postponement of sexual intercourse until adulthood or marriage on the other. It is okay to have sex if you are swept off your feet by the moment; it is not okay to plan for the eventuality of sex. Planning requires foresight and consideration of consequences. Many young adolescents are still very much here-and-now. Their capacity for consideration of all eventualities is only beginning to develop. Remnants of more primitive modes of thought remain well into adolescence. For example, taking the entire range of adolescents, 13–19 years, Sorensen found that nearly one-third of the females believed that pregnancy was impossible if a baby was not wanted. The percentage was even higher among those who had experienced intercourse during the preceding month without using birth control. The "it can't happen to me" sort of repression or a serious failure of reality testing is evident.

TOWARD SOLUTIONS

We have all experienced puberty and have seen brothers, sisters, and friends going through it. Yet, little formal information is available on how puberty is experienced by pubescents. There has been sparse media interest in puberty, and little useful information is avaliable to the individuals caught in the rising tide of sexual hormones. They are often hit with a barrage of physiological information presented as human biology. Reproduction and the reproductive organs are described in detail with glossaries and guides to pronunciation of such terms as menstruation (men stroo-a'shun) and testicle (tes'ti k'l). Drawings tend to be abstract and diagrammatic. The information is rarely directed to the likely feelings, urges, and experiences of the pubescent. One is reminded of the presentations on human reproduction designed for young children which show models of the uterus and ovaries and the path of the ovum with real-life views of the male organs and drawings of spermatozoa, and models of fetuses in various stages of development. For all their accuracy and detail, these displays neither show nor explain the act of copulation nor its potential for pleasure.

We do very little in helping pubescents find their way through the welter of emotional and social experiences which confront them. It's no wonder that many adults have difficulty in discussing matters of puberty with their children. Information about the biological processes of reproduction is not sufficient. While factual knowledge is important, the young person needs to be provided with a better understanding of the emotional accompaniments of puberty. The events of menstruation and seminal emission particularly remain surrounded by taboos. Research can help desensitize these topics and encourage people to talk about what it was, or is, like. In addition to the "hows" and "whens" we need to help the person integrate the information so that the experience of puberty does not leave one with feelings of inferiority, shame, and loss of control. One wonders how many of the less wholesome aspects of stereotyped female and male roles stem from a negative experience of puberty. The quality as well as the amount of sex education needs to be improved. Few topics as important to living are given such little attention in the design of curricula and programs for the young. We must work to reduce the disastrous consequences of associations of sexuality with negative self-identity, with violent behavior, and other forms of pathology. An increased understanding of sexual development is sorely needed.

By early adolescence anatomy is only a small segment of femininity and masculinity. The social meanings associated with the genitalia have been accumulating since birth. The hormonal changes are only an additional part of the cumulative effects of gender identity formation. The years of 11 to 15 are of importance with respect to sexuality because in addition to the maturation of the sex organs, it is during this period that the erotic component begins to be clarified in the sense in which it will be expressed in adulthood. The physical changes of puberty cue both the individual and those around to the prevailing social and class expectations of sexual feelings and behavior. While sexuality does not emerge full blown at puberty, we become sexual in new and different ways.

SUGGESTED READINGS

Connolly, L. Little mothers. *Human Behavior,* June 1975, 17–23.

Feinstein, S. C. and Ardon, M. S. Trends in dating patterns and adolescent development. *Journal of Youth and Adolescence,* 1973, 2, 157–66.

Gadpaille, W. J. *The cycles of sex.* New York: Scribner, 1975.

Gagnon, J. H. and Simon, W. *Sexual conduct: the social sources of human sexuality.* Chicago: Aldine, 1973.

Marshall, D. S. and Suggs, R. C. (eds.) *Human sexual behavior: varia-*

tions in the ethnographic spectrum. New York/London: Basic Books, 1971.

Kogan, B. A. *Human sexual expression.* New York: Harcourt, Brace and Jovanovich, 1970.

Marcus, I. M. and Francis, J. J. (eds.) *Masturbation: from infancy to senescence.* New York: International Universities Press, 1975.

Minkler, M. Sex education in the junior high: a comprehensive approach. *Journal of School Health,* 1972, 42, 487–90.

Sorensen, R. C. *Adolescent sexuality in contemporary America: personal values and sexual behavior, ages 13–19.* New York: World, 1973.

11 *Delinquency, Gangs, and Drug Use*

Gangs of junior high school students—often 30 strong—descend on the shopping center during lunchtime to shoplift and disturb customers. Shop owners claim they have to call the police regularly to thwart the teenagers who enter the stores in large groups, fill their pockets, and leave. When individual students are forceably kept out of the stores, they only return a few minutes later with another ten or fifteen cohorts. They curse at the regular customers, many of whom have stopped coming to the stores on their lunch break.

Daily Democrat, Dec. 16, 1976

Puzzling aspects of delinquency, gang behavior, and drug use become less so when behavior in adolescence is viewed as a means of satisfying the needs for identity, intimacy, and independence coupled with increasing sexual motivation. There are many theories of delinquent behavior. They can be roughly categorized into three groups. One is the socially based concept of a delinquent milieu where behavior considered deviant by the prevailing culture is viewed as normal and acceptable by a particular strata or segment of society. Those theories focus upon the social environment as the determinant of delinquent behavior. Another set of theories proposes that delinquency arises out of disordered family relationships. Broken homes, alcoholic parents, severe economic deprivation, and family pathology are seen as major contributors to delinquent behavior. The poor family situation leads to an absence of control over the child's behavior and contributes to the personality and character deficits which constitute the third set of explanations for delinquency. The young person's ego development, frustration tolerance, and coping ability may be inadequate. These three themes—the social support for illicit behavior, the problem of psychological deprivation, and inadequate personality and character development—are neither contradictory nor mutually exclusive. Even for the same person, these factors may contribute differentially at different times and in various situations. The use of tobacco and marihuana, for example, is often a reflection of relaxed social attitudes rather than of faulty character development. On the other hand, drug use may indicate identification with a deviant group, be an act of defiance, or serve to bolster a fragile personality structure.

The point was made in Chapter 5 that cognitive development, internalized values, and situational factors all contribute to moral behavior. Further, qualities of autonomy and empathy may predict a person's vulnerability to group pressure and sensitivity or insensitivity to the potential consequences of delinquent acts. The development of conscience depends greatly upon the relationships within the immediate family, which in turn are affected by the larger community and society. To understand delinquency, all three levels of analysis are necessary—the personal, the familial, and the societal.

Using these three levels of analysis, it becomes possible to better understand why delinquency becomes a substantial issue in adolescence. At the personal level, puberty brings chaos for some youngsters. Even the well adjusted may suffer temporary setbacks in their feelings, cognitive growth, and social relationships. During childhood, inadequacies in development may pass undetected. Generally only the more aggressive or disruptive children come to the attention of guidance personnel or community agencies. The events of the years from 11 to 15 play an important role in delinquency and psychopathology because, while the antecedents lie in infancy and childhood, puberty contributes added stress and many of the protections of childhood are left behind. Sexual maturation and cognitive growth, primary events of early adolescence, contribute to an awareness and sense of urgency of identity, intimacy, and independence needs as well as increased sexual motivation and feelings. Family relationships often become strained as a result of these needs, and parental controls become less effective. At the societal level, the young person's world is greatly expanded; it includes a wider range of friends and contacts and an increased opportunity for engaging in illegal or destructive behavior. Strong emotions, feelings of frustration, new capabilities, and opportunities for action all make the stage a potentially volatile one. Delinquency in adolescence can be viewed as a means of meeting internal needs and environmental demands.

JUVENILE DELINQUENCY— FINDINGS AND DISCUSSION

There are two general categories of juvenile delinquents: (1) young people who have violated regulations which are not considered criminal offenses for adults, and (2) young people who have been judged by the courts as having committed an act which would be considered a crime if performed by an adult. The offenses of the first category, grouped under the rubric of "in need of supervision," have been termed *status offenses*, as they are based on the age and dependency status of the person.

Status Offenses

Status offenses include truancy, runaway, sexual misconduct, curfew and loitering violations, and incorrigibility. The latter is a broad concept often defined as "being beyond parental control." In 1974, according to the *Uniform Crime Reports* published by the FBI[1] 154,653 youths were arrested in the United States as runaways and 70,167 for curfew and loitering law violations (Table 11-1). These figures do not reflect informal action taken by the police; one can assume that in many instances runaways and curfew violators were simply taken home to their parents. Of those arrested 41 percent of the runaways and 24 percent of the curfew and loitering law violators were under the age of 15 years. Other arrest categories include status offenses such as violation of liquor laws (possession by a minor) and sex offenses (sexual intercourse on the part of an unmarried minor irrespective of consent). It is also possible that minors are more likely to be arrested for particular violations where adults may not—vagrancy and disturbing the peace, for example.

Curfew and loitering law violations do not require great elaboration with respect to causes. Because of their increasing maturity, pubescents begin to stay out later. Often lacking financial resources and places to go, they congregate on the streets and in other public areas such as parks, bus stations, and all-night markets. Their presence at times becomes disturbing to adults and proprietors who then call upon the police. In a similar vein, though perhaps one more indicative of serious problems at home— prompted by increased independence, many youngsters choose to leave home. Sometimes the child is escaping from imaginary over-restrictiveness; in other instances the child is leaving an extremely unpleasant situation in which mistreatment has been common. In the National Health Survey described earlier[2] using self-report rather than arrest records, 6 percent of the boys and girls ranging in age from 12 through 15 years had run away from home once; an additional 2 percent had run away more often. In this survey sex differences were negligible. However, the *Uniform Crime Re-*

Table 11-1.   Number of persons under 15 years of age arrested and percentage of total arrests represented by the under-15 age group (from Crime in the United States, 1974. *Uniform Crime Reports,* FBI, Department of Justice).

Offense	Number arrested	Percentage of total arrests of juveniles and adults
Drunkenness	911,837	.4
Disorderly conduct	544,321	6.8
Narcotic drug laws	451,948	3.3
Other assaults	269,643	8.1
Liquor laws	191,213	4.0
Runaways	154,653	41.5
Weapons: carrying, possessing, etc.	119,189	3.9
Fraud	91,176	1.5
Stolen property: buying, receiving, possessing	76,943	10.3
Curfew and loitering law violations	70,167	24.5
Vandalism	61,621	42.1
Prostitution and commercialized vice	53,309	.3
Gambling	45,900	.6
Sex offenses (except forcible rape and prostitution)	44,375	7.8
Forgery and counterfeiting	39,741	2.4
Offenses against family and children	34,902	4.7
Suspicion	33,363	10.1
Vagrancy	32,802	3.3
Arson	10,756	38.1
Embezzlement	5,891	1.4
All other offenses (except traffic)	757,040	10.0

ports showed that 57 percent of all runaway arrests involved females. The picture was quite different on curfew and loitering law violations: males constituted four out of five of those arrested.

Anyone who has spent time working with the Juvenile Court and probation or parole systems is aware that a majority of girls under investigation or supervision are there because they committed status offenses. A frequent one is sexual misconduct. Becoming pregnant is frequently used as evidence of having engaged in sexual intercourse, an act which is illegal for a minor. The potential for discrimination in who gets prosecuted and who doesn't is obvious. Ironically, as status offenses are viewed as separate from criminal acts in many states, legal rights which may serve to reduce or set sentences do not apply.

The motives underlying status offenses vary. In some cases these offenses are preludes to more serious involvement in criminal activity. They may also indicate personality disturbance. However, in many cases status offenses reflect situational factors that do not lead to further criminal activity or indicate pathology. Some truants simply do not like school and many runaways are leaving an intolerable situation.

Serious Crime

The incidence of arrest for serious crimes against persons (murder, manslaughter, forcible rape, robbery, and aggravated assault) and property (burglary, larceny, and motor vehicle theft) shows a substantial increase in the early adolescent years (Table 11-2). While constituting about 6 percent of the arrests for violent crime (crimes against persons) those under 15 years constitute 22 percent of the arrests for serious crimes against property. In later adolescence and adulthood the rate of crime against persons increases, while crimes against property decrease. This pattern may in part be attributable to the lessened difficulty of obtaining weapons as one gets older and increased strength provided by physical maturation—a factor of considerable import in assault and forcible rape. Stealing automobiles does not require the same degree of muscular strength.

Criminal Offenses of a Lesser Nature

In looking at the actual *number* of arrests (see Table 11-1) drunkenness is by far the most frequent, followed by disorderly conduct and narcotic drug law offenses. The pattern of a majority

Table 11-2. Arrests for serious crimes against persons and property by age, U.S., 1974 (adapted from Crime in the United States, 1974, *Uniform Crime Reports*, FBI, Department of Justice).

			Age		
Offense charged	10 and under	11–12	13–14	15	16
Violent crime					
Murder and nonnegligent manslaughter	10	31	165	264	395
Forcible rape	42	115	614	624	891
Robbery	571	2,019	7,394	6,999	8,894
Aggravated assault	814	1,676	5,433	4,796	6,528
Total violent crime	1,437	3,861	13,606	12,683	16,708
Percent distribution	.5	1.3	4.6	4.3	5.7
Grand total all ages = 294,617	17 years and older = 83.6%				
Property crime					
Burglary—breaking and entering	8,849	17,220	47,888	35,851	38,173
Larceny—theft	20,384	43,662	101,168	66,205	65,207
Motor vehicle theft	417	1,782	13,500	15,212	16,144
Total property crime	29,650	62,664	162,556	117,268	119,524
Percent distribution	2.5	5.3	13.8	10.0	10.1
Grand total all ages = 1,177,584	17 years and older = 58.3%				

of arrests for alcohol and drug use and disorderly conduct are illustrative of the attractions and conflicts of young adolescents. Use of alcohol and pharmacological agents of varying sorts is common in United States society. The attraction is not lost on the young. However, impulsiveness and poor self-control make moderation difficult, leading to drunkenness and arrest. Disorderly conduct may reflect rebelliousness mixed with boisterousness characteristic of the age. However, alcohol use may also contribute to the high rate of arrests in that many persons become more noisy and unruly when intoxicated.

The percentage column of Table 11-1 provides additional insight into juvenile delinquency by indicating the degree to which those under 15 years contribute to the total number of arrests of minors and adults for each activity. While arson is not the most frequent offense, of all persons arrested for arson, 38 percent were below age 15. Vandalism is also a category in which a large proportion of arrests were of pubescents. In the 1970 U.S. population census, the 10- to 14-year-olds constituted slightly over 10 percent of the entire population. Thus, young adolescents are disproportionately represented in the criminal arrest categories of arson and vandalism. These percentage figures give an overall view of the relationships between crime and the life cycle.

Vandalism and arson. Lacking the size, strength, and skill or techniques for satisfying needs, a youngster may choose a less direct means of expressing power over others by damaging their property. Much of our law, police activity, and social values centers on the importance of property, be it land, buildings, or goods, and these become a major focus of rebellious youth. Property possesses symbolic aspects of power. The juvenile gets back at adults or shows self-assertion by burning down the school or defacing public buildings. Alienation and a sense of powerlessness may underlie the expression of destructive impulses. In many instances a group facilitation factor is operating; in the company of others, people will sometimes do things they would not do if alone. Young adolescents spend a great deal of time with friends and are strongly influenced by their peers. Compared with younger children, they have more freedom and less supervision, yet have fewer demands upon their free time than most adults. Hence excitement and daring, as well as opportunity, play a part in destructive activity. The issue becomes one of people with too little judgment and too much time eventually getting into trouble.

In psychoanalytic theory the revitalized sexual impulses at puberty are believed to be accompanied by destructive impulses com-

Graffiti

The defacement of walls and buildings had been going on for years in low-income neighborhoods with gang names and warnings announcing territorial claims: However, little general attention was paid to the phenomenon until the rise of the graffiti kings in the early 1970s. These were mostly inner-city youngsters who used aerosol paint cans to transform drab subway cars and city walls into bold identity displays. A vast majority of the graffitists were young adolescents. The names displayed were self-chosen nicknames incorporating the identity and fantasies of the artist: Taki 183, Pepin I, Nova, Turok 161, Cay 161, and Stay High 149. The 3 digits usually indicated the street of the writer's residence. The favorite writing surface of New York's young graffitists was the subway car—painted late at night when the trains were in the yards.

The flamboyant script was a clear expression and assertion of identity. "I have put my name," declared Super Kool, "all over the place. There ain't nowhere I go I can't see it. I sometimes go on Sunday to Seventh Avenue 86 Street station and just spend the whole day watching my name go by." Japan said, "You have to put in the hours to add up the names. You have to get your name around." From Mike 171, "There are kids all over town with bags of paint waiting to *hit* their names." Norman Mailer commented on these, "An object is hit with your name, yes, and in the ghetto, a hit equals a kill . . . You hit your name and maybe something in the whole scheme of the system gives a death rattle. For now your name is over their name, over the subway manufacturer, the Transit Authority, the city administration. Your presence is on their presence, your alias hangs over their scene."[3] Sal 161 had been induced by a summer workshop program to turn his talents from subway cars to canvas. He elaborated "When you have it on canvas you don't risk getting written over. But somehow I just can't come to grips with seeing my identity hanging on a wall, just seems to look better on the side of a train."[4] Writing in *New York* magazine, Richard Goldstein[5] claimed that most of the subway graffitists were rather ordinary 14- or 15-year-old males. An exception was Charmin 65—nee

Virgin I, who made her reputation by hitting the Statue of Liberty. The New York subway graffiti movement finally succumbed to intense pressure from city government and transit police who threatened to use trained attack dogs in pursuing vandals.

Philadelphia youth had their own style. Bobby Kidd artistically sprayed a police car; Tity Peace Sign put his name on the side of an elephant in the Philadelphia Zoo; and Cornbread decorated a TWA jet which took off bearing his nickname on the wings. From one Philadelphia youth, "In a way I think what we've all done is wrong. I wouldn't want anyone writing on my house, I know. But maybe we just don't understand yet what we've done or why we did it." Cool Earl explained, "I started writing to prove to people where I was. You go someplace and get your name up there and people know you were there, that you weren't afraid."[6]

In Los Angeles, Louis Torres, a relatively straight (by his own description) Chicano created his first *placa*, a statement written in spray paint in distinct angular letters:

> "Hell," I thought, "no wonder they do it." Forced to cope with an existence that provides virtually no outlet for creative, personal expression, no wonder they (now *we*) make *placas* . . . A blank wall in the barrio invites a writer to imprint part of himself for all to see. My *placa*, for a time at least, will endure.

Torres' description published in the *Los Angeles Times*[7] led to a flurry of irate letters from readers who feared that the seductive blank wall may be the side of their own house or place of business. Some communities, recognizing the deeper impulses, have taken advantage of territorial feelings in adolescents by enlisting their cooperation in painting over graffiti and replacing it with murals, or other forms of street art. One ninth grader, thus engaged, admitted having contributed to the graffiti and said, "We used to do it for fun when we were high. We would be loaded and would just come out at night and start writing our names or spraypainting on the walls." He went on to express a sense of shame and pointed out that "We couldn't bring people to come

(continues)

and visit our neighborhood because of the writings. That is why we want to clean it up."[8]

The vast majority of the spectacular graffiti was produced by young males, further evidence that, in general, the process of identity formation is expressed in different ways for boys and girls. Identity confirmation for the graffiti kings involved display combined with daring. The production of graffiti is vandalism. It is the damage of property of others. It also very vividly illustrates the theme of both individual and group identity, a dominant feature of the adolescent years. Cornbread took up public decoration when he decided not to join a gang, "There isn't much choice of what to do . . . I did it because there was nothing else. I wasn't goin' to get involved with no gangs or shoot no dope, so I started writin' on buses. I just started with a magic marker an' worked up."[9] The association between property, territory and power plays a role in graffiti as well. Defacement of property is a strike at the more powerful. Granted that the shopkeeper is probably not an immensely powerful person, the symbolic aspects are important to the adolescent. Markings not only serve to express defiance but also serve to impose one's own claims. In the words of Ley and Cybriwsky[10] "He who is king of the walls claims also to be king of the streets and master of their use. The walls are more than an attitudinal tabloid; they are a behavioral manifesto."

Graffiti is no joy when it appears on the newly-painted walls of one's dwelling, or when an entire neighborhood corridor is defaced with the identity scribblings of its youthful residents. Nevertheless, like the pubescent's messy room, the markings of graffitists reveal much about their concerns and motives. The outcome is not always negative. The dull, gray, thundering subway cars were a joy to behold as they roared through bearing the exultant, exuberant identities of "rather ordinary 14 or 15-year-olds."

prising a part of the id component of personality. Destructive acts of arson and vandalism reflect the inadequacy of the person's character structure (ego and superego) in controlling the destructive urges of the id. Clinical studies have also alluded to aspects of sexual arousal; that acts of arson and vandalism possess symbolic aspects of the sexual act.

No single explanation suffices for all, and often more than one factor is operating in any given instance of arson and vandalism. The fact remains that their incidence is high among the pubescent group, hence attempts at prevention by reducing contributing factors such as boredom, alienation, and poor impulse control are well directed to this group, particularly males. Females commit acts of vandalism and arson also, but generally less often and to a reduced degree.

Petty theft. In a recent nationwide survey on shoplifting in super-markets, drugstores, and discount houses it was found that juveniles accounted for about half of those apprehended. More females were caught, but more males were formally prosecuted, a remnant of the double standard, where males are more harshly punished than females. Arrests of shoplifters are greatest just after school lets out in the afternoon, and the most frequently seized shoplifter in a single category was a 13-year-old boy with his shirt-tails out—to cover pocketed merchandise.[11]

AN EXPLANATION OF DELINQUENCY—ACTING OUT

The concept of acting out has been offered by mental health professionals as an explanation for much delinquent behavior. The term was first used by Sigmund Freud to refer to the nonverbal expression of unconscious conflicts. Rather than attempting an internal adjustment, the person acts on impulse against environmental forces, persons, or restraints. Looking back at the discussion of cognitive development and the notion of equilibration, a disjuncture between internal representations and external reality was seen as a potential source of growth in that individuals are thereby motivated to bring their own views more in line with reality, becoming less egocentric. The person who acts out continues to operate in an egocentric mode in accord with his or her own impulses and desires. The failure of internal change often occurs when the disparity between internal representations or needs and external reality is very great.

Another hypothesis about acting out is that it reflects both an inability to tolerate frustration and the reliance on motor activity as a means of communication. Verbal abilities play a substantial role in the organization, expression, and control of emotions. Thus a person with a limited capacity for verbal expression is more likely to use nonverbal modes of discharging tension. Studies of delinquents support this hypothesis; verbal abilities of these individuals often are found to be below average. Jerome Singer[12] has pointed out how a limited capacity for fantasy is likely to be associated with an active attempt to achieve gratification, even when those attempts may be illegal or immoral. A teenager with a limited repertory of interests and cognitive capacities is more likely to act directly upon sexual and aggressive urges.

It is possible that televised violence contributes to acting out on the part of some viewers. Young adolescents watch television three or four hours per day. A steady diet of violence can reduce inhibitions to aggression. While network officials and some researchers debate the effect of televised violence on behavior, those who work with delinquents are less hesitant in making a connection. A reporter recently commented on how often incarcerated youth would describe their acts saying "I did it just like on ——!" naming a violent, often police-related, show. A young person who watches two or three hours of TV a night will have probably witnessed 12,000 murders by the time he or she reaches adulthood.[13]

Acting out may also result in punishment, thereby providing relief of guilt over inner thoughts, feelings, and desires. In these instances the impulses motivating "getting into trouble" and bringing punishment may remain beyond awareness. Psychoanalysts might explain the motives of a young boy who runs away, steals a car, and gets into a police chase, as an avoidance of unconscious incestual desire. Leaving home took him away from the object of desire, mother or sister; while getting caught and being punished relieved the guilt stirred by the unconscious wish.

In other cases one need not invoke explanations involving the unconscious. The delinquent act may reflect conscious hostility toward authority stemming from feelings of powerlessness. For example, anger toward school personnel may be expressed in vandalism against school property.

For girls, sexual promiscuity is a major channel of acting out. Parental and social prohibitions may be flaunted in a show of defiance. At the same time a girl may be desperately attempting to satisfy yearnings for intimacy and self-worth. As with acts of vandalism, sex can reflect an attempt to assert control over others and to earn the affection of peers as well. Sexuality involves very complex motives and a promiscuous person may be operating in accord with any number of them. Directing one's affections outside the family circle may contribute to a sense of independence and, at a more unconscious level, may be a defense against incestuous longings. A father who has behaved seductively toward his daughter may foster her early sexual involvement with others as a defense against feelings aroused at home. Another girl may have fantasies about having a baby who will love her unquestionably and satisfy the longing which went unfulfilled by her own parents. Sexual seductiveness is part of the female role and in many cases sexual involvement reflects neither rebellion nor frustration. Instead, sex and motherhood may represent the only means by which a young woman feels she can demonstrate her worth, value, and identity as a female.

As noted earlier in Chapter 5, delinquents are often aware of the immorality of their behavior, but do not seem particularly concerned about it. Kohlberg[14] found that in comparing delinquents and a matched group of nondelinquents, the former were more likely to show premoral or preconventional levels of reasoning, where "rightness" is a matter of force and social pressure. Much of their thinking was that of Stage 2, the moral judgment level characteristic of 8- to 10-year-olds. Adolescents functioning on an externally based morality will be highly subject to immediate environmental influences. Further, the commission of delinquent acts may consolidate a deviant identity.

A childhood history of inconsistent rearing practices, overindulgence, insufficient discipline, and a general over-charging of sexual and aggressive impulses has been suggested as producing a low frustration tolerance conducive to impulse action or acting out. These features may also contribute to an inadequate development of a sense of individual identity, thus leaving the person more vulnerable to peer influence.

GANGS

The prime age of gang memberships is middle- and late-adolescence and may extend into adulthood. However, pubescents sometimes are found participating in gang activities, and gang members often serve as idols or role models. Most gangs are male. Friendship patterns described in Chapter 8 showed boys as more likely to form larger groups while girls formed friendship pairs, triads, and foursomes. Few female gangs have been found to be as organized, long-lived, and destructive as male ones. The term *gang* refers to a group of persons acting together for some purpose, usually criminal. As one youth worker has pointed out, while minority cliques are often referred to as gangs, those of white suburbanites are called clubs or teams. Whatever they are called, these groups often play an important part in the environment and social lives of adolescents. It is important to note that a majority of adolescents, even males, are not gang members. For example, East Los Angeles is infamous for its rough gangs and bloody battles; yet most authorities agree that probably no more than 15 to 20 percent of the local youth identify with these groups.[15]

Much gang behavior possesses a territorial quality. Commenting on East Los Angeles, Leo Cortez, a youth worker, states:

> What most people don't understand is that the kids out here,
> the gang members, don't consider themselves criminals . . .
> even when they kill, national standards just don't apply. Because,
> here a gang member regards himself as a soldier, you understand?
> Even if he's only patrolling a few square blocks. No matter how
> small his turf is, he still regards himself as a patriot . . . protect-

ing his homeland. Because that's all he's got, all he's ever had
. . . And the leader is his general, directing the battle against
enemies . . . so, if somebody hurts one of their 'homeboys' (a
fellow gang member, or neighbor), then they *have* to retaliate.
Because they're at war. And, after all, what's a war crime?[16]

Gang membership offers an identity, a set of associates, independence from family, and a chance to defy authority. Gang warfare enables the adolescent to demonstrate that he is a man. The
attractions of the gang probably bear an inverse relationship to
the availability of other means of meeting basic identity needs, an
assumption borne out by the association of gang activity with reduced socio-economic resources and opportunities for participation in the larger society. The gap between expectations and reality
in socio-economic level remains great and may even be increasing,
particularly for urban groups. A downward trend in the economy
contributes to increasing frustration and the reduced likelihood of
seeing one's way to a more prosperous future. Fewer and fewer
means of meeting needs for identity and self-worth are available
under these circumstances. Further, one sees other segments of
society who continue to flourish, thus making a mockery of one's
own misfortune.

Incidents of violence may result from the intensification of
frustration. However, other factors contribute as well. Drugs are
available to greater numbers and increasingly younger persons.
Ironically, preventive measures by authorities have contributed
to increased violence. Gang rumbles and "fair ones" (weaponless
fights) are conspicuous and result in arrests. Increased gang sur-
veillance has also led to the incarceration of leaders. The result
has been for younger members to take the initiative and to rely
on individual assaults—hit-and-run attacks with lethal weapons
leading to a dramatic increase in street killings. The following
quotation from Lieber[17] illustrates the trend:

Leaderlessness explains why jitterbugs (younger gang members) make decisions regarding violence, but it doesn't explain
their preference for deadly quick "hits." In fact, gang members
seem confused by the trend to homicide. The corner boys mainly

respond obtusely when I ask about their roles in the war. One, a slight smooth-faced 15-year-old, shyly admits to being a night shooter, a fact which troubles him. He knows he'll die: "I'll be standin' on my corner. The car'll pull up to me and the window'll roll down. That's the last thing I'll see."[18]

The preference for the quick hit may reflect the unavailability of other means of attack. Gang violence will not be eliminated by police crackdowns which simply lead to leaderlessness and a shift from group activity to sporadic hit-and-run tactics. Other means of demonstrating one's emerging manhood and seeing a passage to the future must be available before the undesirable aspects of gangs can be eliminated. This is not to say that law enforcement ought to be suspended in gang-ridden neighborhoods. The residents in those areas deserve and require protection. However, improved enforcement in and of itself will not be sufficient in markedly reducing the problems posed by gangs—problems stemming directly from the unmet basic needs of adolescence.

DRUG USE

Alcohol

A series of California studies have shown that by the seventh grade nearly three-fourths of the boys and one-half of the girls had consumed alcoholic beverages. A smaller group, 16 percent of the boys and 11 percent of the girls had used them ten times or more.[19,20] In an Oregon city among ninth graders about 80 percent of both boys and girls had tried alcohol; 37 percent of the boys and 26 percent of the girls admitted to consuming it 16 times or more.[21] A survey of seventh and eighth graders on an Indian Reservation in Wyoming found that while a majority of youngsters perceived that drinking was a source of getting into trouble, both boys and girls approved of it for people in general. Over 90 percent claimed they had tried alcoholic beverages and 80 percent considered themselves drinkers.[22] It is possible that the high rates reported from all these studies reflect a degree of exaggeration and bravado on the part of the respondents; however, it clearly indicates the accepting attitude that many young people hold toward alcohol.

Tobacco

While a majority of young adolescents do not smoke, the numbers who do increase with age. The national health survey[23] revealed an upturn in smoking at age 14 for both sexes, from an average of 5 percent of the 13-year-olds to 11 percent of the 14-year-olds and 18 percent of the 15-year-olds. Another study in an urban setting found that 16 percent of the boys and 10 percent of the girls in the ninth grade were regular smokers.[24]

Marihuana

Since 1968 a yearly anonymous survey has been taken in a populous suburban and light-urban Northern California county. In the most recent result 49 percent of the ninth-grade males had used marihuana one or more times in the preceding year. Included in that group were the 30 percent who had used it ten or more times.[25] These figures are probably higher than the national average, and in general there is a greater use of drugs among males than females. Table 11-3 shows the results of a sample of households throughout the nation. While the percentages are relatively low in early adolescence, it is evident that a substantial number of pubescents have at least experimented with marihuana.

Inhalants

Among children of elementary and junior high school age there are intermittent fads of inhalation of toxic substances—glue, gasoline, lighter fluid, and aerosol sprays. Inhalation produces varying degrees of euphoria and intoxication. Many of these substances are extremely dangerous and can cause organic damage and death. In one study the majority of glue sniffers were found to be 13-year-old boys with a history of delinquency and broken homes.[26] A survey of urban ninth graders indicated that 15 percent of the boys and 11 percent of the girls had experimented with inhalants. Contrary to their use of other drugs, the use of inhalants by ado-

Table 11-3. Marihuana use among youth, 1971–1974 (from Marihuana and Health, *U.S. National Institute on Drug Abuse,* 4th annual report to the U.S. Congress, 1975, Department of Health, Education and Welfare).

	Percent ever used, by year			Percent current use—used during last month, by year		
	1971	1972	1974	1971	1972	1974
All	14	14	23	6	7	12
Age						
12–13	6	4	6	2	1	2
14–15	10	10	22	7	6	12
16–17	27	29	39	10	16	20
Sex						
Male	14	15	24	7	9	12
Female	14	13	21	5	6	11

lescents declines with age, the practice being most common among 10- to 14-year-old boys, with older adolescents disdaining the practice.[27] The advantages of getting high with inhalants are that it is more spontaneous, costs less, and doesn't require outsiders, as is the case in obtaining alcohol and other drugs. One group of pubescent boys indicated that sniffing was *their* own thing with drinking for adults and dope for hippies.[28]

Other Illicit Drugs

Amphetamines (stimulants) and barbiturates (depressants) may be found on almost any secondary school campus. Table 11-4 shows rates of use reported by 365 boys and 378 girls in the ninth grade (high school freshmen) in an urban setting.[29] There undoubtedly are regional differences in rates of use. Figures on heroin use by this age group were not available. However, one can assume that where these drugs are accessible and used by adults, the young adolescents also will show increasing use. It is very dif-

Table 11-4.   Percentage of urban ninth graders, by sex, reporting one or more uses of specific psychoactive substances (adapted from K. G. Johnson, J. H. Donnelly, R. Scheble, R. L. Wine, and M. Weitman. Survey of adolescent drug use. I. Sex and grade distribution. American Journal of Public Health, 1971, 61, 2418–2432).

Drugs	Males (N = 365)	Females (N = 378)
Sedatives and tranquilizers	17.8	16.1
Amphetamines	9.8	7.4
Narcotics	7.7	7.1
Barbiturates	5.7	3.4
Hallucinogens	4.9	2.1
Cocaine	2.6	0.6

ficult to keep track of the burgeoning multiplicity of psychoactive substances—powerful concoctions with fanciful names such as Angel Dust, an animal tranquilizer.

The Marihuana Commission has published a report indicating an association among alcohol, tobacco, and marihuana.[30] Those who use one are more likely to use the others as well. The sequence of use or causal association is not clear. However, the studies indicated that a majority of marihuana users do not go on to hard drugs but instead forsake marihuana for alcohol. Research on psychedelic drugs seems to have declined with the passing of the sixties, evidence of the cultural factors of fashion in drug use and research on it.

Comment

Drug use, like delinquent acts and gang associations, may fulfill adolescent needs for self-assertion and self-expression and provide peer acceptance and approval as well. In its more virulent aspects, one sees the role of drugs in creating the mystique of the "crazy," the drugged individual (usually male) who is extremely unpredictable and dangerous. Many gang members use drugs to fortify their courage in the ongoing warfare. Alcohol and amphetamines become parts of preparation for crimes such as theft, robbery, burglary, and rape. Here the role of such substances is primarily that of overcoming fear.

The reduction in self-consciousness and increase in sociability provided by marihuana or alcohol serves intimacy needs. The shared use may possess a ritual quality—passing marihuana cigarettes, the bottle, or sharing a six-pack is a gesture of friendship and amicability. The role of drugs in reducing sexual inhibition is probably not lost on young people either. Alcohol and other psychoactive substances also serve as sources of substitute gratification. A person with a poorly developed sense of identity who feels outcast and friendless may find solace in drugs which dull his or her sense of alienation and inadequacy by stimulating fantasies of power, pleasure, and general well being. Heroin is a drug of this type, as is cocaine. Yet both have very different properties; heroin is a narcotic or depressant and it dulls the senses producing withdrawal, while cocaine, a stimulant, produces excitement.

Habitual users of alcohol, narcotics, and other drugs such as barbiturates (downers) and amphetamines (uppers) show many of the characteristics as well as behaviors found among other delinquents. There is a very high frequency of drug use and abuse among urban dwellers from disordered families where both high availability and peer group enticement combine to make alcohol and narcotics a way of life. In general, addicts (adults as well as juveniles) are found to be immature, irresponsible, insecure, and egocentric.[31] However, drug use in the urban centers may also represent conformity to the prevailing standards of the street serving needs for acceptance and enhancing reputation.[32] The various needs served by drugs exist in adults as well as adolescents. It is about the time of puberty that the individual becomes more conscious of personal psychological needs and becomes aware of the degree to which these are not met. A degree of frustration is inevitable, as neither the environment nor the pubescent's skill may be sufficient in satisfying the broad complex of identity, independence, and intimacy needs interlaced with sexuality and an increasing complexity of life. This is not to say that younger children do not suffer from psychological deprivation when these needs are not met; they do, and inadequate rearing and care is by far the most significant source of difficulty in meeting the demands of puberty. However, the awareness and increased sensitivity of early adolescence coupled with increased access accounts for much of the upsurge in drug use in the early adolescent years. Another aspect to be explained is the increasing involvement of younger persons. A partial explanation may be the declining age of puberty itself, which initiates adolescence sooner than was the case in the past. Drug use has become an integral part of U.S. society. Advertisements in virtually all media push pills as a means of dealing with the slightest discomfort or stress. Alcohol and tobacco use is continuously associated with glamour and sophistication. While not yet a part of establishment media, in the counterculture, marihuana has become a symbol of rejection of the establishment, rebellion, and camaraderie among youth—motives which appeal strongly to many young adolescents. Thus, the use of marihuana and other illicit drugs, particularly the psychedelics such as LSD and peyote, have developed a glamour of their own, promoting an image and role of daring rebellion—an idealism contrasted to the alleged sodden hypocrisy of adults—and the revelation of spiritual features and forces.

Each social class has come to have its drugs—heroin to dull the pain of the ghetto, LSD for those seeking enlightenment, beer as the honest beverage of the working folk, wine for the more genteel, and cocaine for the avant-garde. The message has become—"mix them up, experience it all"—an invitation hard to resist if given the chance, and young people often do have the chance. Their choices reflect availability. In many states, all it takes is someone over 18 willing to purchase the booze. Glue remains available despite attempts at control. Home medicine cabinets are often cornucopias of amphetamines and barbiturates. Inhaling fumes of gasoline, turpentine, and aerosol cans serves those who are desperate or beginning experimentation. Drug use by the young follows from the attitudes and use of drugs by the populace at large. It cannot be singled out and eliminated without an alteration in overall patterns. Recall that while a majority of arrests of youth under 15 involved drunkenness, these arrests constituted less than ½ of 1 percent of all arrests for drunkenness. These youngsters are imitating their elders. There is a strong association between adolescent drinking and parental drinking.[33] Ironically, while drug use in adolescence in many cases reflects rebellion and assertions of independence, it also appears to reflect a modeling of the adult culture by young people.

In order to deal with drug abuse, realistic education which deals honestly with both the pleasures and hazards of drug use must be provided. It is also necessary to critically evaluate factors contributing to the drug flow: the source of their availability and those benefitting from their manufacture and use, as well as factors of social policy, environmental qualities, and values in general which perpetuate an ever-increasing reliance upon mind- and behavior-altering substances.

SUGGESTED READINGS

Blum, R. H. and associates. *Horatio Alger's children*. San Francisco: Jossey-Bass, 1972.

Coffey, A. R. *Juvenile justice as a system; law enforcement to rehabilitation*. Englewood Cliffs, N.J.: Prentice-Hall, 1974.

Comstock, G. A.; Rubinstein, E. A.; and Murray, J. P. (eds.) *Television and social behavior; reports and papers, Volume 5: television's effects: further explorations*. National Institutes of Mental Health, DHEW publication # HSM 72–9060, 1972.

Glueck, S. and Glueck, E. *Of delinquency and crime; a panorama of years of search and research*. Springfield, Ill.: C. C. Thomas, 1974.

Goldmeier, H. Vandalism: the effects of unmanageable confrontations. *Adolescence*, 1974, 9, 49–56.

Haskell, M. R. and Yablonsky, L. *Crime and delinquency*. Chicago: Rand-McNally, 1970.

Khanna, J. L. (ed.) *New treatment approaches to juvenile delinquency*. Springfield, Ill.: C. C. Thomas, 1974.

Muuss, R. E. Legal and social aspects of drug abuse in historical perspective. *Adolescence*, 1974, 9, 495–506.

Platt, A. M. The rise of the child-saving movement: a study in social policy and correctional reform. *The Annals*, Jan. 1969, 21–38. Reprinted in Skolnick, J. H. and Currie, E. (eds.) *Crisis in American Institutions*. Boston: Little, Brown, 1970, pp. 442–63.

12 *Psychopathology*

> Mental health problems do not affect three or four out of every five persons but one out of one.
>
> William Menninger

It is almost a psychiatric cliché that if adults behaved like adolescents, they would be called crazy. Yet while the turmoil of adolescence at times borders on the pathological, many symptoms of anxiety and depression are transitory responses to temporary stress. On the average, adolescents do not display more pathological symptoms than the public at large; hence indications of disturbance are not all that normal and should not be ignored. In one longitudinal study, young adolescents who showed a cluster of symptoms of impaired school performance and social functioning plus a turbulent family situation did not "grow out of it." Follow-up showed continuing personality disturbance in these cases.[1]

Suicide and schizophrenia represent desperate attempts to cope with overwhelming stress. Neurotic reactions and eating disorders are also symptomatic of less-than-adequate means of coping. In many instances a person's motives may be mixed, as in the case of a young delinquent who may be virtually suicidal in taking risks when acting aggressively. It is often difficult to determine whether a drug overdose was an accident or deliberate self-destruction.

SUICIDE

In contrast with the acting out which characterizes many delinquent acts, suicide involves the turning inward of aggression and
represents the culmination of feelings of alienation and a final
withdrawal from interpersonal relationships. However, elements
of acting out may be present when self-destruction is perceived
as a means of getting back at others. The major issues of puberty
are interwoven throughout the description of the dynamics of suicide: fragments of egocentric thought, problems of identity and
intimacy, concerns both on the part of parents and adolescents
about sexuality and the expression of independence, and hostile
feelings. The suicidal person often has a history of disruption in
personal relationships; and the developments of early adolescence
may further exacerbate feelings of unworthiness, alienation, and
a general inability to cope with life. Self-destruction among the
young shows a marked increase following puberty. In 1974 there
were 188 reported suicides committed by persons between the ages
of 5 and 14 years with 4258 reported in the 15- to 24-year-old group
in the United States. This represents an increase in rate from 0.5
to 10.9 suicides per 100,000 persons in the specified populations,
a twentyfold increase.[2] Estimates of *attempted* suicide range as
high as 1 out of every 1000 adolescents.[3]

Although suicide is commonly associated with depression among
adults, this is less often the case with younger persons; depression
is far more frequent in middle-age. Suicide attempts among adolescents have been traditionally viewed as impulsive acts. However, this assumption has been seriously challenged.[4] Many attempts are premeditated and one adolescent in every ten who
attempts suicide will later complete it.[5] Precipitating factors may
range from the loss of a loved one to being pregnant; but more
often than not, the youngster has a history of problems and comes
from a home environment which is chaotic and unstable.

About three times as many adolescent girls as boys attempt suicide. However, two to three times as many adolescent boys actually
kill themselves. At all ages males who attempt suicide are more

inclined than females to use lethal modes such as guns or hanging.[6] The statistics may be artificially low, since many deaths judged to be accidental may have in fact been intentional. Rates have been rising for females and nonwhite males, although they still remain below that of white males.

The route to suicide in adolescence has been described by Teicher as a three-stage process.[7] The first stage is a preadolescence marked with problems which serve to isolate the person from meaningful relationships, in short, problems of intimacy. The second stage is an escalation of stress and further isolation resulting from an inability to establish a firm sense of identity and independence. These issues are increasingly critical in adolescence. Friendship and peer relationships are extremely important in meeting both the intimacy needs of preadolescence and adolescence and the development of identity and the expression of independence. A young loner characterized by low self-esteem may be a prime candidate for suicide. Another factor contributing to stress may be the parents' apprehension about their child's developing sexuality and expressions of hostility. Their own reaction of secretly wishing the youngster dead and gone may be communicated in indirect ways. While the pubescent has a realistic concept of death, recognizing it as the final cessation of bodily activities, fragments of egocentric thinking remain. Revenge, manipulation, and expression of rage are often contributing motives, and fantasies about grieving parents may precede or accompany the suicide attempt. The third stage, the final dissolution of relationships with others and the subsequent suicide attempt, is generally brought on by some specific event of rejection or deprivation such as the loss of a loved one or a major disappointment. While these are often perceived as the cause of the suicide attempt, Teicher doubts their major role as causal factors and emphasizes the insidious aspects of suicide as a response to an ongoing pattern of development rather than a simple response to a single event. In many instances the suicide attempt stems from the adolescent's view of a complete breakdown of meaningful social relationships.[8]

Social class alone is not a good predictor of suicide. People at all social levels are vulnerable. However, there is a higher rate in transitional sections of a community which usually are run-down and impoverished. Neighborhoods which are poor but stable show lower rates.[9] Cultural factors play an important role. In Japan where suicide does not have the connotations of cowardice and craziness as it does in the United States, it is the number one cause of death among persons below the age of 30. Suicide rates drop in wartime (when one can raise esteem by serving one's country) and increase in times of social unrest and economic depression (when unemployment becomes a problem). Economic factors and a sense of alienation may contribute to the above-average rates of suicide among adolescent blacks, Native Americans, residents of San Francisco's Chinatown, and New York Puerto Ricans.[10,11]

In terms of prevention, Berg[12] has listed a number of points to be considered by teachers, public health personnel, club leaders, and other adults who deal with adolescents. All suicide attempts should be taken seriously. They indicate serious problems and failures in communication. The person may not be crazy or be intent on dying, but a problem exists and it is important not to let the attempt compound feelings of isolation. Berg also points out that because a person was at one time suicidal, this may not always be the case. Each person to some degree will at some time consider the possibility of suicide. That does not mean the thought will be acted upon. Clues suggesting an impending attempt by an adolescent are a sudden or unexplained neglect of schoolwork; a decrease in ability to communicate; disturbances in sleep or appetite; psychophysiological complaints such as headache, nervousness, etc.; and changes in social behavior including the sudden use of alcohol or drugs, promiscuity, or violent outbursts. Low esteem and self-deprecation, depression, or the occurrence of hallucinations and delusions are also danger signals.

An adult noticing danger signs should speak to the adolescent who appears troubled or confused. Pointing out a behavioral change is more sensible than suggesting that the young person may be suicidal. Chances are that the family situation is a contributor to the problem and thus a teacher or counselor may need to call on other community resources. The important point is to let the adolescent know that someone cares and to put her or him in touch with someone with whom problems and feelings can be discussed openly and honestly. If a suicide attempt is made it is important that upon the return to school and other social life, the person's feelings of isolation be reduced and communication with him established. Discussion of suicide in junior high classes on health or social problems may be helpful. Talking about suicide can reduce much of the stigma as well as fear and misapprehension of the suicide attempt. Young adolescents often have little understanding of the emotional turmoil they are experiencing. Sharing of feelings and exploration of the sources of emotions may reduce the sense of being the only sufferer around. When suicide does occur the community will often attempt to avoid discussion and hush up the incident. However, students will talk about it anyway, but in ignorance and fear. Open and honest discussion with competent adults is a better alternative.

PSYCHOSIS

Severe personality disturbances characterized by a lack of contact with reality, often involving delusions and hallucinations, are called psychoses. Hospitalization is ordinarily required. There are three major categories of psychoses: (1) schizophrenia, (2) paranoid disorders, and (3) affective (mood) disturbances. Schizophrenia is the most common of the three and is more likely than the other two to be diagnosed in adolescence, increasing dramatically from age 15. An early term for the disorder was *dementia praecox* (precocious or early derangement) a label which reflected the belief that adolescents were particularly susceptible. The term "dementia praecox" has been discarded and schizophrenia is now used. The characteristic symptoms are disordered thinking, a poor relation to reality, restricted feelings toward persons and the environment in general, and inadequate control of emotion, thought, and behavior.[13] The roots of schizophrenia are likely to reach back into childhood, but the adolescent period is when a psychotic reaction is more likely to be observed. The pressure of maturation and of a more complex environment disrupt previously established but weak or inadequate means of coping. However, contrary to earlier impressions, schizophrenia is not an exclusive disorder of adolescence, and some have argued that it peaks about ten years after puberty.[14]

Arieti[15] has vividly described the role of puberty in the development of prepsychotic personality. One example is the schizoid personality; the person who is detached and unemotional because of earlier unpleasant relationships. The extent of emotional detachment may increase after puberty. School demands, sexual desires, the need to find a place in the world, all put a strain on one's character armor or self-protection. Feelings of being assaulted or pushed around lead to a desire to withdraw. The world may be seen as populated by millions of authorities ready to criticize. At puberty the person begins to project feelings formerly directed toward family members to others in the society. The projection goes something like this: if family relationships have been bad, the world is going to be bad. Sexual urges can be expected to remain unsatisfied as will other needs and desires. If the conscious realization which occurs in early adolescence contains a sense of hopelessness, a state of panic or desperation may ensue. In a competitive society like the United States, a person who withdraws is likely to fail and each failure leads to successive retreats. The accompanying aloofness and detachment may at the beginning not be recognized by the casual observer and may be seen as poise or sophistication. Further, the dynamics of withdrawal may be subtle and show up as a decline in schoolwork. Symptoms may be intermittent rather than continuous.

Another example of a prepsychotic personality is the stormy individual who vacillates from compliance to explosive outbursts of aggression.[16] Underlying the behavioral instability is essentially a problem of identity, of the person's not having a concrete sense of who he or she is; thus there is both a searching for self and a vulnerability to external influences. In both cases, schizoid and stormy, the onset of psychosis is hastened by experiences which damage a person's self-esteem and produce high levels of anxiety.

The occurrence of paranoid disorders is much more characteristic of the later teen and adult years than of early adolescence. With respect to depression, a prevailing psychiatric view has been that it is quite rare in the childhood and early adolescent years. The general symptoms of depression are a sad and despairing mood, a decrease of mental productivity, and a reduction of drive. Other accompaniments are feelings of helplessness; a preoccupation with one's health; and feelings of depersonalization, self-accusation, and self-deprecation. Although the symptoms of depression observed among adults are rarely seen in the young, it is possible that depression takes a different form. In the adolescent, depression may underlie an inability to be alone, boredom, restlessness, and a constant search for new activities. Feelings of isolation, alienation, and emptiness may impel a young person to acting out or sexual promiscuity as attempts to alleviate depression. Again, the clue to pathology is the persistence of the symptoms. Most adolescents express boredom and show a sometimes frantic search for activity. However, if such symptoms persist, the possibility of depression should be considered. Other potential indicators of depression are an inability to concentrate, persistent fatigue, bodily preoccupation, and complaints about health.[17]

NEUROSIS

People are described as neurotic when their means of coping with normal life stresses and demands prove inadequate and they feel threatened and anxious. They may not require hospitalization but are often guilt-ridden, ineffective, unhappy, and in need of therapy. The neuroses include anxiety attacks, phobias, obsessions and compulsions, hysterical or conversion and disassociative reactions, hypochondriasis, neurasthenia (chronic fatigue and apathy), and depression. These conditions reflect an overreliance upon the normal ego defense mechanisms of repression, denial, reaction-formation, projection, displacement, etc. Defense mechanisms are coping responses, means of protecting one's self image. They are learned in childhood and are fairly well established by preadolescence. Puberty puts a stress upon one's coping system. The increase in sexual feelings and the desire for independence with its implicit threat of a loss of dependency and perhaps love, may be perceived as direct threats to the self. Indications of stress are frequent and to some degree normal among pubescents; recall the descriptions of movement, finger-snapping, and nail-biting. Unfortunately, there are those who have not acquired adequate means of dealing with the stress of puberty and rely even more heavily on defense mechanisms to the point of maladaptation. Nevertheless, it is rare for a well-structured neurotic reaction to be observed prior to the later teen years. One explanation is that the young adolescent directs much of his or her conflict outward, rather than showing the high degree of internalization of anxiety characteristic of neurosis. The young adolescent is more likely to display single and short-lived neurotic reactions. These may be quite dramatic—fainting, seizures, temporary blindness, for example. They may be distinguishable from more severe and persistent pathology only by their brief duration.[18]

Rates of incidence are difficult to determine. However, one nationwide survey made in the early 1960s found that children aged 10–14 showed the maximum out-patient usage of mental health clinics of any age group. Treatment rates were characterized by a sharp rise for boys around the age of 9 and again at 14; and for girls, a slight rise at 10 with a marked increase at 15.[19] The most common diagnosis was a transient situational personality disturbance—an assessment based on the assumption of a disturbance brought about by situational factors that was expected to pass with time. Others[20] have questioned the validity of this diagnosis, suggesting that in some cases the symptoms were indicative of a more lasting disturbance. Among neuroses diagnosed, the most frequently observed were anxiety reactions in both sexes and an increasing incidence with age of depression in girls.

Characteristics of early adolescent development may interfere with attempts at therapy—rebelliousness and other assertions of independence often displayed with hostility or a failure to cooperate may sharply reduce a therapist's effectiveness; and the therapist is not able to rely on cognitive insight to the degree possible in adulthood. A matching of individual and type of therapy may be even more critical in adolescence than in adulthood, given the wide variations and asynchronies of cognitive and emotional maturation.

EATING DISORDERS

The eating disorders of severe obesity and *anorexia nervosa,* a loss of appetite, are not common. Yet when they do occur they are often first manifested during puberty and adolescence. Obesity is a condition where body weight exceeds the limitations of skeletal and physical requirements. Its causes are multiple; however, the immediate problem is burning fewer calories than are ingested. Thus, a combination of overeating and inactivity may contribute to becoming fat. Obesity refers to a continuous and extreme condition of overweight, distinct from the transitory weight gain preceding and associated with the height spurt.

A popular notion about obesity is that overeating is a response to stress, that the obese person copes with anxious or fearful feelings by eating. However, while this may explain the dynamics of obesity in some, it is not a satisfactory explanation for others. Schachter[21] found that the obese did not eat more under stress produced by examinations, work pressure, or personal problems. Based on these and other observations, it appears that many persons who are obese lack awareness of the distinctions among their own various body states. Failure to adequately distinguish between hunger and satiety may be accompanied by failures to distinguish among other states as well. In one study a group of obese adolescents showed very vague and global perceptions of the emotional states of others. They were shown pictures of people in widely interpretable scenes (Thematic Apperception Test) and asked to give an account of what might be transpiring in the scene.

They could accurately describe the picture, but showed very little projection of feeling or thought into the figures depicted. When pressed about their own feelings, they became withdrawn. It was also very difficult to get them involved in any activity, and to eat was to *do* something.[22] For the obese, eating is often influenced by external cues such as time of day, and the presence of food and its appearance, odor, or quality. The reverse is true for normal-weight persons whose eating is based upon internal indicators of hunger.[23]

Anorexia nervosa, a loss of appetite or consistent refusal to eat, is an affliction almost solely restricted to adolescence. Accompanying symptoms are hyperactivity and general bodily dysfunction brought about by metabolic imbalance resulting from starvation.[24] Anorexia nervosa may occasionally occur at other periods of transition, for example, upon leaving home in late adolescence or early adulthood. While more common among females, it also occurs in males. Cultural norms proclaiming the value of being slender probably contribute to the sex difference and the anorexic's failure to eat, but such factors are not adequate in fully explaining occurrence of the disorder. Like obesity, anorexia may be an accompaniment of some other disturbance such as depression or psychosis, and often, obesity precedes anorexia.[25] In its primary form, where weight is the central issue, there is an almost constant preoccupation with thinness, a sort of weight phobia. As with the obese, anorexics avoid responding appropriately to internal cues. They appear different from the obese in their presumed ability to exercise control over eating and are often quite rigid and effective in demanding that parents not keep food in the house or serve only specified amounts. However, the appearance of control is illusory and its rigidity betrays the desperation of one who is not in control at all—an observation further supported by the occurrence of eating binges on the part of some anorexics.

Hilde Bruch,[26] who has done much research on eating disorders, has described anorexics and the obese as having failed to achieve a sense of ownership of their own body. Not only are they inept at distinguishing internal states, but they lack awareness of being a self-contained and self-directed organism and are likely to view themselves as a product of someone else's action, or at the mercy of external events. In addition, both seriously overweight and seriously underweight adolescents frequently exhibit disturbances in sexual development. The anorexic girl may be attempting to literally starve away her secondary sex characteristics. The obese girl may succeed in losing them among mounds of flesh. For the male, fatness often carries with it a feminine connotation. Among obese girls, Bruch found some who wanted to be male; and size was associated with being of the male gender, or of a hermaphroditic third sex. Bruch also points out that among both obese and anorexic patients, a reconstruction of early development frequently reveals a disregard of their individuality and their expressed needs and discomforts. Parents may have been either overindulgent or overly rigid. Both treatments lead to a situation where the child's own cues are ignored. Hunger, in common with other sensory and subjective experiences, has a learned component. Under certain conditions of stimulus deprivation, monkeys show disturbances in eating patterns. While the obese or anorexic person may not have been deprived of sensory experience and are likely to have been adequately clothed, fed, and sheltered, they may have been deprived of the opportunity to develop self-awareness and a sense of identity.

Treatment programs in the past have shown little success. One difficulty is that some therapies perpetuate the same pattern of someone else acting upon the person—telling her what to do and giving or withholding food. While insight into one's problems may be necessary, in the case of both the obese and the anorexic, it is often insufficient. Under these conditions the adolescent needs help in developing initiative, which in turn is based on feelings of competence and adequacy. Principles of biofeedback and behavior modification have been applied with some success in taking the first step of alerting persons to their own self-initiated feelings, thoughts, and behavior. Development of discrimination and acting upon one's own sensations are important aspects of increasing willpower and self-control. Following increased awareness and action, it is also desirable to monitor environmental feedback in evaluating the appropriateness of the action taken. The simple act of putting on a sweater when cold, while appearing trivial, is part of a larger set of acts which arise as a result of this three-step process. The same applies to the decision to eat or not to eat. The twin problems of obesity and anorexia nervosa serve to illustrate the importance of learning—even in a process as basic as eating.

With puberty, the demands and stresses of existence are increased. Faulty development in terms of self-expression and understanding becomes more apparent. Like the acting-out adolescent, the obese and the anorexic are unable to translate thoughts and feelings into realistic and appropriate behavior—behavior not merely desired by others but beneficial to the self as well. Successful treatment requires a great deal of new learning on the part of the person at a time when he or she may be least amenable to the intervention of adults. Nevertheless, young people are often responsive to those they trust. Also, therapy groups involving peers show promise as a tool in the treatment of eating disorders as well as other adjustment problems. Needless to say, while improved treatment techniques are desirable, prevention is more sensible.

COMMENT

The onset of adolescence as well as other phases of life are periods prone to challenge earlier adaptations. Puberty is one of the first major challenges, bringing with it an end not only to environmental protection but to naiveté as well. Childhood innocence has often been construed as an absence of sexuality. We know this is not a correct assessment. However, childhood is possessed of an innocence of another sort—a less than full awareness of the content and meaning of one's own thought. It is this increasing awareness which may play a role in the development of psychopathology in adolescence. A frequent predictor of schizophrenia is the lack of ability of the pre- or early adolescent to relate or participate in the informal and intimate group life of peers. Harry Stack Sullivan[27] to whom we referred in Chapter 8 on social relationships has emphasized the therapeutic aspects of friendship during the years from about 9 to 12. A chum provides a relatively uncomplicated experience of love. Love, according to Sullivan, exists when the satisfactions and security of the loved one are as important as one's own. In preadolescence the capacity for love has an opportunity to develop and may compensate in many respects for its absence in family relationships. Beyond puberty, interpersonal relationships are complicated by sexual connotations and drives.

The period of preadolescence and early adolescence has been characterized by many as a time when one's potential is at its peak expression. Whether that potential is realized will to a large extent depend upon the stresses of adolescence and adulthood and the ability of the person to meet those challenges. Hence it appears that, while not causal in and of themselves, the developments accompanying puberty are often pivotal in the expression of major behavior disturbances: delinquency, suicide, the neuroses, schizophrenia, and psychophysiological problems exemplified by eating disorders.

The actual incidence of delinquency and psychopathology is very low among pubescents. Not all symptoms require treatment; many are transitory, stemming from the asynchrony of development which characterizes the phase and makes adjustment difficult. However, a person with temporary difficulties needs love, support, and understanding, too. Short periods of messiness and obstinacy, anger, acting out, moodiness, withdrawal, arrogance, or grandiosity are the rule during adolescence and characterize a normal phase of development for which the best response is tolerance. Occasionally they are indicators of more severe disturbance. It is their persistence which is significant. Adults should be alert to long-lasting and generalized indicators of maladjustment in order to provide remedial action in those few cases where it is necessary.

SUGGESTED READINGS

Finch, S. M. and Pozanski, E. O. *Adolescent suicide.* Springfield, Ill.: C. C. Thomas, 1971.

Jacobs, J. *Adolescent suicide.* New York: Wiley, 1971.

Hafen, B. Q. (ed.) *Self destructive behavior: a national crisis.* Minneapolis, Minn.: Burgess Publishing, 1972.

Hardy, R. E. and Cull, J. G. (eds.) *Problems of adolescents: social and psychological approaches.* Springfield, Ill.: C. C. Thomas, 1974.

Weiner, I. B. *Psychological disturbance in adolescence.* New York: Wiley, 1970.

Werkman, S. L. Psychiatric disorders of adolescence. In Arieti, S. and Caplan, G. (eds.) *Handbook of Psychiatry,* Vol. 2. New York: Basic Books, 1974, pp. 223–33.

Zubin, J. and Freedman, A. M. (eds.) *The psychopathology of adolescence.* New York: Grune & Stratton, 1970.

13 *Visible People*

Let us put our minds together and see what
life we will make for our children.
>> Poster from Akwesasne Notes,
>> Mohawk Nation

I hope the invisible people have become more visible and that the reader's own recollections of puberty have been revived, refreshed, and expanded. Puberty is an important period of life. The rites of ancient origin with their themes of death and rebirth epitomize the awesome quality of sexual maturation and the potential for reproduction, making it one of life's more significant events. In modern society this quality is overlooked or repressed in the service of other motives, primarily those of prolonging childhood and adolescence. However, even in a culture which emphasizes an adult potential requiring years of preparation, the pubertal phase remains an important one. The young person is still very much a developing organism with respect to physical and cognitive change. The outcome of these changes are corollary alterations in behavior, interests, and attitudes. The turn toward peers, for example, reflects motivations stimulated by physical maturity and a general drive toward competence and expansion of personal relationships. Mood changes are explicable on the basis of both hormonal and cognitive factors, as is the increase in sexual and aggressive impulses. The hormones stimulate physical growth and maturational events linked with sexual identity and sexuality, e.g., menstruation and genital growth. Increased cognitive awareness provides the ability for interpretation and action associated with these changes.

Of equal importance to physical maturation is the social context in which it occurs. A major social development in Western society has been the increasing segregation of children.[1] Children have come to be seen not as miniature adults but as a group with special needs and interests. Clear ideas about pastimes, ways of dress, modes of speech, and kinds of toys appropriate for the very young are shared throughout the culture. The process of separation, which began initially with the sons of wealthy men, has extended to all children and led to the evolution during the last century of the adolescent. In fact, American society is becoming extensively stratified by age. A new category termed *youth*, which is intermediate to adolescence and adulthood, has evolved as a result of the postponement of marriage, child-bearing, and occupational commitment among persons in their early twenties. The older years are being divided up into life stages as more attention is focused on the psychological developments of adulthood. Fashions, media, and music also have become specialized according to the age of audience and participants.

With the evolution of a stage of adolescence, the pubescent became a marginal person, separate by virtue of being neither child nor adolescent. Marginality during transitional periods is a dominant theme in many cultures. Mary Douglass[2] drawing upon a cross-cultural analysis, describes how transition is linked to risk and danger:

> Danger lies in transitional states; simply because transition is neither one state nor the next, it is undefinable. The person who must pass from one to another is himself in danger and emanates danger to others. The danger is controlled by ritual which precisely separates him from his old status, segregates him for a time

and then publicly declares his entry to his new status. Not only
is transition itself dangerous, but also the rituals of segregation
are the most dangerous phase of the rites.[3]

The theme of marginality pertains to pubescents. In a sense we
perceive that they cannot be held fully responsible for their behavior. In numerous societies of Africa, Oceania, and parts of the
Western Hemisphere, pre- and early adolescents were provided
the support and control of extended family or bush schools. However, the pubescent was outcast in some American Indian tribes
where the adolescent boy lived alone in the woods or mountains
and the girl was subject to isolation during menstruation. In Medieval Europe the transition from a dependent, supervised existence to a more autonomous one was gradual if it occurred at all.
Technological societies contain pubescents in school where they
are supervised, trained, and, in general, kept busy. When constraints are relaxed, the unkempt aspects, obscenity, and lawless-
ness which often characterize an outcast may be sporadically observed in the dress, habits, speech, and acts of pubescents.

Recognizing the separateness of particular stages of life has its
benefits and its penalties. As an example, consider the adult communities in which residence is restricted to persons of retirement
age. "Leisuretown" has many amenities and advantages for the
elderly. However, a sense of participation in the larger world cannot help but be lost in an environment in which the young are
absent. In a similar sense the dangers of alienation and illusion
increase in more constricted and narrow niches of self-definition.
Tom Wolfe[4] in a set of witty characterizations titled *The Pumphouse Gang* described surfers, who, over-the-hill at age 21, chose
suicide over retirement. The world beyond the life of the beach
existed for them but was seen as so different and strange as to be
intolerable. As a result of their isolation and the making of their
own culture, adolescents have often come to be viewed with dis-
may, disdain, and sometimes outright fear by adults. Edgar Z.
Friedenberg[5] in his essay titled "The Image of the Adolescent
Minority" has articulated the stereotype of the erotic, imprudent,
sexually aggressive, excitable, and dangerous male teenager, elab-

orating how adults project their own secret wishes and fantasies onto adolescents. If not perceived as dangerous, adolescents are often considered inept; and in the case of teenage girls, treated as invisible or, if characterized at all, show up as sex kittens or caretakers of children.

A serious result of the segregation of children and adolescents from adults is the loss of learning which occurs—learning based on modeling and on the informal exchange of information. There is a grandmother data loss; the youngster no longer has the benefits of grandmother's experience because of limited contact with her. Grandmother is not perceived as being a reliable and useful source of knowledge, wisdom, and information. Further, she herself may have internalized this view and be unable or unwilling to communicate her information in a useful and meaningful manner. These failures culminate in a general devaluation of potential lessons from the past. With the decline of informal systems of education, we become ever more reliant upon institutions, particularly the school, for the transmission of knowledge. More people are formally educated for a longer period of time than has ever been the case in our history. However, as these advances have been made, little note has been taken of the accompanying losses of informal education resulting from age separation. This is not to argue for a removal of educational functions from the school to the home or other segments of the community. The school is in many respects a more thorough and efficient system. However, education should be a function of home, the media, and various community institutions and members as well. It is too important a matter to leave to any single agency or channel of communication.

Means of reducing the potential for alienation in transition can be provided within the family, community, and school. A continuation of close family relationships with gradually increasing responsibility for self-direction and accountability by the young adolescence is a major aid. Further, the incorporation of the adolescent into meaningful community activities which allow the expression and development of new skills is of help. Tutoring of younger children, being a playground assistant, serving in a home for the aged, working at odd jobs, are among the many possibilities for increasing the participation of adolescents. Expanding the junior high to meet the needs and interests of a wide variety of youths rather than promoting only the interests of the college-bound would be another positive step in providing teenagers with a sense of identity and competence. Not all approaches will work with all young people. A degree of patience exceeding normal levels is sometimes required on the part of adults. Rationality, consistency, and kindness go a long way in clarifying communication and in indicating and establishing mutual respect. The burden of achieving these rests with the adult who has the benefit of hindsight unavailable to the pubescent.

It is difficult to put up with the tumult and emotional excesses of early adolescence. Thus, it takes an aware and courageous adult to resist the available inducements and arguments (which are many) for leaving adolescents to go their own ways. All the obvious events of the stage point in that direction. The establishment of independence, intimacy, and identity takes a turn toward age-mates rather than adults, but that this must exclusively be the case does not follow. To assume that the young teenager has the resources to take full responsibility for life choices is a serious mistake. Parents who throw up their hands and psychologically leave the scene make a grievous error. Gradually increasing opportunities for independence and responsibility from childhood on through adolescence will best serve adjustment. Responsibility is a learned characteristic, not one which is acquired automatically upon the achievement of sexual maturity—a fact which pubescents themselves must learn. Such learning is likely to be enhanced by continued interaction with adults and a sharing with them of awareness of responsibility and its rewards.

The author's purpose has been to provide the reader with knowledge and information about the process of puberty and its impact on individual development, and not to argue for isolated institutions for pubescents. It is hoped that a more detailed understanding of the phase will lead to better relationships among adults and young adolescents. Many of the crises of puberty are a direct result of change, not in hormones, but in status—change having to do with how one is perceived and responded to by others. Pubescents have their particular sets of needs. In attempting to best meet these needs we must be careful not to overlook the importance of participation, contact, and familiarity with the larger society.

FREEDOM TO THINK

In addition to the need for inclusion in the larger society there is another need which on the surface appears contradictory to social participation. That is the need for protection from many of the stresses experienced by adults in order that a more full and rich cognitive and emotional development may occur. Persons who at an early age must bear the full brunt of a hostile and difficult world or of excessive emotional demands within the family, often show a premature closure in their intellectual development. They may be extremely practical or wise to the ways of the streets and quite competent in dealing with concrete issues, but this may be accompanied by a deficit in the abstract realm and limitations in conceptualizing realistic possibilities beyond the immediate ones. Orientation toward the future may also be restricted. Intellectual development benefits from a degree of freedom from the immediate demands of survival. In order to develop the capacities for increased awareness and abstract thought, a young person needs time alone or unbothered for contemplation, for fantasy, daydreaming, and thought. Just as the learning of new language is difficult after puberty, the development of other cognitive abilities may show similar types of critical period limits. If the early stage of the capacity for abstract thought is not established in adolescence, it may be extremely difficult to acquire at a later age.[6]

Varying degrees of environmental pressure may contribute to social-class differences in cognitive abilities. The direction and elaboration of mental growth is likely to differ by social class not only as a result of formal schooling but also as a result of variations in freedom from those emotional and economic demands which might interfere with the development of specific abilities. Freedom from having to deal with necessity does not automatically produce a more intelligent person. It contributes to a set of intellectual abilities which will differ from those fostered by day-to-day involvement with job responsibilities, such as the care of younger siblings, maintaining family solidarity in the face of food and rent demands, substandard housing, and all the other problems of poverty. Yet, even in the poverty situation, for some families there may be a strong cultural tradition favoring the development of reflective and abstract intellectual abilities—an example which comes to mind is that of many impoverished Jews of Eastern Europe who for centuries lived under very stressful environmental conditions yet continued a tradition of scholarly study, essentially religious in nature. In contrast, many children born in opulence and educated formally in the abstract ways of logic and higher mathematics fail to show patterns of abstract intellectual thinking in their daily activities. While the luxury of time which can be bought with money may be a contributing factor, it is not a sufficient one for the development of abstract abilities. Cognitive development reflects a combination of cultural tradition, personal values of parents which a child internalizes to varying degrees, and the young person's own temperament reflecting genetic endowment. A desirable goal is to provide each and every young person with a chance for the realization of his or her potential, and to extend our understanding and appreciation of alternate modes of intellectual development and elaboration.

Development requires both a degree of conflict and the capacity to cope with crisis. The most immediate need is for emotional support. Economic pressures and tradition affect coping and adaptation by their influence upon the quality and character of relationships among adults and children in the community and within the family. The freedom to think can be blocked by those who dominate, belittle, and degrade children's attempts to express beliefs, solve problems, and deal intellectually with their world. If thinking leads to embarrassment, humiliation, or punishment, a young person soon learns to inhibit curiosity and questioning, and instead becomes compliant, obedient, and dependent; or sullen and resentful and devoid of spontaneity. Neither result contributes to a positive mode of living. The need for social participation and the freedom to think are not contradictory. The middle range is broad. A teenager can contribute much to the welfare of family and community without having to bear the full burden of support, either financially or emotionally.

The pubescent is on a threshold. The threshold itself is well worth considering. There are many things to come: vocational choice, commitment to a mate—at least for a time, an increasing concern with the world beyond the self. The vast and even more complex world of late adolescence and adulthood lies ahead.

Glossary

adrenal: a gland situated near the kidney which produces a number of important hormones.

anal stage: the second of Freud's psychosexual stages of development, characterizes the 1- to 2-year-old's preoccupation with anal activities and interest in feces.

androgens: a family of hormones influencing bone and muscle growth. Androgens are produced by the adrenals and the gonads of both sexes. Testicular testosterone, an androgen produced by the testes, contributes to increasing muscle size and strength and skeletal differentiation characteristic of the male.

anorexia nervosa: a loss of appetite or refusal to eat.

circumcision: the removal of all or part of the foreskin on the penis.

clitoris: a small organ located in front and above the vaginal opening which is sensitive to tactile stimulation and plays an important role in sexual arousal and orgasm.

cognition: the means by which one acquires, stores, and utilizes knowledge. The mental processes of perception, learning, problem solving, and memory. An individual's thoughts, knowledge, interpretations, understanding, or ideas about self and environment.

cognitive: pertaining to cognition.

coital: pertains to coitus.

coitus: sexual intercourse.

concept: a general idea derived from observing similarities among different objects or events.

conservation: a term used by Piaget indicating the recognition that quantitative attributes of objects (mass, number, area, volume, etc.) remain unchanged unless something is added or taken away from them.

deduction: reasoning from the general to the particular, from the universal to the specific, or from given premises to their necessary conclusion.

deductive: pertaining to deduction.

ego: the self. In Freudian theory the rational, reality-oriented segment of personality (see *id* and *superego*).

ejaculation: often used to refer to seminal emission, the discharge of seminal fluid from the penis.

equilibration: adjustment based on feedback in maintaining a balance between organism and environment.

genitalia: the reproductive organs, e.g., vagina, clitoris, scrotum, penis.

genitals: synonymous with genitalia.

genital stage: the fourth and final stage of Freud's psychosexual stages of development. Expected to occur in adolescence, it is characterized by a turning toward heterosexual modes of sexual gratification outside the family. The individual obtains pleasure from sexual contact with other persons.

gonad: a gland producing the reproductive germ cells; ovary or testis.

gonadal: pertaining to the gonads.

hedonism: the doctrine that pleasure is the sole or chief good in life, and that moral duty is fulfilled in the gratification of pleasure-seeking instincts or dispositions.

hedonistic: pertaining to hedonism.

hormone: a chemical substance produced in the body which has a specific effect on the activity of a certain organ.

hypothesis (plural -es):   a supposition provisionally adapted to explain certain facts. A possible explanation or prediction about some phenomenon.

hypothetical: involving a formal hypothesis or condition, assumed without proof for the purpose of reasoning.

id: one of the three structures of personality in Freudian theory; includes the unconscious basic biological impulses or instincts and the desire for immediate gratification (see *ego* and *superego*).

identification: the process of assuming the characteristics, mannerisms, goals, and behaviors of another and making them one's own.

ikonic thought: characterized by concrete mental images or representations (as contrasted with symbolic thought).

induction: reasoning from a part to a whole, from particulars to generals, or from the individual to the universal.

inductive: pertaining to induction.

innate: inborn, native, natural, not acquired.

intentionality: term used by Piaget to refer to the recognition of intent; that design or purpose plays a part in the interpretation of the meaning and significance of an act.

labia: the folds over the vaginal opening.

libido: a term used in Freudian theory to refer to sexual energy.

longitudinal study: a survey of the same person or persons over time.

menarche: the first menstrual period.

menses: pertains to menstruation.

menstruation: a monthly (approximately) discharge of blood and tissue from the womb of a mature female.

oral stage: the first stage of Freud's psychosexual stages of development which covers the first year of life, characterized by activity involving the sucking reflex and reflecting a preoccupation with immediate gratification of desires. The mouth is where the action is.

ovary: the sexual gland of the female.

penis: the male organ of copulation, homologous to the clitoris in the female.

personality: the characteristic behavior and psychological makeup of a person as a whole. The characteristic qualities of an individual person.

phallic stage: the third of Freud's stages of psychosexual development. Gratification is associated with the genitals from approximately age two to six years, and sexual attraction develops toward the opposite-sex parent.

phenomenon (plural: phenomena): an occurrence, event, or happening.

proposition: an expression of anything which is capable of being believed, doubted, or denied; a statement or verbal expression which is either true or false.

prostate: a gland near the genitals in the male which stores semen and spermatozoa.

qualitative: pertaining to quality, type, or attribute.

quantitative: pertaining to quantity or amount.

secondary sex characteristics: accompaniments of gonadal maturation —breast and hip enlargement in females, shoulder and beard growth in males, genital and underarm hair.

semantic: pertaining to meaning in language.

seminal emission: the discharge of seminal fluid from the penis.

seminal vesicles: a pair of semen-producing glands near the male genitals.

superego: one of the three structures of personality according to Freudian theory, synonymous with conscience and ego-ideal—

what one feels one ought to be, the ideal self. Represents the moral and ethical aspects of personality (see *ego* and *id*).

superordinate: a more universal category, as including several particulars.

symbolic thought: representation of the world through arbitrary symbols which need not correspond to perceptual reality.

testis (plural -es): the sexual gland in the male.

uterus: the hollow muscular organ in the female which is the abode and place of nourishment of the developing fetus, the womb.

vagina: the female organ of copulation; the genital canal and the walls of the canal leading from the uterus to the outside of the body.

variable: a property, quantity, or characteristic which may vary.

Notes

CHAPTER 1

1. G. Stanley Hall, *Adolescence: its psychology and its relation to physiology, anthropology, sociology, sex, crime, religion and education*, 2 vols. New York: D. Appleton and Company, 1904.
2. P. L. Adams, Puberty as a biosocial turning point. *Psychosomatics*, 1969, *10*, 343–9.
3. B. Sommer and C. Northcutt, *Survey of the experience of puberty, 1974*, unpublished data.
4. K. Lewin, Field theory and experiment in social psychology: Concepts and method. *American Journal of Sociology*, 1939, *44*, 868–97.
5. F. Redl, Adolescents—just how do they react? In G. Caplan and S. Lebovici, eds., *Adolescence: psychosocial perspectives*. New York: Basic Books, 1969, pp. 79–99.
6. R. Kohen-Raz, *The child from 9 to 13: the psychology of pre-adolescence and early puberty*. Chicago: Aldine-Atherton, 1971.
7. W. A. Schonfeld, The body and the body-image in adolescents. In G. Caplan and S. Lebovici, eds., *Adolescence: psychological perspectives*. New York: Basic Books, 1969, pp. 27–53.
8. E. Hurlock, *Adolescent development*, 4th edition. New York: McGraw-Hill, 1973.
9. P. Blos, *On adolescence*. New York: Free Press of Glencoe, 1962.
10. P. Blos, The child analyst looks at the young adolescent. *Daedalus*, 1971, *100* (4), 961–78.

CHAPTER 2

1. R. E. Muuss, *Theories of adolescence*, 3rd edition. New York: Random House, 1975.
2. P. Ariès, *Centuries of childhood*. New York: Knopf, 1962.
3. J. J. Rousseau, *Émile*. London, 1911.
4. J. F. Kett, *Rites of passage; adolescence in America 1790 to the present*. New York: Basic Books, 1977.
5. J. F. Walzer, A period of ambivalence: eighteenth century American childhood. In L. deMause, ed., *The history of childhood*. New York: The Psychohistory Press, 1974, pp. 351–82.
6. Kett, *Rites of passage*.
7. D. Bakan, Adolescence in America: from idea to social fact. In J. Kagen and R. Coles, eds., *Twelve to sixteen: early adolescence*. New York: Norton, 1971, pp. 73–89.
8. G. Stanley Hall, *Adolescence: its psychology and its relation to physiology, anthropology, sociology, sex, crime, religion and education*, 2 vols. New York: D. Appleton and Company, 1904.
9. Kett, *Rites of passage*.
10. B. A. Whiting, ed., *Six cultures: studies of child rearing*. New York: Wiley, 1973.
11. W. E. Precourt, Initiation ceremonies and secret societies as educational institutions. In R. W. Brislin, S. Bochner, and W. J. Lonner, eds., *Cross-cultural perspectives on learning*. New York: Wiley, 1975, pp. 231–50.
12. A. van Gennep, *Les rites de passage*. Paris, 1909.
13. M. Eliade, *Birth and rebirth; the religious meanings of initiation in human culture*. New York: Harper & Brothers, 1958.
14. E. Norbeck, D. E. Walker, and M. Cohen, Interpretation of data: puberty rites. *American Anthropologist*, 1962, *64*, 463–85.
15. Eliade, *Birth and rebirth*.
16. Ibid.
17. G. W. Harley, Notes on the Poro in Liberia. *Peabody Museum of American Archeology and Ethnology*, 1941, *19*, No. 2, pp. 13–14.
18. F. Barth, *Ritual and knowledge among the Baktamen of New Guinea*. New Haven: Yale University Press, 1975.
19. Eliade, *Birth and rebirth*.
20. M. R. Allen, *Male cults and secret initiations in Melanesia*. London & New York: Cambridge University Press, 1967.

21. B. Bettelheim, *Symbolic wounds: puberty rites and the envious male*, New revised edition. New York: Macmillan, 1962.

22. G. D. Spindler, The education of adolescents: an anthropological perspective. In D. Ellis, ed., *Adolescents: readings in behavior and development*. Hinsdale, Ill.: Dryden Press, 1970, pp. 152–61.

23. G. Mount, University of California, Riverside, unpublished manuscript, 1976.

24. M. E. Opler, Cause and effect in Apachean agriculture division of labor, residence patterns, and girl's puberty rites. *American Anthropologist*, 1972, 74, 1133–46.

25. V. Bullough, *The subordinate sex; a history of attitudes toward women*. Baltimore: Penguin, 1974.

26. H. E. Driver, Girl's puberty rites and matrilocal residue. *American Anthropologist*, 1969, 71, 905–8.

27. Mount, 1976.

28. L. H. Clark, The girl's puberty ceremony of the San Carlos Apaches. *Journal of Popular Culture*, 1976, 10, 431–48.

29. C. J. Frisbie, *Kinaaldá; a study of the Navaho girl's puberty ceremony*. Middletown, Conn.: Wesleyan University Press, 1967.

30. S. N. Otoo, The traditional management of puberty and childbirth among the Ga people, Ghana. *Tropical Geographical Medicine*, 1973, 25, 88–94.

31. T. O. Beidelman, Pig (gudawe): an essay on Ngulu sexual symbolism and ceremony. *Southwestern Journal of Anthropology*, 1964, 20, 359–92.

32. P. Kloos, Female initiation among the Maroni river Caribs. *American Anthropologist*, 1969, 71, 898–905.

33. G. Eichinger Ferro-Luzzi, Women's pollution periods in Tamiland (India). *Anthropos*, 1974, 69, 113–61.

CHAPTER 3

1. J. Horn, Physical fitness, 10 years later. *Psychology Today*, July 1976, Newsline, p. 26.

2. H. E. Jones, Adolescence in our society. In *The family in a democratic society: anniversary papers of the Community Service Society of New York*. New York: Columbia University Press, 1949, pp. 70–82.

3. J. Wilmore, Department of Physical Education, University of California, Davis, personal communication, 1975.

4. B. T. Donovan, Neural control of puberty. *Journal of Psychosomatic Research*, 1972, *16*, 267–70.

5. J. M. Tanner, Growing up, *Scientific American*, 1973, 229, 35–42.

6. V. L. Bullough, *The subordinate sex*. Baltimore: Penguin, 1974.

7. A. F. Goldfarb, Puberty, *Clinical Obstetrics and Gynecology*, 1968, *11*, 769–79.

8. E. O. Reiter and H. E. Kulin, Sexual maturation in the female. Normal development and precocious puberty. *Pediatrics Clinics of North America*, 1972, *19*, 581–603.

9. R. E. Frisch and R. Revelle, Height and weight at menarche and a hypothesis of menarche. *Archives of Diseases in Childhood*, 1971, *46*, 695–701.

10. K. Bjolén and M. W. Bentzon, Seasonal variations in the occurrence of menarche in Copenhagen girls. *Human Biology*, 1971, *43*, 493–501.

11. R. W. Hillman, P. Slater, and M. Nelson, Jr., Season of birth, parental age, menarcheal age and body form; some interrelationships in young women. *Human Biology*, 1970, *42*, 570–80.

12. Frisch and Revelle, 1971.

13. R. E. Frisch, Weight at menarche: similarity for well-nourished and under-nourished girls at differing ages and evidence for historical constancy. *Pediatrics*, 1972, *50*, 445–50.

14. H. K. A. Visser, Some physiological and clinical aspects of puberty. *Archives of Disease in Childhood*, 1973, *48*, 169–82.

15. J. M. Tanner, *Growth at adolescence*. Oxford, England: Blackwell, 1962.

16. J. M. Tanner, Sequence, tempo, and individual variation in growth and development of boys and girls aged twelve to sixteen. In J. Kagen and R. Coles, eds., *Twelve to sixteen: early adolescence*. New York: Norton, 1971, pp. 1–24.

17. Tanner, 1973.

18. Goldfarb, 1968.

19. B. MacMahon, Age at menarche. *National Center for Health Statistics. Vital and Health Statistics*, Series 11: Data from the National Health Survey, no. 133.

20. J. Scanlon, Self-reported health behavior and attitudes of youths 12–17 years. *National Center for Health Statistics. Vital and Health Statistics*, Series 11: Data from the National Health Survey, no. 147.

21. Ibid.
22. M. Mead, Cultural determinants of sexual behavior. In W. C. Young, ed., *Sex and internal secretions*, Vol. 2, 3rd edition. Baltimore: Williams & Wilkins, 1967, p. 1466.
23. E. Hurlock, *Adolescent development*, 3rd edition. New York: McGraw-Hill, 1967.
24. P. H. Mussen and M. C. Jones, Self conceptions, motivations, and interpersonal attitudes of late and early maturing boys. *Child Development*, 1957, 28, 243–56.
25. M. C. Jones and P. H. Mussen, Self conceptions, motivations, and interpersonal attitudes of early and late maturing girls. *Child Development*, 1958, 29, 491–501.
26. M. C. Jones, N. Bayley, J. W. Macfarlane, and M. P. Honzik, eds. *The course of human development*. Waltham, Mass.: Xerox College Publishers, 1971.
27. D. Weatherly, Self-perceived rate of physical maturation and personality in late adolescence. *Child Development*, 1964, 35, 1197–1210.
28. H. Peskin, Pubertal onset and ego functioning. *Journal of Abnormal Psychology*, 1967, 72, 1–15.

CHAPTER 4

1. J. Mishima and K. Inoue, A study on development of visual memory. *Japanese Psychological Research*, 1966, 8, 62–72.
2. D. Friedrich, Developmental analysis of memory capacity and information-encoding strategy. *Developmental Psychology*, 1974, 10, 559–63.
3. E. M. Edmonds, Some developmental characteristics of schematic concept formation. *Journal of Psychology*, 1974, 86, 293–6.
4. T. Trabasso, H. Rollins, and E. Shaughnessy, Storage and verification stages in processing concepts. *Cognitive Psychology*, 1971, 2, 239–89.
5. H. J. Klausmeier, E. S. Ghatala, and D. A. Frayer, *Conceptual learning and development: a cognitive view*. New York: Academic Press, 1974.
6. J. F. Richard, E. Cauzinille, and J. Mathieu, Logical and memory processes in a unidimensional concept differentiation task by children and adults. *Acta Psychologica*, 1973, 37, 315–31.
7. B. Inhelder and J. Piaget, *The growth of logical thinking from*

childhood to adolescence; an essay on the construction of formal operational structures. New York: Basic Books, 1958.

8. D. Elkind, L. Medvene, and A. S. Rockway, Representational level and concept production in children and adolescents. *Developmental Psychology*, 1970, 2, 85–9.

9. G. K. Nelson and H. J. Klausmeier, Classificatory behaviors of low-socioeconomic-status children. *Journal of Educational Psychology*, 1974, 66, 432–8.

10. T. C. O'Brien and B. J. Shapiro, The development of logical thinking in children. *American Educational Research Journal*, 1968, 5, 531–42.

11. J. E. Taplin, H. Staudenmayer, and J. L. Taddonio, Developmental changes in conditional reasoning: linguistic or logical? *Journal of Experimental Child Psychology*, 1974, 17, 360–73.

12. J. J. Roberge and D. H. Paulus, Developmental patterns for children's class and conditional reasoning abilities. *Developmental Psychology*, 1971, 4, 191–200.

13. E. A. Peel, *The nature of adolescent judgment.* London: Staples Press, 1971.

14. Ibid., p. 35.

15. Inhelder and Piaget, *The growth of logical thinking from childhood to adolescence.*

16. J. Langer, Werner's comparative organismic theory. In P. Mussen, ed., *Carmichael's manual of child psychology*, Vol. 1, 3rd edition. New York: Wiley, 1970, pp. 733–71.

17. J. Piaget, Piaget's theory. In Mussen, *Carmichael's manual of child psychology*, Vol. 1, pp. 703–32.

18. L. S. Vygotsky, *Thought and Language*, Translated by E. Hanfmann and G. Vakar. Cambridge: M.I.T. Press, 1962.

19. Ibid., p. 38.

20. J. S. Bruner, On cognitive growth II. In J. S. Bruner et al., eds., *Studies in cognitive growth.* New York: Wiley, 1966, pp. 30–67.

21. J. M. Tanner, Relation of body size, intelligence test scores, and social circumstances. In P. H. Mussen, J. Langer, and M. Covington, eds., *Trends and issues in developmental psychology.* New York: Holt, Rinehart & Winston, 1969, pp. 182–201.

22. R. Kohen-Raz, Problems of assessing relationships between physiological and mental development at adolescence. In S. R. Berenberg, ed., *Puberty: biologic and psychosocial components.* Leiden, Netherlands: H. E. Stenfert Kroese, 1975, pp. 191–197.

23. W. D. Wall, Intelligence and cognition. In S. R. Berenberg, ed., *Puberty: biologic and psychosocial components*. Leiden, Netherlands: H. E. Stenfert Kroese, 1975, pp. 186–8.

24. H. Peskin, Pubertal onset and ego functioning. *Journal of Abnormal Psychology*, 1967, 72, 1–15.

25. R. G. Niemi, ed., *The politics of future citizens*. San Francisco: Jossey-Bass, 1974.

26. A. M. Orum, R. S. Cohen, S. Grasmuck, and A. W. Orum. Sex, socialization and politics. *American Sociological Review*, 1974, 39, 197–209.

27. J. Adelson, B. Green, and R. P. O'Neil, Growth of political ideas in adolescence: The sense of community. *Journal of Personality and Social Psychology*, 1966, 4, 295–306.

28. J. Adelson, The political imagination of the young adolescent. In J. Kagan and R. Coles, eds., *Twelve to sixteen: early adolescence*. New York: Norton, 1972, pp. 106–143.

29. J. Gallatin and J. Adelson, Legal guarantees of individual freedom: a cross-national study of the development of political thought. *Journal of Social Issues*, 1971, 27, 93–108.

30. Adelson, Green, and O'Neil, 1966.

31. Adelson, 1971.

32. Ibid.

CHAPTER 5

1. H. D. Fishbein, *Evolution, development and children's learning*. Pacific Palisades, Calif.: Goodyear, 1976.

2. L. Kohlberg, Stage and sequence: the cognitive developmental approach to socialization. In D. A. Goslin, ed., *Handbook of socialization theory and research*. Chicago: Rand-McNally, 1969.

3. E. Turiel, Developmental processes in the child's moral thinking. In P. H. Mussen, J. Langer, and M. Covington, eds., *Trends and issues in developmental psychology*. New York: Holt, Rinehart & Winston, 1969, pp. 92–133.

4. L. Kohlberg and C. Gilligan, The adolescent as a philosopher: the discovery of the self in a post conventional world. In J. Kagan and R. Coles, eds. *12 to 16: early adolescence*. New York: Norton, 1971, pp. 144–79.

5. L. Kohlberg, Moral development and the education of adolescents.

In R. F. Purnell, *Adolescents and the American high school*. New York: Holt, Rinehart & Winston, 1970.

6. Kohlberg and Gilligan, 1971.

7. Kohlberg, 1970.

8. J. E. Tapin, H. Staudenmeyer, and J. L. Taddonio, Developmental changes in conditional reasoning: linguistic or logical? *Journal of Experimental Child Psychology*, 1974, 17, 360–73.

9. J. Loevinger and R. Wessler, *Measuring ego development*. San Francisco: Jossey-Bass, 1970.

10. S. Freud, *Civilization and its discontents*. Garden City, New York: Doubleday, 1958.

11. J. Aronfreed, The concept of internalization. In D. A. Goslin, *Handbook of socialization theory and research*. Chicago: Rand-McNally, 1969, pp. 263–323.

12. R. R. Sears, E. E. Maccoby, and H. Levin, *Patterns of child rearing*. Evanston, Ill.: Row, Peterson, 1957.

13. H. Hartshorne, M. A. May, and F. K. Shuttleworth. *Studies in the nature of character*. New York: Macmillan, 1930.

14. R. F. Peck and R. J. Havighurst, *The psychology of character development*. New York: Wiley, 1960.

15. R. Hogan, Moral conduct and moral character: a psychological perspective. *Psychological Bulletin*, 1973, 79, 217–32.

16. Fishbein, *Evolution, development and children's learning*.

17. D. Baumrind, Current patterns of parental authority. *Developmental Psychology*, 1971, 4, (1, part 2).

18. Ibid.

19. Hogan, 1973.

20. U. Bronfenbrenner, *Two worlds of childhood: U.S. and U.S.S.R.* New York: Basic Books, 1970.

21. J. C. Condry, Jr., M. L. Siman, and U. Bronfenbrenner, Characteristics of peer- and adult-oriented children. Unpublished manuscript, Cornell University, 1968. Cited in Bronfenbrenner, *Two worlds of childhood: U.S. and U.S.S.R.*, p. 105.

CHAPTER 6

1. T. Parsons, Family structure and the socialization of the child. In T. Parsons and R. F. Bales, eds., *Family, socialization and the interaction process*. New York: Free Press of Glencoe, 1955, pp. 35–131.

2. D. Bakan, *The duality of human existence.* Chicago: Rand-McNally, 1966.

3. J. H. Block, Conceptions of sex role; some cross-cultural and longitudinal perspectives. *American Psychologist,* 1973, 28, 512–26.

4. J. Money and A. A. Ehrhardt, *Man and woman, boy and girl: the differentiation and dimorphism of gender identity from conception to maturity.* Baltimore: Johns Hopkins University Press, 1972.

5. C. Etaugh and B. Brown, Perceiving the causes of success and failure of male and female performers. *Developmental Psychology,* 1975, 11, 103.

6. C. Leibel, J. Schwartz, and B. Sommer, Study of interests of early adolescents. Unpublished manuscript, 1975.

7. W. Emmerich, Developmental trends in evaluations of single traits. *Child Development,* 1974, 45, 172–83.

8. E. C. Stefic and M. Lorr, Age and sex differences in personality during adolescence. *Psychological Reports,* 1974, 35, 1123–6.

9. J. Macfarlane, K. Allen, and M. P. Honzik, *A developmental study of the behavior problems of normal children between twenty-one months and fourteen years.* Berkeley, Calif.: University of California Press, 1954.

10. Leibel, Schwartz, and Sommer, 1975.

11. W. H. Rivenbark, Self-disclosure patterns among adolescents. *Psychological Reports,* 1971, 28, 35–42.

12. R. P. Littlefield, Self-disclosure among some Negro, white, and Mexican-American adolescents. *Journal of Counseling Psychology,* 1974, 21, 133–6.

13. R. G. Wiggins, Differences in self-perceptions of ninth grade boys and girls. *Adolescence,* 1973, 8, 491–6.

14. Libel, Schwartz, and Sommer, 1975.

15. H. Witkin, D. Goodenough, and S. Karp, Stability of cognitive style from childhood to young adulthood. *Journal of Personality and Social Psychology,* 1967, 7, 291–300.

16. J. A. Sherman, *On the psychology of women; a survey of empirical studies.* Springfield, Ill.: C. C. Thomas, 1971.

17. D. P. Waber, Sex differences in cognition: a function of maturation rate? *Science,* 1976, 192, 572–4.

18. E. E. Maccoby and C. N. Jacklin, *The psychology of sex differences.* Stanford, Calif.: Stanford University Press, 1974.

19. J. Ernest, et al., Mathematics and sex. Published by *Mathematics Department University of California,* Santa Barbara, January 1975.

20. E. Fenema and J. Sherman, Sex-related differences in mathematics learning: myths, realities and related factors. Paper presented at a symposium on women and mathematics, *American Association for the Advancement of Science*, Boston, 1976.

21. J. Scanlon, Self-reported health behavior attitudes of youths 12–17 years. *National Center for Health Statistics. Vital and Health Statistics*, Series 11: Data from the National Health Survey, no. 147, DHEW publication no. (HRA) 75-1629, 1975.

22. Wiggins, 1973.

23. Scanlon, 1975.

24. R. C. Barnett, Sex differences and age trends in occupational preference and occupational prestige. *Journal of Counseling Psychology*, 1975, 22, 35–8.

25. R. G. Simons and M. Rosenberg, Functions of children's perceptions of the stratification system. *American Sociological Review*, 1971, 36, 235–49.

26. J. E. Teahan, The effect of sex and predominant socioeconomic class school climate on expectations of success among black students. *Journal of Negro Education*, 1974, 43, 245–6.

27. L. E. Patterson, Girl's careers: expression of identity. *Vocational Guidance Quarterly*, 1973, 21, 269–75.

28. U.S. Census Bureau, reported in the *Sacramento Bee*, 4/27/76, p. 1.

29. E. L. Moerk, Age and epogenic influences on aspirations of minority and majority group children. *Journal of Counseling Psychology*, 1974, 21, 294–8.

CHAPTER 7

1. E. H. Erikson, *Childhood and society*, 2nd edition. New York: Norton, 1963.

2. W. Kilpatrick, *Identity and intimacy*. New York: Delacorte Press, 1975.

3. R. W. White, Motivation reconsidered: the concept of competence. *Psychological Review*, 1959, 66.

4. E. Douvan and J. Adelson, *The adolescent experience*. New York: Wiley, 1966.

5. R. Bailey and K. G. Bailey, Self perceptions of scholastic ability at four grade levels. *Journal of Genetic Psychology*, 1974, 124, 197–212.

6. P. Katz and E. Zigler, Self-image disparity: a developmental approach. *Journal of Personality and Social Psychology*, 1967, *5*, 186–95.

7. D. Elkind, *A sympathetic understanding of the child six to sixteen.* Boston: Allyn and Bacon, 1971.

8. C. H. Cooley, *Human nature and the social order.* New York: Charles Scribner's Sons, 1902, p. 152.

9. R. P. Beech and A. Schoeppe, Development of value systems in adolescents. *Developmental Psychology*, 1974, *10*, 644–56.

10. D. Chabassol and D. C. Thomas, Sex and age differences in problems and interests of adolescents. *Journal of Experimental Education*, 1969, *38* (2), 16–23.

11. Beech and Schoeppe, 1974.

12. J. Scanlon, Self-reported health behavior attitudes of youths 12–17 years. *National Center for Health Statistics. Vital and Health Statistics*, Series 11: Data from the National Health Survey, no. 147, DHEW publication no. (HRA) 75-1629, 1975.

13. Ibid.

14. E. A. Rubinstein, G. A. Comstock, and J. P. Murray. *Television and social behavior, Volume 4: Television and day-to-day life: Patterns of use.* Rockville, Md.: National Institute of Mental Health, 1972.

15. Gottlieb and Sybil, cited in J. L. Singer, *The inner world of daydreaming.* New York: Harper & Row, 1975.

16. Singer, *The inner world of daydreaming.*

17. Ibid.

18. Ibid.

CHAPTER 8

1. H. S. Sullivan, *The interpersonal theory of psychiatry.* New York: W. W. Norton, 1953.

2. D. P. Ausubel, *Theory and problems of adolescent development.* New York: Grune & Stratton, 1954.

3. M. Gold and E. Douvan, eds., *Adolescent development: Readings in research and theory.* Boston: Allyn & Bacon, 1969, pp. 171–8.

4. Ibid.

5. E. Douvan and J. Adelson, *The adolescent experience.* New York: Wiley, 1966.

6. Muuss, *Theories of adolescence*, pp. 46–9.

7. Ausubel, *Theory and problems of adolescent development*.

8. Sullivan, *The interpersonal theory of psychiatry*.

9. G. E. Gardner, The mental health of normal adolescents. In G. Murphy and A. J. Bachrach, eds., *An outline of abnormal psychology*. New York: Random House, 1954, pp. 183–98.

10. Ibid., p. 198.

11. C. E. Bowerman and J. W. Kinch, Changes in family and peer orientation of children between the 4th and 10th grades. *Social Forces*, 1959, 37, 206–11.

12. B. A. Burk, S. M. Zdep, and H. Kushner, Affiliation patterns among American girls. *Adolescence*, 1973, 8, 541–6.

13. J. B. Landsbaum and R. H. Willis, Conformity in early and late adolescence. *Developmental Psychology*, 1971, 4, 334–7.

14. J. B. Kernan, Her mother's daughter? The case of clothing and cosmetic fashions. *Adolescence*, 1973, 8, 343–50.

15. J. S. Coleman, The adolescent subculture and academic achievement. *American Journal of Sociology*, 1960, 65, 337–47.

16. M. Roff, S. B. Sells, and M. M. Golden, *Social adjustment and personality development in children*. Minneapolis: University of Minnesota Press, 1972.

17. N. Cavior and P. R. Dokecki, Physical attractiveness, perceived attitude similarity, and academic achievement as contributors to interpersonal attraction among adolescents. *Developmental Psychology*, 1973, 9, 44–54.

18. C. Gordon, Social characteristics of early adolescence. In J. Kagan and R. Coles, eds., *12 to 16: early adolescence*. New York: Norton, 1971.

19. J. Remick, *Adolescent rites*. Unpublished manuscript.

20. W. M. Madsen, *The Mexican-American of South Texas*, 2nd edition. New York: Holt, Rinehart & Winston, 1973.

21. J. Lopez, personal communication.

22. W. Labov, Rules for ritual insults. In D. Sudnow, ed., *Studies in social interaction*. New York.: Free Press, 1972, pp. 120–69.

23. Ibid., p. 133 and p. 137.

24. A. Dundes, J. W. Leach, and A. Özkök. The strategy of Turkish boy's verbal dueling rhymes. In J. Gumperz and D. Hymes, eds., *Directions in sociolinguistics: the ethnography of communication*. New York: Holt, Rinehart & Winston, 1972, pp. 130–60.

25. W. J. Lively and D. B. Bromley, *Person perception in childhood and adolescence.* London: Wiley, 1973.

26. C. Hendrick, C. M. Franz, and K. L. Hoving, How do children form impressions of persons? They average. *Memory and Cognition*, 1975, 3, 325–8.

27. E. C. Martin, Reflections on the early adolescent in school. In Kagan and Coles, *12–16: early adolescence.*

28. F. Redl, Adolescents—Just how do they react? In G. Caplan and S. Lebovici, eds., *Adolescence: psychosocial perspectives.* New York: Basic Books, 1969, pp. 79–99.

29. A. Gesell, F. L. Ilg, and L. B. Ames, *Youth: the years from ten to sixteen.* New York: Harper, 1956.

30. Cited in Ibid., p. 182.

CHAPTER 9

1. M. M. Smith, L. L. Standley, and C. L. Hughes, *Junior high school education; its principles and procedures.* New York: McGraw-Hill, 1942.

2. W. T. Gruhn and H. R. Douglass, *The modern junior high school,* 3rd edition. New York: The Ronald Press, 1971.

3. National Education Association, Addresses and Proceedings, 1899, pp. 659–60. Cited in Smith, Standley, and Hughes, *Junior high school education.*

4. F. F. Bunker, The junior high school movement—its beginnings. Washington, D.C.: W. F. Roberts, 1935, p. 3. Cited in Smith, Standley, and Hughes, *Junior high school education.*

5. Cited in Gruhn and Douglass, 1971.

6. W. Van Til, G. F. Vars, and J. H. Lounsburg, *Modern education for the junior high school years.* Indianapolis and New York: Bobbs-Merrill, 1961.

7. J. H. Hansen and A. C. Hearn, *The middle school program.* Chicago: Rand-McNally, 1971.

8. W. M. Alexander, E. L. Williams, M. Compton, V. A. Hines and D. Prescott. *The emergent middle school.* New York: Holt, Rinehart & Winston, 1968.

9. Hanson and Hearn, *The middle school program.*

10. D. E. Overly, J. R. Kinghorn, and R. L. Preston. *The middle school: humanizing education for youth.* Washington, Ohio: Charles A. Jones, 1972.

11. A. W. Howard and G. C. Stoumbis, *The junior high and middle school: issues and practices.* Scranton, Pa.: Intext Educational Publishers, 1970, pp. 45–6.

12. Alexander et al., *The emergent middle school.*

13. C. P. Heffner, The student as teacher. *Theory into Practice,* 1974, *13,* 371–5.

CHAPTER 10

1. A. C. Kinsey, W. B. Pomeroy, and C. E. Martin, *Sexual behavior in the human male.* Philadelphia: W. B. Saunders, 1948.

2. A. C. Kinsey and associates, *Sexual behavior in the human female.* Philadelphia: W. B. Saunders, 1953.

3. M. G. Schofield, J. Bynner, P. Lewis, and P. Massie, *The sexual behavior of young people.* Boston: Little, Brown, 1965.

4. R. C. Sorensen, *Adolescent sexuality in contemporary America: personal values and sexual behavior, ages 13–19.* New York: World, 1973.

5. Ibid.

6. Ibid.

7. J. H. Kellogg, *Plain facts for old and young; embracing the natural history of hygiene,* revised. Burlington, Iowa: I. F. Segner & Co., 1888.

8. Sorensen, *Adolescent sexuality in contemporary America.*

9. J. H. Gagnon and W. Simon, They're going to learn in the street anyway. *Psychology Today,* 1969, *3,* 46–47, 71.

10. S. M. Dranoff, Masturbation and the male adolescent. *Adolescence,* 1974, *9,* 169–76.

11. A. Freud, Adolescence. In R. S. Eissler, A. Freud, H. Hartman, and M. Kris, eds., *The Psychoanalytic Study of the Child,* 1958, *13,* 255–78. New York: International Universities Press, 1958.

12. P. Blos, *On adolescence.* New York: Free Press of Glencoe, 1962.

13. Committee on Adolescence, Group for Advancement of Psychiatry. *Normal adolescence.* New York: Charles Scribner, 1968.

14. A. Freud, *The ego and mechanisms of defense,* revised edition. New York: International Universities Press, 1966.

15. J. H. Gagnon and W. Simon, *Sexual conduct: the social sources of human sexuality.* Chicago: Aldine, 1973.

16. H. K. A. Visser, Some physiological and clinical aspects of puberty. *Archives of Diseases of Childhood,* 1973, *48,* 169–82.

17. J. Money and A. A. Ehrhardt, *Man and woman, boy and girl: differentiation and dimorphism of gender identity from conception to maturity*. Baltimore: The Johns Hopkins University Press, 1972.
18. B. A. Kogan, *Human sexual expression*. New York: Harcourt, Brace, Jovanovich, 1970.
19. Money and Ehrhardt, *Man and woman, boy and girl*.
20. Gagnon and Simon, *Sexual conduct*.
21. Ibid.
22. L. Whisnant and L. Zegan, A study of attitudes toward menarche in white middle-class American adolescent girls. *American Journal of Psychiatry*, 1975, *132*, 809–14.
23. J. J. Paonessa and M. W. Paonessa, The preparation of boys for puberty. *Social Casework*, 1971, *52*, 39–44.
24. Sorensen, *Adolescent sexuality in contemporary America*.
25. Ibid.
26. J. H. Meyerowitz and J. S. Malev, Pubescent attitudinal correlates antecedent to adolescent illegitimate pregnancy. *Journal of Youth and Adolescence*, 1973, *2*, 251–8.

CHAPTER 11

1. Crime in the United States, 1974. *Uniform Crime Reports, Federal Bureau of Investigation*, Department of Justice, U.S. Government Printing Office.
2. J. Scanlon, Self-reported health behavior attitudes of youths 12–17 years. *National Center for Health Statistics. Vital and Health Statistics*, Series 11: Data from the National Health Survey, no. 147, DHEW publication no. (HRA) 75-1629, 1975.
3. N. Mailer, The faith of graffiti, *Esquire*, May 1974, p. 77.
4. Some artful dodgers find a different line. *New York Times*, May 1976.
5. R. Goldstein, The thing has gotten completely out of hand. *New York*, March 26, 1973, p. 35.
6. S. Padwe, The aerosol autographers: why they do it. *Today Magazine, Philadelphia Inquirer*, 5/2/71, p. 12F.
7. L. Torres, On being seduced by a flat, white wall. *Los Angeles Times*, 2/6/76.
8. T. Kumbula, Kilroy was here—among others. *Los Angeles Times*, 9/8/74, page II, 2.

9. S. Padwe cited in D. Ley and R. Cybriwsky, Urban graffiti as territorial markers. *Annals of the Association of American Geographers,* 1974, *64,* 491–505.

10. D. Ley and R. Cybriwsky, Urban graffiti as territorial markers. *Annals of the Association of American Geographers,* 1974, *64,* 491–505.

11. Shirttail statistics on area shoplifters. *Daily Democrat,* Woodland, Calif. 7/7/76, pg. 7A.

12. J. L. Singer, *The inner world of daydreaming.* New York: Harper and Row, 1975.

13. S. Bathen, Teen offenders' reasons varied. *Sacramento Bee,* 8/39/76, pg. 1.

14. L. Kohlberg, The development of moral character and moral ideology. In M. L. Hoffman and L. G. Hoffman, *Review of child development research, Vol. I.* New York: Russell Sage, 1964.

15. B. Stumbo, East L.A. gangs: youth worker struggles for peace in the barrios. *Los Angeles Times* 9/19/76, Part II, p. 1.

16. Ibid.

17. J. G. Lieber, Gunfights in the graveyard. *The Nation,* 1/18/75, pp. 42–47.

18. Ibid., p. 44.

19. *Adolescent Medicine,* 1974, *6,* 1–2.

20. R. H. Blum and associates, *Horatio Alger's children.* San Francisco: Jossey-Bass, 1972.

21. K. G. Johnson, J. H. Donnelly, R. Scheble, R. L. Wine, and M. Weitman. Survey of adolescent drug use. I—Sex and gender distribution. *American Journal of Public Health,* 1971, *61,* 2418–32.

22. W. C. Cockerham, Drinking attitudes and practices among Wind River reservation Indian youth. *Journal of Studies on Alcohol,* 1975, *36,* 321–6.

23. Scanlon, 1975.

24. Johnson et al., 1971.

25. U.S. National Institute on Drug Abuse, *Marihuana and health,* 5th annual report to the U.S. Congress, 1975.

26. P. W. Lewis and D. W. Patterson, Acute and chronic effects of voluntary inhalation of certain commercial volatile solvents by juveniles. *Journal of Drug Issues,* 1974, *4,* 162–75.

27. Johnson et al., 1971.

28. J. H. Harris, A participant observer study: the everyday life of a group of delinquent boys. *Adolescence*, 1974, *9*, 31–48.

29. Johnson et al., 1971.

30. H. Wechsler and D. Thum, Teen-age drinking, drug use and social correlates. *Quarterly Journal of Studies on Alcohol*, 1973, *34*, 1220–7.

31. G. N. Braught, D. Brakarsh, D. Follingstad, and K. L. Berry. Deviant drug use in adolescence: a review of psychosocial correlates. *Psychological Bulletin*, 1973, *79*, 92–106.

32. H. Feldman, American way of drugging; street status and drug users. *Society*, 1973, *10*, 32–8.

33. Bombed generation, in keeping up with youth, *Parade, Sacramento Bee*, 3/14/76, p. 19.

CHAPTER 12

1. J. G. Masterson and A. Washburne, The symptomatic adolescent: psychiatric illness or adolescent turmoil? *American Journal of Psychiatry*, 1966, *122*, 1240–8.

2. Monthly Vital Health Statistics Report, 2/3/76, *National Center for Health Statistics*.

3. J. D. Teicher, Children and adolescents who attempt suicide. In B. Q. Hafen, ed., *Self destructive behavior: a national crisis*. Minneapolis, Minn.: Burgess Publishing, 1972, pp. 119–29.

4. I. B. Weiner, *Psychological disturbance in adolescence*. New York: Wiley, 1970.

5. D. E. Berg, A plan for preventing student suicide. In Hafen, *Self destructive behavior*, pp. 225–34.

6. J. Barter, Self-destructive behavior in adolescents and adults: similarities and differences. In Hafen, *Self destructive behavior*, pp. 113–18.

7. Teicher, 1972.

8. J. Jacobs, *Adolescent suicide*. New York: Wiley, 1971.

9. R. H. Seiden, Studies of suicidal behavior. In Hafen, *Self destructive behavior*, pp. 153–91.

10. Teicher, 1972.

11. J. C. Coleman, *Abnormal psychology and modern life*, 5th edition. Glenview, Ill.: Scott, Foresman, 1976.

12. Berg, 1972.
13. Weiner, *Psychological disturbance in adolescence.*
14. Ibid.
15. S. Arieti, *Interpretation of schizophrenia.* New York: Robert Brunner, 1955.
16. Ibid.
17. J. M. Toolan, Depression and suicide. In Arieti and Caplan, *Handbook of psychiatry,* Vol. 2, pp. 294–305.
18. S. L. Werkman, Psychiatric disorders of adolescence. In S. Areiti and G. Caplan, eds., *Handbook of psychiatry,* Vol. 2. New York: Basic Books, 1974, pp. 223–33.
19. B. M. Rosen, A. K. Bohn, and M. Kramer, Demographic and diagnostic characteristics of psychiatric clinic outpatients in the U.S.A., 1961. *American Journal of Orthopsychiatry,* 1964, 24, 455–67.
20. Weiner, *Psychological disturbance in adolescence.*
21. S. Schachter, Discussion of the presentation of Dr. H. Bruch, Eating disorders in adolescence. In J. Zubin and A. M. Freedman, eds., *The psychopathology of adolescence.* New York: Grune & Stratton, 1970, pp. 197–202.
22. S. Nathan and D. Pisula, Psychological observations of obese adolescents during starvation treatment. In N. Kiell, ed., *The psychology of obesity.* Springfield, Ill.: C. C. Thomas, 1973, pp. 125–38.
23. Schachter, 1970.
24. Werkman, 1974.
25. Coleman, *Abnormal psychology and modern life.*
26. H. Bruch, Eating disorders in adolescence. In Zubin and Freedman, *The psychopathology of adolescence.*
27. H. S. Sullivan, *Conceptions of modern psychiatry.* New York: Norton, 1953.

CHAPTER 13

1. P. Ariès, *Centuries of childhood,* translated from French by R. Baldick. New York: Vintage Books, 1962.
2. M. Douglass, *Purity and danger; an analysis of concepts of pollution and taboo.* London: Routledge & Kegan Paul, 1966.
3. Ibid., p. 116.

4. T. Wolfe, *The pumphouse gang*. New York: Farrar, Straus & Giroux, 1968.

5. E. Z. Friedenberg, The image of the adolescent majority. In E. Z. Friedenberg, *The dignity of youth and other atavisms*. Boston: Beacon, 1965, pp. 66–78.

6. D. Elkind, Borderline retardation in lower and middle income adolescents. In R. M. Allen, A. D. Cartazzo, and R. P. Toister, eds., *Theories of cognitive development*. Coral Gables, Florida: University of Miami Press, 1973, pp. 57–85.

Author Index

Adams, J. F., 141
Adams, P. L., 229
Adelson, J., 66, 68, 69, 107, 108, 235, 238, 239
Alexander, W. M., 241, 242
Allen, M. R., 230
Allen, K., 237
Ames, L. B., 137, 140, 241
Ardon, M. S., 176
Ariès, P., 230, 246
Arieti, S., 69, 207, 246
Aristotle, 16
Aronfreed, J., 84, 236
Ausubel, D. P., 239, 240

Bailey, K. G., 238
Bailey, R., 238
Bakan, David, 30, 87, 230, 237
Barnett, R. C., 99, 238
Barter, J., 245
Barth, F., 230
Bathen, S., 244
Baumrind, D., 80, 236
Bayley, N., 233
Beech, R. P., 239
Beidelman, T. O., 231
Bentzon, M. W., 232
Berenberg, S. R., 49
Berg, D. E., 205, 245, 246
Berry, K. L., 245
Bettelheim, B., 25, 30, 231

Bjolén, K., 232
Block, J. H., 87, 92, 237
Blos, Peter, 9, 117, 229, 242
Blum, R. H., 200, 244
Bohn, A. K., 246
Bowerman, C. E., 240
Brakarsh, D., 245
Braught, G. N., 245
Brody, E. B., 141
Bromley, D. B., 241
Bronfenbrenner, Urie, 81, 236
Brown, B., 237
Brown, J. K., 30
Bruch, Hilde, 211, 212, 246
Bruner, Jerome, 64, 70, 234
Bullough, V., 231, 232
Bunker, F. W., 145, 241
Burk, B. A., 240
Bynner, J., 242

Cauzinille, E., 233
Cavior, N., 240
Chabassol, D., 239
Claparède, E., 63
Clark, LeVerne H., 28, 231
Cockerham, W. C., 244
Coffey, A. R., 200
Cohen, M., 230
Cohen, R. S., 235
Coleman, J. S., 240, 245, 246
Coles, R., 141

Compton, M., 241, 242
Comstock, G. A., 200, 239
Condry, Jr., J. C., 236
Connolly, L., 176
Cooley, C. H., 239
Cortez, Leo, 192
Cottle, T. J., 117
Cull, J. G., 215
Cybriwsky, R., 188, 244

Deaux, K., 102
DePalma, D. J., 84
Dokecki, P. R., 240
Donnelly, J. H., 244, 245
Donovan, B. T., 232
Douglass, H. R., 241
Douglass, Mary, 217, 246
Douvan, E., 107, 108, 238, 239
Dranoff, S. M., 242
Driver, H. E., 27, 29, 231
Dundes, A., 130, 240

Edmonds, E. M., 233
Ehrhardt, A. A., 49, 237, 242
Eichinger Ferro-Luzzi, G., 231
Eliade, M., 23, 30, 230
Eliot, Charles W., 144
Elkind, D., 53, 70, 111, 117, 234,
    239, 247
Emmerich, W., 237
Erikson, Erik, 105, 106, 107, 109,
    118, 120, 161, 238
Etaugh, C., 237
Evans, E. D., 141

Feinstein, S. C., 176
Feldman, H., 245
Fenema, E., 238
Finch, S. M., 214
Fishbein, H. D., 235, 236
Flavell, J. H., 70
Foley, J. M., 84
Follingstad, D., 245
Francis, J. J., 177
Franklin, Benjamin, 143
Franz, C. M., 241

Frayer, D. A., 233
Freedman, A. M., 215
Freud, Anna, 160, 161, 242
Freud, Sigmund, 105, 122, 159, 160,
    189, 236
Friedenberg, Edgar Z., 218, 247
Friedman, R. C., 102
Friedrich, D., 52, 233
Frisbie, C. J., 231
Frisch, R. E., 36, 232

Gadpaille, W. J., 102, 176
Gagnon, J. H., 176, 242, 243
Gallatin, J. E., 118, 235
Gardner, R. W., 118, 240
Gesell, A., 137, 140, 241
Ghatala, E. S., 233
Gilligan, C. J., 235, 236
Glueck, E., 200
Glueck, S., 200
Gold, M., 239
Golden, M. M., 240
Goldfarb, A. F., 232
Goldmeier, H., 200
Goldstein, Richard, 186, 243
Goodenough, D., 95, 237
Gottlieb, A., 239
Grasmuck, S., 235
Green, B., 235
Greif, E. B., 84
Gruhn, W. T., 241
Grumbach, M. M., 49

Hafen, B. Q., 215
Hall, G. Stanley, 3, 20, 229, 230
Hamburg, B., 141
Hansen, J. H., 153, 241
Hardy, R. E., 215
Harley, G. W., 230
Harris, J. H., 245
Hartshorne, H., 78–79, 236
Haskell, M. R., 200
Havighurst, R. J., 78, 236
Hauck, B. B., 103
Hearn, A. C., 153, 241
Heffner, Carole Papirtis, 148, 242
Hendrick, C., 241
Hillman, R. W., 232

Hines, B. A., 241, 242
Hoffman, M. L., 84
Hogan, R., 84, 236
Honzik, A., 237
Horn, J., 231
Hoving, K. L., 241
Howard, A. W., 153, 242
Hughes, C. L., 241
Hurlock, Elizabeth, 7, 8, 229, 233

Ilg, F. L., 137, 140, 241
Inhelder, Barbel, 58, 70, 233, 234
Inoue, K., 233

Jacklin, C. N., 103, 237
Jacobs, J., 215, 245
Johnson, K. G., 244, 245
Jones, H. E., 231
Jones, M. C., 233

Kagan, J., 141
Karp, S., 95, 237
Katz, P., 239
Kellogg, J. H., 156, 242
Kernan, J. B., 240
Kett, Joseph F., 17, 30, 230
Khanna, J. L., 200
Kilpatrick, W., 107, 238
Kinch, J. W., 240
Kinghorn, J. R., 153, 241
Kinsey, A. C., 154, 242
Klausmeier, H. J., 233, 234
Kloos, P., 231
Kogan, B. A., 177, 243
Kohen-Raz, R., 7, 8, 118, 229, 234
Kohlberg, Lawrence, 72–75, 191,
    235, 236, 244
Konopka, G., 141
Kramer, M., 246
Kulin, H. E., 232
Kumbula, T., 243
Kurtines, W., 84
Kushner, H., 240

Labov, W., 240
Landsbaum, J. B., 240
Langer, J., 234
Leach, J. W., 130, 240
Leibel, C., 237
Leiber, J. G., 193
Levin, H., 236
Lewin, Kurt, 7, 229
Lewis, P. W., 242, 244
Ley, D., 188, 244
Lieber, J. G., 244
Littlefield, R. P., 237
Livesly, W. J., 241
Locke, John, 18
Loevinger, J., 84, 236
Lopez, Jorge, 240
Lorr, M., 237
Lounsburg, J. H., 241

Maccoby, E. E., 103, 236, 237
Macfarlane, J. W., 233, 237
MacMahon, B., 232
Madsen, W. M., 240
Mailer, Norman, 186, 243
Malev, J. S., 243
Malina, R. M., 49
Marcus, I. M., 177
Marshall, D. S., 176
Martin, C. E., 242
Martin, E. C., 153, 241
Massie, P., 242
Masterson, J. G., 245
Mathieu, J., 233
May, M. A., 78–79, 236
Mayer, F. E., 49
Mead, Margaret, 46, 233
Medvene, L., 53, 234
Meyerowitz, J. H., 243
Minkler, M., 177
Mischel, T., 70
Mishima, J., 233
Moerk, E. L., 238
Money, J., 49, 237, 243
Moore, Vernon K., 100
Moriarty, A., 118
Mount, G., 231
Murray, J. P., 200, 239
Mussen, P. H., 233
Muuss, R. E., 7, 8, 118, 141, 201,
    230, 240

Nathan, S., 246
Nelson, G. K., 234
Nelson, Jr., M., 232
Niemi, R. G., 235
Norbeck, E., 230
Northcutt, C., 229

O'Brien, T. C., 234
O'Neill, R. P., 235
Opler, M. E., 231
Orum, A. M., 235
Otoo, S. N., 231
Overly, D. E., 153, 241
Özkök, A., 130, 240

Padwe, S., 243, 244
Paonessa, J. J., 243
Paonessa, M. W., 243
Parsons, Talcott, 87, 236
Patterson, D. W., 244
Patterson, L. E., 100, 238
Paulus, D. H., 234
Peck, R. F., 78–79, 236
Peel, E. A., 55, 57, 70, 234
Peskin, H., 47, 65, 233, 235
Piaget, Jean, 58, 59, 62, 63, 70, 72, 74, 161, 233, 234
Pisula, D., 246
Platt, A. M., 201
Pomeroy, W. B., 154, 242
Pozanski, E. O., 214
Precourt, W. E., 31, 230
Prescott, D., 241, 242
Preston, R. L., 153, 241

Rank, Otto, 122
Redl, Fritz, 7, 229, 241
Reiter, E. O., 232
Remick, Jack, 128, 240
Revelle, R., 36, 232
Richard, J. F., 233
Richart, R. M., 102
Rivenbark, W. H., 94, 237
Roberge, J. J., 234
Rockway, A. S., 53, 234
Roff, M., 240
Rollins, H., 233

Rosen, B. M., 246
Rosenberg, B. G., 103
Rosenberg, M., 238
Rousseau, Jean Jacques, 17, 230
Rubinstein, E. A., 200, 239

Scanlon, J., 232, 238, 239, 243, 244
Schachcter, S., 210, 246
Scheble, R., 244, 245
Schoeppe, A., 239
Schofield, M. G., 154, 242
Schonfeld, W. A., 7, 8, 229
Schwartz, J., 237
Schweitzer, Albert, 140
Sears, R. R., 236
Seiden, R. H., 245
Sells, S. B., 240
Serei, C., 31
Shapiro, B. J., 234
Shaughnessy, E., 233
Shaw, M. E., 153
Sherman, J. A., 237, 238
Shuttleworth, F. K., 236
Silverman, I., 153
Siman, M. L., 236
Simmons, R. G., 238
Simon, W., 176, 242, 243
Singer, Jerome, 115, 190, 239, 244
Slater, P., 232
Smith, M. M., 241
Sommer, B., 229, 237
Sorensen, R. C., 125, 154–158, 177, 242, 243
Spindler, G. D., 26, 31, 231
Standley, L. L., 241
Staudenmayer, H., 234, 236
Stefic, E. C., 237
Stern, L. O., 102
Stoller, R. J., 103
Stoumbis, G. C., 153, 242
Stumbo, B., 244
Suggs, R. C., 176
Sullivan, Harry Stack, 120, 141, 213–214, 239, 240, 246
Sutton-Smith, B., 103
Sybil, B., 239

Taddonio, J. L., 234, 236
Tanner, J. M., 8, 49, 232, 234

Taplin, J. E., 234, 236
Teahan, J. E., 100, 238
Teicher, J. D., 204, 245
Thomas, D. C., 239
Thompson, L. J., 153
Thum, D., 245
Toolan, J. M., 246
Torres, Louis, 187, 243
Trabasso, T., 233
Turiel, E., 84, 235

Van de Wiele, R. L., 102
Van Gennup, A., 22, 23, 230
Van Til, W., 241
Vars, G. F., 241
Visser, H. K. A., 232, 242
Vygotsky, L. S., 63–64, 70, 234

Waber, D. P., 97–98, 237
Walker, D. E., 230
Wall, W. D., 235
Walzer, J. F., 230
Washburne, A., 245
Weatherly, D., 233

Wechsler, H., 245
Weiner, I. B., 215, 245, 246
Weitman, M., 244, 245
Werkman, S. L., 215, 246
Werner, H., 62
Wessler, R., 84, 236
White, R. W., 107, 238
Whisnant, L., 243
Whiting, B. A., 230
Wiggins, R. G., 94–95, 237, 238
Williams, E. L., 241
Willis, R. H., 240
Wilmore, J., 231
Wine, R. L., 244, 245
Witkin, H., 95, 96, 237
Wolfe, Tom, 218, 247

Yablonsky, L., 200
Young, F. W., 31

Zdep, S. M., 240
Zegan, L., 243
Zigler, E., 239
Zubin, J., 215

Subject Index

Absolutism, 11–12
Abstract thought, 51, 54, 55–57, 59, 63, 67
Acne, 44
Acting out, 189–92
Adolescence, 5, 16–21
Adolescent rites, 129
Adrenal gland, 40
Affective disturbances, 206
Affiliation patterns, 126
Agency (defined), 87, 90
Alcohol, 184–85, 194–95, 197, 198, 205
Alienation, 83
American Girl, 100
Amphetamines, 196, 197
Anal stage, 135, 160
Androgen, 40, 91, 163
Angel Dust, 197
Anorexia nervosa, 172, 210–13
Anovulatory cycles, 40
Anxiety, 202
Arson, 185, 189
Asceticism, 161
Asynchrony, 10
Athletic performance, 92
Autistic thought, 117
Autonomy, vs. empathy, 79–81, 179
Awareness, 51

Barbiturates, 196
Berkeley Growth Study, 47

Body image, 46
Boy Scouts, 100
Boys' Life, 100
Bush school, 24

California Growth Studies, 92–93
Cambridge Growth Study, 48
Canon law, 6
Career planning, 100–2
Catholic Church, 72
Character development (male vs. female), 90
Character education (moral development), 81
Child labor legislation, 19
Circumcision, 25
Climate, 36
Cliques, 108, 121, 192
Coitus, 155, 166, 168, 171, 175
Communion(defined), 87, 90
Competence (defined), 107
Compulsory education, 19
Concept formation, 52, 54
Concrete operations, 58–62
Concrete thought, 57
Conformity, 80–81, 127
Conscience, 76–77
Conservation (recognition of), 60
Continuity, vs. discontinuity, 11, 12–13, 51, 64–65
Contraceptives, 174

Cooperation, human propensity for, 79
Crime, 181–85, 243
Critical weight hypothesis, 36–37
Cultural Relativism, 11–12
Curfew, 181, 182

Daydreams, 114–15, 116
Defense mechanisms, 208–9
Deliquents, 78
Dementia praecox, 206
Denver Growth Study, 48
Depression, 202, 203, 209
Discontinuity, vs. Continuity, 11, 12–13, 51, 58, 64–65, 83
"Disturbing the peace," 181
Dominance, sexual, 86
Drug use, 179, 194–200, 205
    alcohol, 184–85, 194–95, 197, 198, 205
    amphetamines, 196
    Angel Dust, 197
    barbiturates, 196
    marihuana, 179, 196–98, 244
    Nat'l. Inst. on Drug Abuse, 195, 244
    PCP (Angel Dust), 197
    psychedelics, 197, 199
    tobacco, 179, 195

Early maturation, 46–48
Eating disorders, 202, 210–13
Effectance motivation, 107
Ego, 76, 77, 105, 159, 161, 162, 179, 188, 208
Egocentrism, 79, 109, 112
Ejaculation, 6, 42, 170, 175
Embedded Figures Test, 95–97
Empathy, vs. autonomy, 79–81, 179
English Common Law, 72
Equilibrium, disruption of, during development, 62, 161, 162
Erection, penile, 33, 42, 164
Erotic development, 159–70
    females, 168–70
    males, 164–68

Estrogen, 35, 163
External focus of control, 174

Fantasy, 114–17
Field dependence, 95–97
Field independence, 95–97
Formal operations. *See* Abstract thought
Friendship, 121, 192

Gangs, 108, 192–94
Gender identity, 91
Genital mutilation, 26
Genital stage, 160
Girl Scouts, 100
Gonadotropins, 34
Gonads, 34
Graduate Record Examination, 88–89
Graffiti, 186

Hedonism, 73, 77
High school, 144
Homosexuality, 157–59
Hormones, 34, 90, 163, 217
    androgens, 40, 91, 163
    changes in, 91
    estrogens, 35, 163
    progesterone, 35, 163
    testosterone, 35, 86
Hypothalamus, 34

Id, 77, 159, 161, 162, 188
Identification, in development of conscience, 76–77
Identity, 104, 105, 108, 119, 122, 178, 180, 193, 198
    formation of, 105–11
    gender, 91
Ikonic thought, 64
Independence, establishment of, 122–24, 178, 180, 220
Information processing, 52
Inhalants, 195

Intellectualization, 161
Intermediate school, 145
Intimacy, 107, 119–21, 122, 123, 178, 180
Intuitive thought, 59
IQ tests, 57

Junior high school, 9, 142–43, 220
  curriculum, 146–47
  history, 145
  identity problem, 151
Juvenile Court, 20, 182

Kinaaldá, 28

Lactation, 86
Latency, 160, 161–62
Latin grammar school, 143
Life crises, 105, 106
Logic, development of, 52, 54–57, 59, 63
Loitering, 181, 182
Looking-glass self, 111

Marginality, of pubescents, 7, 217–18
Marihuana, 179, 195, 196, 197, 198, 244
Mastery, development of, 107, 161
Masturbation, 19, 155–57, 164–69, 172
Mathematics, 98
Maturation, 10, 33, 65, 98
Mechanical performance, 91–92
Media, 113, 116, 190
Memory capacity, 52
Menarche, 6, 23, 40, 170
  age, 36
  environmental influences, 36
  genetic factors, 36
  nutrition, 37
  racial differences, 40
Menopause, 91
Menstruation, 23, 25, 27, 29, 30, 33, 35, 48, 86, 168, 170, 175

Mexican-Americans, 129
Middle school, 151–53
Moral behavior, 73, 79
Moustache, 43
Muscular development, 86

National Education Association, 144, 145, 241
National Health Survey, 1966-1970, 40, 98–99
Neurosis, 202, 208–10
Nocturnal emissions, 48

Oakland Growth Study, 47
Obesity, 210–13
Oral stage, 160
Orgasm, 165–66
Ovary, 37, 91

Palomillas, 129
Paranoid disorders, 206
PCP (Angel Dust), 197
Penile erection, 33, 42, 164
Person perception, 132–33
Petty theft, 189
Phallic stage, 160
Pituitary, 34, 39
"Playing the dozens," 129
Political ideology, 66–69
"Prairie City," 78
Pregnancy, 86, 171, 173–75
Progesterone, 35, 163
Promiscuity, 101, 205, 208
Psychedelic drugs, 197, 199
Psychoanalytic theory, 76, 185
Psychosexual development, 160
Psychosis, 206–8
Psychosocial development, 106
Puberty
  definition, 5–6
  developmental phase designations, 8
  legal age, 6
  onset, 36
  precocious, 163
  recollections, 4
  timing and cognitive function, 47

Puberty rites, 23, 216
  boys: Africa, 23–24; Australia, 25;
    New Guinea, 25; North Amer-
    ica, 25
  girls: Africa, 29; Apache, 28;
    India, 29; Pacific, 29; South
    America, 29
Pubescence, definition, 6
Punishment, 77, 190

Reductionism, vs. wholism, 11, 13–14
Releasing factor, 34
Reversibility, capacity for, 59–60
Rites of passage, 22–29
Rod-and-Frame Test, 95–97
Roman Law, 6
Runaway, 181, 182

Schizophrenia, 202–6
School reform, 18
Sebaceous glands, 44
Sensory-motor stage, 59
Sex characteristics
  female, 37–40
  male, 41–44
Sex differences
  cognitive, 95–98
  life cycle, 90–92
  personality, 92–95
  in vocational planning, 98–102
Sex hormones. *See* Hormones
Sex play, 155
Sex roles, 85

Sexual intercourse, 155, 166, 168,
    171, 175
Sexuality, development, 159–70
  female, 168–70
  male, 164–68
Sexual promiscuity, 191, 205, 208
Short-term memory, 52
Skeletal maturity, 40–41
Socialization, differences, for males
    and females, 87, 90
Social learning, 77
Sports participation, 92, 113
Status offenses, 180–83
Stress, indicators, 4
Suicide, 208, 203–6
Superego, 76, 77, 159, 162, 188

Television, 113, 116, 190
Testosterone, 35, 86
Tobacco, 179, 195
Truancy, 181

Uniform Crime Reports, 181–82, 243
USSR, 81–83

Vagrancy, 181
Vandalism, 185, 188, 189, 191
Venereal disease, 171, 173
Verbal ability, 95, 97–98
Visual-spatial ability, 95, 97–98
"Vospitanie," 81